GORDON GILL

A MÉTIS MAN'S DREAM

FROM TRAPLINES TO TUGBOATS IN CANADA'S NORTH

NEIL GOWER

◆ FriesenPress

One Printers Way
Altona, MB R0G 0B0
Canada

www.friesenpress.com

ISBN
978-1-03-914549-8 (Hardcover)
978-1-03-914548-1 (Paperback)
978-1-03-914550-4 (eBook)

1. BIOGRAPHY & AUTOBIOGRAPHY, CULTURAL,
ETHNIC & REGIONAL, INDIGENOUS

Distributed to the trade by The Ingram Book Company

TABLE OF CONTENTS

MAPS

Courtesy Freeworldmaps.net

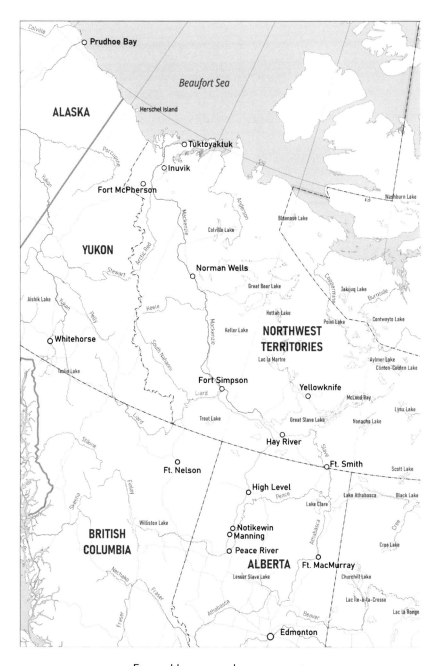

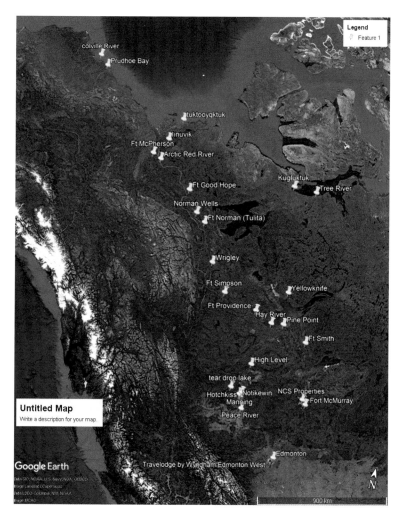

Gordon's personal Google Map of places worked and lived.

WORDING NOTE

THE USE OF WORDS describing Indigenous Peoples' lives, and history is rife with confusion, insensitivity, and differing opinions. Changes in approach appear fairly regularly. It does seem like a bit of a minefield. We have tried to be sensitive and up to date. Initially, we tried to use the word metis in different ways to show origins, ancestors, political affiliation and the like. (See Chapter 8 for more detail). This led to confusion and awkwardness. Therefore, for ease of reading, we have primarily used the capital-M "Métis," with the accent *aigu*, throughout, although arguably this technically may refer only to Métis descendants of Indigenous, French Catholic stock from Red River (the present-day Winnipeg area of Manitoba)[1].

Further, we have used the words "Indian," "Métis/Metis/metis," "half-breed," and "native" in the context of Gordon's voice and time. He calls himself a "Native." These are the words of Gordon's lifetime, which he uses still. The word "Indian" is also used in a legal, historical, or descriptive context, arising from the common use of that word, and as defined by the Indian Act of Canada. The descriptor Aboriginal, while formerly acceptable, has been used only as part of a quotation or in an historical context.

The reference to the Northwest Territories (NWT) can also be confusing. Its use in this work changes depending on the time frame of the narrative. Originally, the whole of the "northwest of Canada," outside of a small part of the Red River valley and the lands now occupied by British Columbia, was part of the NWT. Over time, especially with the passing of Manitoba Act of 1870, and the creation of the Yukon Territory in 1989 and the prairie provinces of Saskatchewan and Alberta in 1905, the NWT was reduced to that (still huge) area north of the 60th parallel of latitude,

----

1 AlbertaMetis.com; Queen's University Office of Indigenous Initiatives, for example. There seems to be no consistency! The Métis Nation of Alberta versus the Metis Settlement Appeal Board. Quotations, book titles and the like are used with, or without, the accent over the e, as in the original source, as much as possible.

east of the Yukon border, and west of northern Quebec. The eastern arctic territory of Nunavut was separated from the NWT in 1999. To add to that confusion, the postal description of the NWT is now NT, which is also a common acronym for Northern Transportation Company Limited, which plays such an important role in this narrative.

The occasional use of the capitalized N in the words "the North" is because, for those who know it, the North is a place, no matter the names, and boundaries and borders put on a map. Northerners are people from that place, often no matter where they now live.

Finally, we have generally used metric measurements, as is common in Canada now. However, Gordon still talks "imperial" and his words therefore use miles. References to miles can roughly be "metricked" by multiplying by 1.6. The opposite calculation can be done by dividing the kilometre, very roughly, in half. A foot is about a third of a metre. Where it seems particularly important, the metric/imperial detail is given.

PROLOGUE

Tugboat "Malta" on calm water, Hay River, NWT.

THE SMALL TUGBOAT LURCHED, the big waves relentlessly pushing its flared bow up in the air, then pounding it down into the next trough, its wires and steel whining in the wind. The tug rolled and heaved, twisting under the swallowing force of the crashing waves of Great Slave Lake. The cold wind and heavy seas brutalized the little ship in the never-never land of northern freeze-up.

The boy, just sixteen and terrified, was coming home from his summer job as a cook's helper and deckhand on the MV *Malta*, part of the Department of Public Works' northern fleet. In his short lifetime, he had lived not on the water but in the bush and muskeg of northern Alberta.

The boy knew poverty and hard work and what it meant to be a half-breed. He knew the ways of trapping, but he didn't know the forceful anger of an easterly blowing over a hundred and sixty kilometres or more of open water from the east arm of the huge northern sea. He had never seen the big lake—so deep it was unfathomable—in a storm.

The captain had started the final run for home, sixty-five kilometres across the southwest corner of Great Slave to their home harbour at Hay

River. He was in charge of the tug, but the master of the dredging vessel insisted on pushing past the captain's reluctance to enter the big lake. The dredge master was the boss of the dredge, the house barge, and the scows that made up the *Malta*'s "tow" and he was pushing hard to get home. And then it was too late to turn back. If the captain did try to turn back to regain the protection of Wrigley Harbour, where the Mackenzie River started its long journey to the Arctic Sea, they'd capsize for sure. The very small tug, with its heavy, dragging load, pushed on, into the face of the raging, tormenting storm.

Like a bucking bronco, the small vessel reared up and slammed down—*womp, womp, womp*—waves crashing over the bow, its deck too close to the rushing water. The tug forced forward, its little engine no match for the October storm. The wind and waves pushed hard on the flotilla lined out behind the tug. The boat rose once more, the cables connecting to the tow over the aft pipe railing strained to the breaking point. Then, with a lurch and a *bang*, the cables broke. The house barge was lost. Floundering, the connection to its lifeline broken, it blew away before the wind. Then, with a *crack*, the farthest mud scow snapped its line, and then the next strained and bucked until—*crack!*—its towing cable snapped too. The scows disappeared into the night, pushed by the torrents until they settled on a beach somewhere. The boy held on for dear life, terrified and asking God, "What next? When will it stop?"

The boy stood with the captain in the wheelhouse. The dredge was still attached, dead in the water, weighing down and dragging the little vessel as it struggled to make little headway.

For hours, twenty-eight in all, the captain urged and sweated the little tug on, pushing, steering, begging. The dredge master and his crew huddled in the galley below the wheelhouse. Two men at a time roped themselves onto the two cots there to try to sleep. The captain and the dredge master weren't talking. One had got them into this mess, and the other was doing his darnedest to get them out.

Down in the hold, the engineer focused on keeping the engines pushing and beating. Without them, they were lost. The boy went there sometimes. There was less sway, and the nausea wasn't so bad down in the hold. But the boy couldn't sit still. He climbed to the wheelhouse often and stood there in his life jacket, holding tight. He watched the captain pilot the boat and thought he was going to die. Sometimes he stayed to keep the mate company, who manned the wheel when the captain couldn't take any more pounding and peering into the storm, and had to get some rest.

The pulsing, freezing water filled the inner parts of the dredge, and, pulled down by the weight, the dredge slowly settled lower and lower in the raging seas until it could take no more. It sank there, out in the big lake within a mile of the outer buoy at Hay River. The *Malta*'s cable to the dredge miraculously held fast and pulled tight. It was not going anywhere, anchored like that.

Quickly, a deckhand chopped at the death cable with an axe until it too snapped. The tug, released from that grip, struggled into the protection of the harbour.

The boy didn't die. His name is Gordon Gill.

INTRODUCTION

Granny Justine and Grampa Noel L'Hirondelle with grandson.

NOEL L'HIRONDELLE was Iroquois Cree, born in 1883 near Edmonton before there was an Alberta. In 1916, he moved his small family away from the Roman Catholic missions near Lac Ste. Anne to the deep northern bush. He and his wife Justine had already lost two of their children, and the stories of the fate of other Indigenous children in the hands of the government and the churches had spread amongst the people. For the "Native" people, the Canadian way was to take their children, by force, if necessary, to a residential school to take the "Indian out of the child." Noel was determined the church would not take his surviving children away from his family.

Noel was Gordon Gill's grandfather. The boy in the tugboat.

Long dead now, Noel and Justine are at the root of this story of an Iroquois Cree Irish English man who rose from lowly work as a cook's helper at fifteen, becoming a welder, a mechanic, a ship's engineer, and a businessman. In turns, Gill created a ship and barge repair company that he led in its evolution to the unique position of a northern shipbuilder, and then, in hard times, he courageously moved and transformed that company into a large, successful crane and heavy-haul operation working Alberta's oil sands.

Gordon's Iroquois great-great-grandparents came west before 1850 as part of the fur-trading voyageur life introduced to Rupert's Land, as the Canadian Northwest was known by the English before there was a country called Canada. Some of his ancestors came from the United States, like Justine's ancestor Thomas Gray. One, Pierre Alexis Marteau L'Hirondelle, who was born in 1825 at Lesser Slave Lake, north of Edmonton, was Gordon's great-great-grandfather on both sides of his family, being at once the father of Justine's mother and Noel's father's father. Thus, they were cousins.

This side of Gill's family was Indigenous, with perhaps some European blood introduced along the way. Gordon's mother's people were in the Lesser Slave Lake area of Alberta before 1820, and in Lac Ste. Anne before 1850, when the country had few white men, all of whom were almost entirely French or Scottish men engaged in the fur trade.

Perhaps it was some genetic history of moving, or perhaps it was the Iroquois' longer history with the white man that impelled Noel to leave the relatively comfortable and populous surrounds of the Indigenous community of Lac La Nonne and the nearby Roman Catholic mission at Lac St. Anne, west of Edmonton. Perhaps it was his distrust of the Catholic Church or some better sense of the future.

Whatever the reason, in 1916, Noel uprooted his family, moving hundreds of kilometres north by horse and wagon, rafting across the mighty

Peace River, and finally ending up north of present-day Manning, Alberta, on the corner of a small gathering of buildings called Notikewin. There, Noel established a trapline and homestead for his growing family. His destination was far removed from the parkland and prairie near Edmonton, and north even of the wide-open Peace Country, which later attracted so many homesteaders and freedom seekers to its bounty.

In doing so, Noel distanced himself, his wife, and their family from his parents and extended family, but he may well have saved his own family an ignominious fate.[2]

Notikewin was where their daughter Armand was born in April 1920. Armand L'Hirondelle is Gordon Gill's mother.

The L'Hirondelles spoke Cree.[3] It was Noel and Justine's language of birth and what their children spoke to them. While Justine did speak some accented English, Noel did not.

But speaking Cree was not the way to get along with the non-Indigenous neighbours, those settlers making their way north. Armande, who added the "e" to her name to appear more feminine and, likely, French, learned to speak English. For the rest of her life, she was reluctant to speak or act "Cree" or show she was "Indian" if non-Indigenous people were around. She kept some traditions, of course, especially while the family lived on the homestead, like moosehide moccasins and mitts, and preserving wild berries and meat. Armande spoke Cree to her parents; she knew the language well. However, she spoke only English in her own home with her white husband, Clarence, and half-white children. In later years, she dyed her hair a reddish colour.

Gordon believes his mother's approach was to wish away her "Nativeness," to transition the L'Hirondelle family from the old to the new, to raise her children, as much as she could, *to act white. The white man's way would*

....

2   While the Canadian government and the churches painted a nice picture of smiling "civilized" (well-dressed) Indigenous children getting a good education in residential schools, the reality was significantly, terribly different. Instead of being ripped from their home and culture, Noel's daughters and grandchildren were "weaned" from theirs. See, inter alia, *A National Crime*, referred to below.

3   Based on the listing of those who took Métis script in *Northwest Half-Breed Scrip—1885*, by Gail Morin, there were many L'Hirondelles who came from the Métis settlements at Red River (present-day Winnipeg area of Manitoba). The name is also spelled L'Hyrondelle. The names Joseph, Josephet, and Justine—like in Gordon's family—are scattered throughout that history.

make life easier and better. It was also the way out of the bush. This was necessary for the betterment of her children. That was where the future, and the money, was.

How much of this was due to Clarence's influence is unknown. Gordon does not recall any incident of anyone in the family being criticized for being "too Indian," or being told to act in a certain way.

Noel's trapline rose into the Chinchaga Hills in the Battle River[4] country of northwest Alberta. Rain and snow that fell on Noel's trapline divided into two watersheds. To the west and north, rivulets and streams create the north-flowing Hay River. In the south and east, all waters—including the Notikewin (formerly the First Battle River)—move to join what locals call the "Mighty Peace." These two drainage basins take semi-circular routes, west and east, then circle back to the north until they meet again in the body of the Great Slave Lake[5] in the NWT. From there, the Mackenzie River carries them to their new life in the Arctic Ocean.

Born near the trapline at Notikewin as a half-breed and the son and grandson of trappers, Gordon became a man of northern rivers and especially Canada's usually forgotten "near" north. The strength of those rivers flows through Gordon Gill's life and his spirit. Those rivers, their actions, and their effect made his life's work.

Battle River country was filled with not much more than bushland and rivers. It was a land of few people. That remains the case. The main town in the area is Manning,[6] which was only founded after the end of the Second World War and even now claims only 1,300 people. Most are engaged, directly or indirectly, in servicing the local forestry, oil and gas, and farming industries.

Dr. Mary Jackson, a medical pioneer who travelled to the Battle River district in 1929 (thirteen years after Noel and Justine), is quoted as saying, "There are great stretches of the district that were unbroken bush when I

4   Not to be confused with the Battle River in central Alberta. The northern Battle River was eventually renamed to avoid confusion with the more southerly Battle River.

5   Great Slave Lake is called Tinde'e by some elders. There is political pressure to rename the Slave River and Lake. *UpHere* Magazine. Sept/Oct 2020. https://www.uphere.ca/articles/big-lake

6   Manning was named after the long-serving Alberta Premier (1943–1968), Ernest C. Manning.

came in."[7] In 1933, Dr. Jackson wrote:

> At present practically the whole population north of the Battle River Prairie is breed, and Cree, Beaver and Slavee [sic] Indian right up to the NWT. They have been driven steadily northward during the last 50 years, and the movement is still going on.
>
> Several half-breeds at Notikewin have sold out in the last few weeks; they will move north to where the moose and deer and furs are still plentiful. They were not made for farming.[8]

If nothing else, the arrogance of the last comment, although likely not unusual at the time, seems stunning. Gordon always says Grandfather Noel was an excellent farmer. Perhaps culture, resiliency, family, training and pure economics had more to do with the number of Indigenous People who moved even farther north. In any event, the movement of the people did happen. The L'Hirondelles were one of the few Indigenous families in the Manning area after Gordon's birth in 1941.

Armande met and married Clarence Gill, who had moved north as a young man to escape the Great Depression ravishing Saskatchewan in the 1930s. Clarence was a loner. He left his Irish English family behind to their business and went looking for opportunity. For the rest of his life, he had little to do with them and, in fact, didn't return to Saskatchewan, even for a visit, until his parents and most of his siblings had passed on.

Clarence worked for Noel as a farmhand and trapper's helper. Eventually, he and Armande set up their own homestead and trapline. It was subsistence at best, but their way of life established the base from which their son—and Noel's grandson, Gordon—started his own adventure, working hard throughout his life, taking the next step and the one after that and the one after that as an entrepreneur and a careful but courageous risk-taker. Gordon travelled alongside and was a part of the many different eras of life in Canada's "near north". The birth and death of those eras are now largely forgotten.

This is a story of Gordon's life and times. We travel with him on his journey through the amazing changes in Canada's North and learn of his

7 Morris Zaslow, *The Northward Expansion of Canada, 1914–1967* (Toronto, ON: McClelland & Stewart, 1988), 37.

8 Zaslow, *Northward Expansion*, 151.

approach and adaptation to that world based on his Métis culture and mindset. It is, first and foremost, the tale of an industrious Indigenous man, and his family, moving on from a trapping lifestyle to join the "boom and bust" marine and mining industries in the NWT and later the height of oil-sands mining in Alberta.

This is an oral history and memoir based on interviews with Gordon Gill in 2021 and early 2022. Gordon's words, recollections, beliefs, and personal touch appear in italics. They are his voice. Those words are soft-spoken but clear, gentle, plain, and direct, just like the man.

SETTING

Clarence's trapline cabin with beaver pelts and stretchers.

CANADA IS A STUNNING COUNTRY, beautiful in a multitude of different ways throughout its regions, from sea to sea to shining, and sometimes ice-covered sea. Spanning the northern part of North America, this is a vast and largely uninhabited land. Much of Canada has barely been touched. Even now, if you look at a map upside down—that is, from the North Pole looking south—Canada's main cities and large towns hang from the American border like a chain of jewels dangling from a necklace. And aside from the prairie farmlands and the Far north (the Arctic Islands and the barren, treeless tundra lands of Canada, north and east of the treeline), the great expansive middle of this country constitutes what some have called the "near north".

This area, made up of boreal forests, meadows, rivers, rock, and myriad lakes, is almost beyond comprehension. Sometimes called Indian Country since it is mostly populated by Indigenous Peoples in various reserves and communities, except for the larger towns and cities of the hinterland, this is a land mostly unknown to Canadians... and the rest of the world. Some 70 percent of Indigenous communities in Canada are located in forested regions, of which 277 million hectares are boreal forest.

The boreal forest in the NWT covers much of its 1,144,000 square kilometres (442,000 square miles), leaving only the Arctic Islands and the northern tundra above the treeline. That part of Canada is largely forgotten except by those who have lived it, tasted its air and waters, and experienced its midnight sun, dark winters, and aurora borealis, the dancing northern lights.

In Canada's northwest lies the city of Edmonton, the capital of the province of Alberta. Canada's northernmost major city, Edmonton still lies less than halfway north of Alberta's southern boundary

North and west of Edmonton, the wide-open grain lands of Peace Country spread across into northern British Columbia and east along the Peace River. Even farther north and a bit west, pushed into the tree lands, is the small town of Manning. This is still, in many ways, the frontier. Farming, both grain and mixed, pushes north a bit each year, but much of the work comes from oil and gas and forestry. This story about the life and spirit of one Métis man is also, by necessity, the story of Canada's northern frontier.

Gordon Gill's story is so intertwined with the effect of mineral and petroleum exploration in the North, and the resulting rise and fall of the northern marine industry that it is impossible to separate them. In addition, the role of government, the often-hit-and-miss nature of northern development, and the vast distances and small population are crucial factors in any such history. In particular, for Gordon, the role of tugboats and barge traffic along the Mackenzie River system and the evolution of northern transport and supply in a rapidly modernizing society had an outsized impact. Inherent and embedded in this story are the choices and forces facing this Indigenous person, and certainly most Indigenous Peoples in northern Canada.

Peripherally, to explain the lack of Indian Reserves in this story—that is, land identified and set aside for those peoples defined as "Indians" under the Indian Act, Canada's legislation governing the relationship between the country and its Indigenous "Treaty" people—there is only one such Treaty in the NWT, although there is the Salt River cross-border reserve area near

Fort Smith, on the Alberta border. Gordon was not a part of the Hay River Dene, never lived on the reserve, and so, while it is nearby, it is not very relevant to this tale. And while Manning, Alberta, was, for example, part of Treaty 8 Territory, Gordon was not part of a Treaty family, as he explains later. The Gills did not live in an Indigenous settlement. For clarity, the Inuit of the Far north are not considered "Indians" and the rest of the NWT—that land north of the 60th degree of latitude between Yukon and Nunavut, where the majority of the people are First Nations, Inuit, or Métis—does not segregate land on that basis.[9]

....

9   The City of Yellowknife is the exception, with about 23 or 24 percent of its population
     identifying as Indigenous. However, Yellowknife, by itself is almost half the population
     of the entire Northwest Territories.

CHAPTER 1:
Traplines and
Moosemeat Sandwiches

Gordon on the Mackenzie Highway

We had it tough but so did a lot of people.

IT IS HARD to take in just how big Canada is. You would need a giant telescope zoomed into Alberta in the west, and then on the boreal forest lands of its northwest, just to find the town of Manning and the tiny hamlet of

Notikewan, 6.5 kilometres north. It, like many, was never much more than a store or two and a gas station, which barely exist anymore.

Here, in the unpopulated, treed expanse northwest of Peace River, Alberta, Gordon John Gill was born. It was a high-sun summer day in June 1941. He was the first and only son of Clarence John Gill and Armande Theresa L'Hirondelle.

Gordon's youthful photos show a healthy, cute kid with a direct look. He looks curious; sometimes, he scowls. As Gordon got older, he took on a darker colour, a heavy head of bushy black hair, and a sturdy build. He looked like a movie hero in some ways, dark and handsome, like Charles Bronson or Anthony Quinn (for older readers) or Colin Farrell and Antonio Banderas (for younger ones). As an adult, Gordon topped out at 5 feet, 10 inches tall. He is a big man, seeming taller than his height. And he is a gentle man.

Mildred, his younger sister by two years, followed, and the family, relatively small for those days and that place, lived on a homestead at Notikewan beside grandparents Noel and Justine L'Hirondelle for a few years.

These people of the land worked hard, developed their farm, and raised their family to be productive and hard-working. While many other farm families in Canada would have known the same types of conditions, here in the farthest reaches of prairie farmland, the L'Hirondelles and Gills and the rest of the families of Armande's siblings were starting out pretty much from scratch in an undeveloped area, away from markets and supports. They were poor, without proper equipment. City people at the time would have taken for granted running water, electricity, paved streets, milk delivery, movie shows, and cars.

Gordon remembers the house they lived in at Notikewin.

> I think I was only four when we left, maybe five years old. I can remember the first house was a one-room stick-built house. The other was a one-room log house. My dad wanted his own land, so, after the war, he bought some land that was opening up then with his VLA [Veterans Land Act][10] loan.

Campbell Ross confirms that. "At war's end, the Peace Country remained as the only major region in Canada still available for homestead

---

10   The author's clarifications to Gordon's oral history, and other quotes used, are indicated in square brackets, as seen here.

farming under the benefits available to veterans… Returning soldiers could obtain for free one half-section [320 acres] of Crown land apiece, with title granted after ten years".[11]

> *When we moved to the farm at Hotchkiss, Dad had skidded part of some building for the kitchen and living room and then added on a bedroom. It was probably 14 feet wide and maybe 32 feet long at the most; it was small, two small rooms. One side was the kitchen and living room and they had a pull-out bed in there for the chesterfield, but when you pulled it out, it came out just about right up against the table, so you can imagine how narrow that room was. And then we had the wood cook-stove on one side of the chesterfield and a wood stove on the other side of that chesterfield. Neither the porch nor the bedroom was heated.*
>
> *We could only put so much wood in the wood heater and it would only burn until 4:00 a.m. Back in those days, we would go to bed early because we did not have much to do, so we would be in bed by 10:00 p.m. Our water barrel would be frozen on top when we got up in the wintertime.*

Gordon's family was Indigenous. His L'Hirondelle grandparents spoke Cree. As Gordon explains: *Even though Noel's ancestry was really Iroquois voyageurs, they married Cree people and adopted their customs and languages.*

The Iroquois Cree grandfather spoke with his daughter in Cree; she spoke with her son in English. Grandson and grandfather literally couldn't and didn't speak the same language, but they were close and communicated well anyway.

> *He [Noel] made me a handsaw for cutting wood one time. He made the handsaw out of willow, with a curved willow branch. God, I wish I would have saved that. Honest to God, it was a work of art. Noel gave the saw to me one time for a Christmas gift, and did I ever put that saw to use.*

Gordon worked hard all his life. He liked work, and he got satisfaction from it. Probably, his parents and grandparents were good examples for

. . . .
11   Ross, *Teaching in Northern Alberta*, 59

him. He says they were honest and responsible people and of good character. Gordon's character emulates theirs; Gordon was always known as an
honest man, a person who did his best and who treated others as he would
want to be treated. And of his own childhood character, Gordon says,

> I think I was a fairly good child. My sister, Mildred, said I was a little
> mean because I would tickle her every once in a while, on the arm. But
> outside of that, I think I was good. In those days in the bush, we could
> not go anywhere and could not get into trouble. But I always worked
> hard to do my best and be helpful. It was just our way.

That way involved determination, pride in a job done well, and adaptability, all in the face of privation. It seems, from afar, to be a life composed
of parts of southern Canadian culture—seen in Clarence and the neighbours and adopted as much as practicable by Armande—and, on the other
hand, that heritage inherited from the L'Hirondelles and observed by the
close living arrangements and the practical needs of living by their wits and
resources in a land with more moose than stores.

Our ways were more the Métis ways. Gordon repeats this thought
often when thinking about his childhood. It was a rural life, not just an
Indigenous one.

> We had a rabid fox come into the yard when Dad was gone trapping. I
> ran out to get the dog in. The fox was biting at the horses, but the horses
> were kicking at the fox and thankfully did not get bit. So, then we were
> stuck in the house. Mom was a pretty brave lady, and she got herself a
> good stick and went out to feed the horses. We had not seen the fox for
> a couple hours. We did not know where the fox was, but we knew it had
> rabies because it was wandering around and trying to bite the horses.
> So, Mom went out and fed our two big work horses, Bill and Dixie, and
> the cow. We heard a couple days later the Landry family down on the
> Third Battle River,[12] about 2 miles from us, killed the fox, so we were
> happy about that.
>
> I trapped on my own on the farm. I had my own little trapline. As I
> got older, I would walk northwest of our home about 2 to 3 miles into
> the bush. I didn't go too often because there were no roads or nothing

12   The Third Battle River is now named the Meikle River.

out there, like no shelter. I was always a little scared of getting caught out there in a blizzard. I'd trap a few squirrels or weasels. I would then skin the squirrels and weasels, and because Dad had a trapline, I was able to sell them with his licence. To be legal, a trapper had to have a trapping licence and have his traplines registered with the government. It was kind of like a title to that area. You had to follow the regulations. I would get approximately $1.25 to $1.50 per hide for squirrels. I had a small pair of snowshoes that my grandpa made for me. I used them on my trapline at the farm. When I got to the age of eleven, my dad had a little bigger pair that worked for me.

I trapped enough squirrels to buy my hockey equipment, a Toronto Maple Leafs jersey, shoulder and knee pads, socks, pants and skates, all from trapping. But I couldn't use them because we lived on the farm. People that live in the towns could go to skating rinks after school, but I couldn't do that.

We were stuck in the bush. There was no way I could play hockey in town with the other kids, so one time, I built my own skating rink, 20-feet wide by 40-feet long. I melted snow to build it, just for a place to skate. That Maple Leafs uniform was a waste of money, but I wanted it so badly.

My dad had a big trapline. It had three cabins, and the main one was on Tear Drop Lake. That was not its official name. I don't know if it even had a name, but we called it Tear Drop Lake. The trapline took in the headwaters of the Chinchaga River in the Chinchaga Hills [which drains north to join the Hay River on its journey to Great Slave Lake]. The trapline also took in some of the headwaters of the Hotchkiss River area [which drains east to join the Notikewin, a tributary of the Peace] and one cabin was on the Third Battle [Meikle] River. My dad used to get thousands of squirrels on his trapline. Dad would also trap lynx, wolves, beaver, and weasels. I remember us getting $3.00 to $4.00 for weasel skins. Beaver skins were the best, worth $100 or more in those days. Dad was away on the trapline for months at a time. We had no way of hearing if he was okay.

Dad sold the furs he brought into the local stores in Notikewan or the one store in Hotchkiss. Some of the trappers actually mailed their furs to the fur auction in Winnipeg, but Dad always needed the money and didn't want to wait for the time it would take to sell at auction.

The biggest chore I had was hauling in wood, and that was my job for as long as I can remember. When I was small, Mother would always help of course, but as I got bigger, I wanted that job. Mother was a strong lady and during the winter while Dad was gone, she would feed and water the cow and horses. Mother did not want me getting hurt or anything.

To tell you the honest truth we had good neighbours, and it was good to see our neighbours. Whileen Yost, she would invite us over and have chocolate cake. To the north of us, Connie Kosiorek, to the east of us was Fritz Reiner and his wife, and they had an adopted son named Gayle Vandemark, and also Jim Ryan and his family. To the south was the Pridys, a wonderful family. We were surrounded by nice people. But they had cars, or trucks, farm equipment, stuff like that, and we didn't. We were the poorest people around, and that made me want to get out of Hotchkiss. I didn't see any future there; it was a dead end. So, I took the chance to leave when I could.

Everyone lived approximately a mile away in each direction. So, we did not visit that often. I enjoyed berry picking and it was important for making jams and jellies and such. We would sometimes go in a wagon pulled by horses, and later, after Dad got an old Ford Model A for a couple years, we got to go in the car. It was old by then; I don't remember the year, but it had a canvas top, and you could see your reflection in the door when it was clean. Dad had no insurance on it or anything, so we never took it into Manning. Up in Hotchkiss, well, nobody bothered patrolling the road in those days.

One time a man with a horse came into the yard with two bodies lying over the horse's back, and we put the bodies in a little mechanic's log shed. What happened is they were trappers on the other side of my dad's trapline; they were further out than my dad. For some reason, these guys did not come in to get their supplies for the beaver hunt. So, *this got people wondering why they did not come in. Some people got the police, you know, the RCMP* [Royal Canadian Mounted Police] *involved and the police went out to check on them, and they found that they both had died. So, the police borrowed my dad's packhorse, and they took the horse out there to bring the bodies back. The bodies had deteriorated quite a bit. They were carried in canvas bags.*

We only had nearby relatives on my mom's side. Our cousins Joyce Hodgson and Jenny Sharp would sometimes come to stay with us. They'd get off the school truck with Mildred and me on a Friday and go back with us on Monday. Our male cousins never came because they were older. Joyce and I were close. When Jenny would come, she would play with my sister Mildred. One time Jenny came out because Mildred begged her; it was some holiday, Easter or something. Jenny's dad had to borrow the truck and pick her up, and he was mad. I think it was probably Mildred's fault she got in so much trouble.

We mostly ate meat and potatoes. Most of the meat we ate was moose. Mother canned [preserving by boiling and sealing in glass jars] *a lot of moose, as we had no way of keeping fresh meat. Only in the wintertime were we able to keep it frozen outside. We also ate a type of grouse we called prairie chickens, which were quite abundant in the bush. We did eat rabbit at times but not that much. Oh, I shouldn't say no—we did eat rabbit in the earlier days. We did actually eat a lot of rabbits; Granny also ate rabbit. Granny and those people in Notikewin did eat a lot of rabbit. We didn't eat any bear meat, and although my dad was a trapper, we never ate very much fresh moose meat. Keeping the meat was the big problem in those days. Because we never had electricity or a fridge or anything. We kept our food in the cellar under the house. For a couple of years, we did use ice to keep the food. We had an icehouse with ice in it. Not even an icebox, you know what I mean?*

Because we were stuck on the farm, we had no means of transportation, and there was nothing happening in those times. They probably had their little clubs going in Manning, but we were on the farm. I think it was more social at that time [even though] *social events were few and far between. Mostly social events were people visiting back and forth.*

One problem was that there was only a little creek at Notikewin. It would go dry in the summer, so there was a lack of water, and people started moving to Manning. I think they started moving buildings from Notikewin to Manning around 1943. I know there was no Manning when I was born.

We had a radio, but it always seemed to have a dead battery, so we used it very little, and when we did listen to it, it was always to listen to country music. We always used the radio in the wintertime. We never used it in the summertime because there were always things to do. And in the wintertime, we saved the battery so we could listen to western music on the Calgary station, and we'd sit there huddled around this little radio and the battery was always on the verge of stopping. They were always dry-cell batteries, so once they were dead, they were never good anymore. So, we never had the radio very much. And no TV whatsoever; never even heard of it back then. On the farm we had no electricity, no running water. Only washroom was a washbasin on a stand and an outhouse.

I played the guitar, and my mother played the guitar and the banjo— oh, and the mouth organ. She could make that mouth organ sing; it was so lovely. I used to put my head against the guitar when she was playing. I recall the sound being so much better. It was so comforting. I was learning to play the guitar a bit. When I was small, I could chord and sing a little bit, stuff like that. I spent a lot of time fiddling around like that. Mother played music but she couldn't read music; it was hard to really learn much except she learned some chords and she could sing pretty good. Dad never sang or played any music or instruments. I learned chords from Mother, and at one time I could play fairly well. And about the time I was starting to get a little bit good at it [when we were in Hay River], they started to bring out tape recorders.

We never had electricity until we moved to Hay River, and we never had running water either.

To live, we had to grow a garden and Mildred and I, as kids, we had to pick weeds. Also do a little planting and dropping in a little potato behind the shovel. In the fall of the year, we would all get together and pick berries. Mother would can the berries and our moose meat, you know, boil it up and preserve it in jars for the winter. One of our biggest jobs as kids was to gather wood for the woodstove. I also cut a lot of wood. My dad cut and piled mountains of firewood to last us through those cold winters. We had no furnace, just the wood stove and a little wood heater.

Granny was the real seamstress; she would make pants and stuff for us and different clothes. Or else Granny would downsize clothes from old clothes and make them smaller into something that would fit me. Granny was really good at that. Between Mother and Granny, they made a lot of our winter clothes. Same with our winter coats. Sometimes we would order through Eaton's or Sears catalogues some of our winter clothes. But you were never sure of what size you were going to get when you ordered through the catalogues or if it would fit when it arrived. Sometimes it would take a couple of months before you got your order from Sears or Eaton's.

We had to walk a little over a quarter of a mile to get to our bus stop. Our shoes and boots were ordered through Sears or Eaton's at the time. A lot of the times we wore moccasins. Winter school days would see us wear moccasins and rubber covers. Sometimes we used to put on Dad's wool socks and go out in the snow in those. In them days they had some pretty good heavy wool socks.

Gordon was taught to knit, although neither he nor Mildred were taught other "Native" crafts, or anything in the way of Indigenous decorations, like beadwork, or working hides, even though his Granny and his mother did that kind of thing.

Granny Justine was accomplished in the arts of working hides and decorative beadwork and Armande too. That work was an important source of cash, and they did a lot of it. However, after the family moved to Hotchkiss and saw less of Granny, Armande stopped tanning hides. It was not a skill taught to Mildred or Gordon. Maybe it was too "Indian," or maybe Clarence didn't bring home moose skins from the trapline, or maybe, as Gordon says: *Tanning moosehides was a terrible amount of work. They were so heavy. It was so hard.*

The neighbours would pick Mom up to go shopping at the general store. That was who bought her eggs and homemade butter and things like that.

We always had a few tame chickens. Mother would sell eggs at the Hotchkiss Store and be getting so much a dozen, and I can remember Mother would say we need one or two more eggs to make another dozen. So, I'd be running to the chicken coop, and we could hear Ray and Whileen Yost coming from a long way away, and we would be sitting in the chicken coop waiting for them to lay just one or two more eggs to make a dozen. We would be thinking, one more egg, one more egg, *and the chicken would let us down. This happened so many times trying to complete a dozen eggs. Selling eggs gave Mother enough money to buy a can of Klick or Spork or something extra, like chocolate bars for Mildred and me. She would eat hers all at once, but I always saved mine by eating just one square a day. It was Cadbury's with the squares that we loved the most.*

Gordon smiles at his little joke about eating "one square" a day. Others would see a surprisingly developed self-discipline for such a youngster.

Money was scarce. Gordon isn't the great Métis hunter you might think of. You'll see that on his moose hunting trips as an adult. But even as a child, Gordon was quite gentle—as he still presents to this day.

One bad thing that I remember is I always used to make bow and arrows; I could make some pretty good bows out of willow, and I'd carve them down and make good arrows from the willows too. Then just for the hell of it, in the spring, there would be some really nice colourful birds that would come in our yard. There would be some oriole birds, very colourful, and for some reason, the birds were very far away and would not come close, so I aimed at one and be damned if the arrow didn't go right through the bird. The prettiest bird, maybe a yellow warbler or something. Geez I felt bad about it and still feel bad about it. That's seventy years ago. So, I felt so bad I went and got a shovel and gave it a little burial.

Trapping squirrels was different. I did not feel so bad because it meant money. My mom and dad let me use the rabbit .22 rifle and geez I was young, but they really schooled me on how to use that .22 rifle. I used it to kill prairie chickens. We had many meals from prairie chickens.

Gordon often thinks about how hard his mother worked. She was stuck on the farm and isolated and her husband was out on the trapline. Early on, she would be able to visit her parents, Noel and Justine, but after Clarence and Armande moved to Hotchkiss, about 20 kilometres away, that would be much rarer. Gordon and Mildred would be at school. They had no car and neither did Noel. She was often alone. And as Gordon has said, they had no running water and not much of a well.

My dad had a wooden box that could hold water and it was watertight. It was made special for hauling water, so we put that on the wagon. He'd either haul water with the horses from the Third Battle River, which was three miles away, down the hill, or sometimes he'd get water from the neighbours, they were a mile and a half away. Every once in a while, he'd go to the river because there was really nice clear water. There were also dugouts to get water at from some other neighbours' places. We were welcome to get water there. We had a well, but it was mainly slough water. The water you got from the neighbours mainly was to go in our well so the well wouldn't go dry, and we would have water for the horses. We used a lot of rainwater for drinking.

Our house in Hotchkiss was just bare walls, no real insulation. The insulation that was in there was shavings from the sawmill and what happens with shavings is you fill it up to the top of the wall, and once the shavings sit there for a while, they settle right down, and you lose a lot of the insulating factor. The bedroom had a very heavy paper on the walls holding the shavings in. The walls and ceiling were never finished. The kitchen was finished with painted rough one-by-fours. The heavy wallpaper in the bedroom was painted as well.

We just had at times three horses, one cow, chickens, a dog and cat and five of Dad's sleigh dogs, and in the end, I found out I was allergic to them. For months on end it seemed like, in the wintertime, every winter, my eyes would puff right up. My eyes were almost even with my face, my throat felt like somebody was always choking me; this went on for a few years. And then, we eventually found out that it was probably an allergy to fur, and then we found out it was probably my dad's lynx robe he made me. He gave me a lynx robe so I would be nice and warm in the wintertime, a cozy nice lynx robe, and that's what I had over top of me when I slept, and that's what made me so sick and we didn't realize it. And then, to top it all off, playing with the cats and the dogs, I was allergic to them also. It was just one thing after the other.

We never got around. We just had a little tractor we could use a little bit, but if we went visiting, we would walk there and walk back. A number of times, we came home in the dark from Whileen's place, and it was just Mother, Mildred, and I, and we never had a flashlight or anything. Every tree looked like a bear. We would always say, "We'll never stay that late again," but sure enough, it would always happen again.

Mother did the cooking on the woodstove when we lived on the farm. She worked so hard. The woodstove had the surface to cook on, but also the oven. She did a lot of baking at times, also. Our woodstove had a hot-water tank—a reservoir on the side which kept water warm. The reservoir would hold about three gallons of water, which never boiled; it was just always nice and warm. Mother would heat the water on the stove and use some of the reservoir water for our baths in a galvanized tub. It was always nice to be the first one in the water because the water was never changed until everyone was bathed. Usually, it was just Mildred and I, and most of the time Mildred would bath first, and I would bath second. Outside, we had a ring of rocks for outside fires, but it wasn't for cooking. There might have been a little bit of cooking over the fire in the summertime when it was too hot to cook inside, but mainly it was done on the inside woodstove.

I have to laugh because the other day, I was talking to Mildred, and we were reminiscing. It seemed like from the age of seven to fifteen, half of our time was spent feeling cheap. [Laughing.[13]] Well, we were the poorest people around; we never had the best things to wear. Granny did most of our clothes; shoes and stuff like that were mainly hand-me-downs from Joyce and Clarence, and Granny made the pants smaller and made them fit.

---

13   *Cheap* probably is the word for poor. Each time Gordon uses that word, he does a kind of nervous laugh.

I can remember when we were kids, homemade swords were a big thing, and I would take homemade wooden swords and all kinds of stuff to school. There were even kids taking BB guns, and they'd get us younger kids to line up in a row and bend over. Then they would shoot us in the butts. Could you imagine today? That sure wouldn't be happening.

And another time I remember feeling so cheap there was going to be a little movie at the Town Hall in Notikewin and it cost us $0.25 to get in and we never had $0.25. But Mother had $0.25 of stamps so she wanted me to go to the post office and give these stamps to the lady and the lady would give me $0.25 so I could go to that show. I felt too cheap to do that so when the kids went to go into the show, I went to the outhouse. So, when the kids all left for the Hall, I said I had to go to the washroom but what I did was I went and hid in the caragana bushes out on the perimeter. So, I sat in there, in the caraganas, until the movie was over because I felt too cheap to change my stamps in for $0.25.

So that's what I mean about being poor. Mildred and I knew about that. These were the best memories to remember, I guess. There were no real best memories that I can remember. I guess when we'd go visit the neighbours. That was always kind of a nice memory.

And our family. The only cousins I knew were on my mother's side. I knew all of them. Aunt Adaline's kids were Joyce Hodgson, Robert, Charlie, Clarence and Lena. Granny basically raised Robert, Charlie, Clarence, and Joyce. Lena was adopted by someone around Slave Lake. After Adaline's husband Henry was killed, in the war, times were really tough for Aunt Adaline. She didn't have a farm or anything and hardly even a house. Adaline went on to have more kids after, almost another family, but mostly she was on her own.

Another child she had was adopted out, that was Kenny LaFoie. That was pretty common in them days, adopting kids out to other families. I didn't really know Kenny or Lena. Adaline had other kids also. One of them was my cousin, Joe Gagnier. Lionel Gagnier was his father and Adaline lived with Lionel for a while. Joe was raised by my granny until the age of six and then he went to Hay River and lived with his dad

Lionel and his stepmother, Christine. He still lives in Hay River.

My mother's sister Florence Sharp had Jenny, Lloyd, Ronnie, Emily, and Lynda. Although these cousins were younger and when you're young like that a few years makes a big difference. I knew them and seen them all the time, but they had their own friends.

I did meet one cousin on my dad's side, Warren Gill, and his dad, Dave Gill, one of my dad's brothers. I only met him once with a two-hour visit; that was it. I met him in Vermillion. I was about twenty-two years old. My dad's brother, my uncle Bill, and his wife lived in Edmonton and arranged the visit when I was down south for school, and we went to Vermillion and had supper with him.

That was all I ever saw of the white side of the family.

Although born to a Caucasian father and an Indigenous mother, culturally Gordon and his sister felt akin to their Native family.

Gill is obviously an English name. Thinking historically and socially, at least if your family wanted to assimilate, and felt that it was better to be "whiter," it was likely a good name to have. In fact, what difference having that name made in Gordon's life, rather than being a L'Hirondelle, a Delorme, a Bourassa, or a Bertrand, is an open question. The same applies to his first job on the tugboats, which his father secured for Gordon, sight unseen. Would there have been different considerations if someone other than a man named Clarence Gill had sought it out?

The Gill name may well have blanketed Gordon's Indigenous background somewhat and reduced the level of discrimination he and Mildred would have faced. His wasn't one of the French-Canadian names of his ancestors, mentioned above, or the older names in the family tree often associated—at least in the minds of many Albertans—with Indigenous or mixed-blood people, names like Calliou or Calihoo, Cardinal, Gladue, and Chartrand.

So, he was a Gill. But there was nary a Gill to be found, other than Clarence, the outsider, anywhere in the area. There were no grandparents, uncles, aunts, cousins, or other Gill relatives. They were all back in Saskatchewan. Thus, until they moved to Hay River, Gordon and his family were embedded with their mom's Indigenous family, the L'Hirondelles and Grays, and their descendants and husbands, who were Indigenous or Métis.

Gordon thinks about the past when prodded. *There is probably lots of good memories like getting picked up by Uncle Les at Christmas time. He would drive us down to Notikewin to Granny's place. We'd get together with all the cousins. We sure appreciated him coming.*

But once I got to Hay River, life totally changed for me. For one thing, we lived in a town.

However, no matter what they faced, Gordon and Mildred and Armande, Florence and the others were not part of "the scandalous procession of Indian children to residential school and on to the cemetery.."[14]

They had nourishing food and fresh air. They were not crammed into unventilated, crowded, dirty, and poorly drained, sited, and built residential schools full of tuberculosis and death. Fifty percent or more of children died in the schools, and many of the rest were demoralized by the educational and "civilizing" goals the school system.[15]

Much has been said and published about the reality of residential schools. Indigenous Peoples have suffered death in these schools or as a result of things like tuberculosis. The lives of "survivors" have often been filled with mental illness, addiction, and demoralization. An inability to adapt to life either as an Indigenous or a white person has left far too many people in jail, homeless, or on the streets. The loss of culture and language and pride is an issue that Canada is only just now trying to deal with. Somehow, the Gill home, the influence of the L'Hirondelle relatives, and the education given to Gordon and Mildred at home helped them meet the world and succeed in it. How much of that is due to nature, to location—not on a reservation and not in or near a city—to whom they married, or just simple upbringing is impossible to know. But it seems that the education at home prepared both Gordon and Mildred to meet the world and succeed in it.

What rings true for someone who has not experienced such a family life is that while the Gills were poor in terms of material wealth, they were quite rich in terms of other things—family, humour, adaptability, and perseverance.

....

14   John Milloy, *A National Crime: The Canadian Government and the Residential School System* (Winnipeg, MB: University of Manitoba Press, 1999), 102.

15   Milloy, "Chapter 5: 'The Charge of Manslaughter': Disease and Death, 1879 to 1946," *National Crime.*

Our culture and traditions were different, and we went the Métis ways. For one thing, in that whole area where we lived, we were probably the poorest people. Back in them days, we didn't feel like we were the only poor people around; there were a lot of poor people and kids, more in the Notikewin area. We had a small two-room house. One cow, but again then my dad was a trapper first. We could not have looked after a whole herd of cattle. We had chickens. Our neighbours had battery-type lights, but we never had anything like that. We had nothing, never even a battery. We were always happy, but it was just we never had much. We were happy with very little. We were just trained that way, I guess. My dad sometimes would sit down at the dinner table, put his hands together and say, "Well, for supper we're having rabbit-track soup, wind pudding, and imaginary pie—all you can eat." That was always good for a laugh, but it was kind of a lesson too.

Along with my sister, Mildred, I went to school in Notikewin until grade six, then attended the Paul Rowe School in Manning for grades seven and eight. Paul Rowe was the principal of the public school. Luckily, we had English names; hers was Mildred June Gill.

Our first school bus was a truck with a low rectangular wooden box with a roof and little windows up toward the roof and rows of wooden benches. It had no heater. We walked about a quarter of a mile to where we got picked up, then we climbed in the back and went along picking other kids up too.

Oh God, and our neighbour May Pridy, she made us little cushions to sit on, nice furry cushions, kind of, and a little handle on it so you could carry them around. We felt so cheap to use them because none of the other kids had them other than the Pridys and sometimes we'd hide them in our coat. But it wasn't just me, it was the Pridy's kids too. We all felt cheap. We all laughed about it because we got on the bus first because we were the farthest away, and then they were the second group to get on; their mother was just trying to be nice, but it made us feel cheap because none of the other kids had them.

They were poor, and they were "half-breeds," and Armande was an "Indian." They felt embarrassed and different and likely insecure. It was an awkward time. Gordon talks of the moose meat his dad brought back from the trapline and how Armande would pack school lunches for Mildred and him. There would sometimes be sandwiches made with homemade berry jam, but often they were moose meat.

He and Mildred would hide the sandwiches, holding them out of sight, so the other kids wouldn't know it was moose meat. The local farm kids always knew what was going on. Gordon laughs now. *They always wanted to trade so we were happy; we got pork or beef or maybe chicken sandwiches. They got the moose meat, which they seemed to like. Or maybe it was just the adventure of it. But it seemed to work even if we were a bit embarrassed to not have chicken or pork or whatever it was that the white kids had.*

Gordon is stoic, focused and forgiving. In all this time together, he has uttered no complaint. He does talk of embarrassment, and feeling poor, and of kidding between the 'Indians' and the others, but ends this part of the interview with:

> *It was a different time. The people were nice. I can remember the water barrel at school only had one dipper for everybody to drink out of. No one complained or made any bad comments about us being Indians or half-breeds.*

CHAPTER 2:
The Welder's Spark

International diesel bulldozer

I remember I was five or six and my dad had a guy clearing some land with an old rickety Caterpillar tractor.

IT WAS ALWAYS BREAKING DOWN. *The driver would always be getting down off the Cat and fixing it, and he would do welding and sharpen the blade. I remember I saw the bright welding lights from the house maybe half a mile away. I was so interested in that and so amazed and so that is when I decided I wanted to be a mechanic and a welder.*

However, the path to these trades was not clear, or easy.

One year my dad had got some land cleared and the wood was piled in rows and then we would set it on fire. After the burn-down, we would start throwing the sticks into the hot coals. Somehow, we ended up with the bucket of drinking water on the other side of the brush pile. So, my dad asked me to go around the brush pile and get the water bucket. But on my way down the brush pile, I thought I seen some dirt in the middle, and I thought to myself I could jump to the middle and then jump again and be on the other side.

Well, what happened was when I jumped to the middle onto what I thought was dirt, it just disintegrated, and underneath was total red-hot coals. I had gumboots [high topped rubber boots] *on, and they were folded down. If my boots wouldn't have been folded down and went up high, I might not have been burnt so bad. My one foot that landed in the middle went into the coals, and my boot filled up with red-hot coals. It all happened so fast; I was able to kick the boot off, but the coals had already burnt into my foot all the way around my ankle. That was tough. I suffered with that for a long time and in them days we could only put on gauze and keep it as clean as we could. Mother would put iodine on it and maybe some Vaseline.*

About a mile and a half from us lived some friends of ours; the lady had been a nurse in the army and my dad had been in the army with her husband Jack. So, we knew them pretty well and she would come and clean my foot every two or three days. Their last name was Wilson, Jack and Edna. They had a son, Robert. So, Edna would come every two or three days, whatever it took to clean my sores and clean off any dead meat that was around the burn. It was raw all the way around. I can still see the deep scars all around my ankle and I'm eighty years old, so it was a pretty bad burn.

I think this happened in the fall of the year, so that whole year was pretty much a waste. I couldn't think straight. I couldn't do nothing. I was in so much agony all the time. I think I was in grade four, approximately ten years old. I missed probably the best of two months of school and when I was in school, I was always in so much pain I couldn't think straight so I pretty much lost the whole school year. I had no shoes to wear because of the bandages on my foot. So, the only shoes that would fit were my dad's army boots and I'm in grade four and I had to wear those big army boots, so every day I felt cheap. [Laughs].

I ended up failing grade four. I could have probably caught up later, but the one thing with me to begin with, I never had much interest in school. My interest from the time I can remember I always wanted to be a mechanic and a welder. Grade school to me was just a waste of time. I already knew I wanted to be a mechanic and a welder. I kind of thought I could just go straight there.

He didn't like school and didn't do well. He was in the middle, hearing but not speaking his mother's and his grandparents' language, but knowing he was not like the other kids either. Change was coming. What would he do? What becomes of kids in the bush who don't know where they belong?

I can't remember what my parents wanted for me; they didn't push me one iota toward education. They knew I wanted to be a mechanic and welder, but they probably always wondered about me because I sure didn't have much interest in school. They probably wondered what I would turn out like. I kept them guessing. Thank goodness they got me out of Hotchkiss; there was just nothing in the area for a young person.

Gordon learned early how to work hard. It was necessary, but he had good examples in his parents and his grandparents; he liked it too.

I used to help around the farm cutting wood with a handsaw that my grandpa made for me. That's one thing I did for entertainment. I cut a lot of wood and as I got bigger that saw became a little too small, so I had to use the saws that were at the farm. My ambitions were always to do with work. Cutting wood and, when I got bigger, I had to clean the barn and a lot of snow shoveling in the wintertime because we never had anything to clear the snow out to the road, so I always had to shovel the snow out to the road; sometimes that was a three-day job done in bits and pieces. The driveway was approximately 600 feet long. If we ever had company coming, one path would be shoveled to the road, and then I would shovel another track for the visitor's vehicle to park. I was always busy.

You know, I never had too many jobs in my life. When I was fourteen, I ended up working for a farmer that had land close to us. His name was Norman Fillio, a bachelor. He was getting up in age and needed help. At the age of fourteen, I drove his tractor lots. Early in the spring of 1956, I was helping him with spring work but when school let out, toward the end of June, and I turned fifteen years old, that is when I went to Hay River. That's when I finished working with him. I really felt bad for Norman. At that time, he was paying me $1.25 an hour [about $13.00 an hour now]. *In those days that was good money.*

Gordon decided at a young age that he wanted to be a tradesman, a mechanic and welder. He kept that idea in his mind, focused on it, and accomplished it. He knew that he had to get his grade ten to go to trade school.

Even with his problems reading, and being a *slow learner* (his words), and suffering two separate serious personal injuries, which interfered with his schooling, Gordon succeeded. Though badly burnt as a youngster, and badly injured in a car wreck while in Yellowknife, Gordon reached those goals he set for himself at such a young age.

Luckily, he was pretty good at math and designing things, and despite having to go away to school, first to Yellowknife and then south to Edmonton and Calgary, Gordon Gill's determination held strong. He succeeded.

Gordon: *I did excellent in my trade classes.*

He became a mechanic and a welder. And from that, he built a small one-truck welding business, operated from a loaned garage, into the first Métis shipbuilder in the NWT and maybe all of Canada. In later chapters, we see how Gordon combined hard work, determination, courage, entrepreneurial spirit, good luck, and his cultural background to succeed in a business dominated by large, politically connected, wealthy, and often international companies. Moreover, he did it twice in two separate, highly competitive industries.

CHAPTER 3:
Home for Christmas

Gordon in his Leafs uniform

For entertainment, our cats and dogs played a big part in our daily lives. My mother would play the guitar and sing. And I would work on the woodpile or shoveling snow.

IF WE HAD A GOOD CARDBOARD BOX, *that was always good to play with. Once the cardboard box broke apart, we'd use it for sliding on or doing some little thing or where we could find a bump, we would be sliding on that piece of cardboard.*

That was our entertainment.

I always wanted a bike. My cousin Clarence ended up giving me his bike when he left home. It was so good to have that, even though I got it only a couple of years before I went to Hay River and started to work. I never had a summer off after I turned fifteen.

Being cooped up in a tiny two-room house was not a lot of fun. We mainly used a coal oil lamp for our main lighting, and a gas lamp was a lot brighter but was only used when Dad came home. Summers were a lot more fun, especially with the long days in the North Country. The sun would come up early, like 4 a.m. or so and set really late, close to midnight, so we had lots of time outdoors.

One good thing about winter was Christmas.

My uncle Les Sharp, for as many Christmases that I can remember, he always arranged to come out with somebody's vehicle. Mainly the merchant in town had a truck for hauling grain and stuff. Les always managed to borrow the truck and get us for Christmas Eve. We would stay overnight or two nights sometimes. We would all stay at my granny's and all pile into what seemed at the time to be a big house but was actually small compared to today's standards and I don't know how we all fit in there. I cannot figure out how we all slept there. But we did. It was always a fun time. It was especially when you got to know your family and to be close to them and understand them better.

My dad came also, but there were a couple of years when Dad did not come home for Christmas. We went anyway, but we would worry about what might have happened to him. Why didn't he get there? That was worrisome. Les would still come and get us and would bring us back home. Then after New Year's, sometimes Dad would show up. I forget what the reasons were, but it must have been good trapping, or something was going good out there in the bush, and that is where he stayed, you know.

I remember Granny had a big table and counter and it would always be filled with grub. Everyone would fill their plate and go find somewhere to sit because it wasn't just us there; my mom's sister, my Aunt Florence Sharp and her family would be there too, eh. Sometimes other people also from Notikewin. So, the house would always be jam-packed full. We always had lots to eat, that was one good thing about having the farm and the trapline and picking berries and the gardens Mom and Granny had.

I can remember one Christmas, Lionel Gagnier, my cousin Joe's dad, he came and joined everybody, and he brought half a pig along with the turkey. With the amount of people and all the eating, the stove was going almost around the clock. Lionel had to go buy a second half a pig. For a lot of us eating the fried pork, this was the best thing ever. Lionel was my mom's sister Adaline's partner for a while. He was so strong, and such a hard worker, and he always had money. It was like a big explosion when he came into the house, with all that food and his big personality. He was French-Canadian from Montreal, I think, and did very well for himself in the Hay River country. He was involved in everything, construction, and dirt work, heavy equipment, loading airplanes, driving piles, all kinds of things.

While Gordon might not have known exactly what he was looking for, he knew Lionel was a great example of it.

Lionel, on top of the half of a pig, brought boxes of frozen fish from Hay River, which was a real treat too. Lionel's son Joe now brings fish to the family reunions and seems to be carrying on with the tradition.

Christmas get-togethers were our family times. It's only in the last fifteen years that we have had family reunions. In a way it is sad because at each reunion there are always people missing who have passed away. If we would have had one in 2020, there would have been two less—my wife Treena and my cousin Lloyd Sharpe both passed away.

CHAPTER 4:
Clarence: The Only
One Out of Step

Clarence at his wood pile

Dad never really was able to work for anyone. He was a
loner and independent and he could be a bit of a hothead.

> DAD QUIT SCHOOL *because the teacher tapped him on the head with a pencil and told him he could do better. "And I will," Clarence said, then got up and left for good. In the old days, if you weren't going to go to school, you had to get out of the house and make your own living. Plus, there were three younger brothers to help his dad in his dray* [transport] *business.*

Gordon's father, Clarence Gill, was in his twenties when he took to the bush country of northwest Alberta in the early 1930s. There were barely roads, but the land was open to trappers and homesteaders. Of Irish and English roots, Clarence grew up in the town of Watrous, Saskatchewan, south of Saskatoon. His father ran a hauling business, but there was not enough work for him as an older brother. He and one brother tried homesteading farther north in Saskatchewan—up near Prince Albert, as Gordon recalls. That was pretty temporary, and after a year or so, Clarence left the province and the family he knew and moved about as far north into the Alberta boreal forests as he could reasonably get.

Clarence's stated intention of farming in Peace Country evolved into a life more focused on his trapline. There was nothing for him, nor many other young men from the southern prairies, in those deep days of the Depression. Especially in dust-bowl Saskatchewan. In Clarence's case, that translated into a life on a small homestead, living off the land, running a trapline and adopting many of the ways of the bush Cree of northern Alberta.

> *Dad came from Watrous, Saskatchewan, to Notikewin, Alberta, with the Hart family and acquired himself a quarter section of land at Hotchkiss, and then his first trapline, which was located west and about 25 miles north of Hotchkiss. Clarence's trapline was next to Noel L'Hirondelle's trapline.*

The three Battle Rivers (*First, Second, and Third*, as Gordon calls them) take their name from the Cree invaders' attack on the local Beaver Indians. The three Battle Rivers now show on maps as the Notikewin, the Hotchkiss, and the Meikle. The hamlet Notikewin comes from a variation of the Cree word, *nôtinikewin* (ᓄᑎᓂᑫᐎᐣ),[16] the "River of the Battle."

....

16   Wikipedia, s.v. "Notikewin River," last edited May 13, 2020 at 03:56 UTC, https://en.wikipedia.org/wiki/Notikewin_River

The three Battle Rivers drain into the Peace River, one of the continent's major and longest-reaching waterways. It was up the Peace River, well into northern British Columbia, that Scottish fur trader and explorer Alexander Mackenzie travelled in his successful but harrowing overland quest to find the Pacific Ocean in 1789.[17] This was a full fifteen years before the much-fabled Lewis and Clark overland expedition reached the Oregon coast for the American government. Even earlier, Mackenzie had reached the Arctic Ocean on the river that bears his name, although its definite northward swing and the end of the route in the Arctic Sea led to its first (European given) name, the River of Disappointment. The Dene People called it the Big River, *Deh-Cho* in South Slavey, and *Deho* in North Slavey.

It was near the First Battle River that Clarence filed for his first homestead.

Gordon was born and lived most of his life between the Peace and the Mackenzie Rivers, the two big rivers of the northwest, both explored from start to finish by Mackenzie. Family lore has it that one of the Calihoo ancestors was a guide or crewman for Mackenzie. In due course, Gordon too lived and played beside various sources for the Mackenzie River and started his business life as a working boatman on the great river itself. Later, his skill as a mechanic translated into a job taking care of tugboat engines, and even later, his welding prowess turned into ship and barge repair, and then shipbuilding for the work on the Mackenzie and the Arctic Ocean beyond. The scent and sense of rivers and their proximity stayed with Gordon all his working life.

The first Battle River Trail was cut into the north Peace area around 1914. In the late 1930s, a winter ice and frozen muskeg road led from there to the Yellowknife goldfields via Hay River for use by "Cat-trains" or, more properly, tractor-pulled trains of heavily laden sleds, often with a caboose at the back. The reference to Cat-trains comes from the extensive use of the powerful tracked vehicles made by the Caterpillar Tractor Company.

The road to Hay River was finished—depending on your definition of finished—somewhere between 1948 and 1950 and paved only in fairly recent years. It is this trail that Clarence used to get to his homestead and trapline, and that both Clarence and Gordon followed years later to Hay

17   Barry Gough, *First Across the Continent: Sir Alexander Mackenzie* (Norman, OK: University of Oklahoma Press, 1997).

River to start their new lives. Called the Mackenzie Highway, it is still the only all-weather road north from the prairie provinces to Canada's northern territories.[18] The trail and the rivers were the only routes in and out of the country, and the source of communication, food, and often employment in a county where nothing came easy.

> *Clarence worked on Noel's farm in the summer, and this is how he met Armande. Dad and Noel did have a little issue—Noel spoke very little English. Dad also worked for Joe Rousseau, the local merchant and fur buyer. He drove truck for him. He had no family in the area and was on his own.*
>
> *Dad began living partly like a Native. We* [Clarence's family] *never had any contact with my dad's family, the "white" side. My dad wouldn't say anything, but I think he felt rejected by his family because a lot of the white folks in Saskatchewan were not receptive to Natives.*
>
> *However, Dad's sister Mildred would send presents from Saskatchewan, which was really special, and we would always wait until Christmas to open them. We could hardly wait to open the gifts because there were always good things in them. Lots of times it was something to wear. That was a good memory.*

In those days, Canada encouraged settlers to go to "new" areas. To gain the right to own the land, Canadian law allowed you to take up unoccupied land for a nominal price of $10—if you cleared a certain amount of land and built a shelter on your homestead. This became the principal method of encouraging settlement in the west, often from overseas or the large families of eastern Canada. This would, thought the governments of the day, create stable communities, populate the West, and deny any sense that the land was empty, especially to American expansionists. The settlers themselves would mean business for the railroads and manufactories of the east and grain and beef for the hungry mouths of the world. In addition, the flood of newcomers, including new Canadians, would overwhelm in

---

18   The Alaska Highway does start in Alberta but traverses the northeast corner of British Columbia into the Yukon. The Liard Highway now runs from the Alaska Highway in northern BC to Fort Simpson, NWT. The Dempster Highway reaches the Far north (Inuvik) from the Alaska Highway at Dawson City, Yukon.

numbers and culture, the old ways of the first peoples living nomadic or semi-nomadic lifestyles in the West.

The government, it seems, wanted immigration and settlement and the creation of permanent homes and communities. A teepee or bush camp with a migrant population was not the desired future of that Canada.

While the government may well have envisioned the eventual placement of solid stone or brick houses every half mile or so, like in Ontario or southern Manitoba, this wasn't the way of the North. For starters, there were no proper supplies or methods of use for the rock and stone needed, nor were there brickyards, and even if there were the proper type of materials and clay, the distances were so great that transport of bricks or appropriate stonework—and workers—was mostly confined to places like towns, which were serviced by the railway.

In the country, houses and other buildings were initially constructed of the locally available logs or if, as was often the case, the local bush was poplar and not fit for building permanent houses, logs were floated down rivers or other waterways. This was one reason that the northern rivers were so important to settlement. Later, lumber would be sawn from logs and housing made from the slats and boards produced that way. Sometimes, the very first shelters were huts made from bush, but in a land of timber and winters that easily hit forty below, log houses went up as fast as possible. (The lower prairies had a lack of wood, so early shelters included tents, caves, and buildings [called soddies] made in whole or in part by slabs of sod cut from the soil, until logs could be floated or otherwise transported to the home site.)

> *To have a parcel of land* [homestead] *meant he* [Clarence] *could build a home and have a place to stay. Back in the day, if you had a trapline or you were a trapper in that Notikewin-Hotchkiss area, you were a somebody. He had a grade-eleven or -twelve education so he was able to help a lot of trappers and homesteaders that couldn't read or write. He would read them their mail and help write their letters.*

Clarence relied on Noel to learn how to survive in the bush. Both ran dog teams that pulled the long sleds (carioles) necessary to carry supplies and the bounty of their catch on the traplines set in the snowy bush of wintertime Alberta. At some point, Clarence sold his farm and trapline and joined the Canadian army, where he served in the Second World War. He was trained in Regina and made a couple of trips home to the North. He was assigned to eastern Canada but didn't get overseas.

After serving in the army during the war, Clarence returned to Notikewan and took up another homestead and trapline, this one at Hotchkiss. He was able to get two quarter sections of land through the Canadian government's Veterans' Land Act.

Gordon's only real sense of his dad as an army man is a couple of photos of a man in uniform and one little joke his dad told: *My dad told us that his mother and father came to Calgary to see him parade with the Calgary Highlanders and his mom called out, "My son, the only one in step."*

That same understated, quiet sense of humour comes out in Gordon. He doesn't worry, he says, and he doesn't take himself too seriously.

Lying north of 57 degrees latitude, the Gill place was farther from the American border (at 49 degrees latitude), than it was from the NWT, where the southern border stretches along the 60th parallel from Alaska to Hudson's Bay, which is now part of the border of Nunavut. This was no agricultural paradise, ready for the plow. While Gordon views the area being settled for its prime soil, it was not the natural open farmland like that in Peace Country or farther south in the parkland and prairie of the western provinces. Clarence cleared bits of the land, from time to time, chopping trees and hand sawing the 3.7-metre (12-foot) willows that grew in clumps there. Mostly, he used horses to pull the stumps. Sometimes he would hire a man with a small bulldozer tractor to do some clearing. However, the farm was never the prime source of funds; trapping and driving truck were more Clarence's style. It doesn't seem that the farm was very productive, but rather a source of subsistence living, by way of cow's milk, chickens and eggs, the garden, wild berries for the picking, and the like. In due course Clarence sold this farm and moved his family farther north, after which he worked strictly for wages.

Clarence and Armande raised their two children in what would now be called "primitive" conditions. Life in the bush was especially primitive by Canadian standards of today and by urban standards of that day. As Gordon has said, never on that farm did they have running water, electricity, plumbing, or an inside toilet.

Neither did they have any real farm equipment of a scale to effectively cultivate, seed, and harvest enough land to make it worthwhile.

> *Dad had a small little tractor with a disc and a small set of harrows for the farm. The rest of the work he had to have done by the neighbours, seeding the crops, breaking land, harvesting; stuff like that had to be done by others.*

Take a closer look at the photo of Clarence at his woodpile, axe in hand. There is an attitude and a look of independence and insouciance, perhaps. Clarence was barely 5 feet, 5 inches tall.

There is also the hat or cap—the old-time kind, which snaps down onto the brim—always, according to Gordon, worn at an angle to his face. It pointed off to one side, as if it were looking at you from a different place. Clarence also always wore armbands, like old-time bankers and bookkeepers did, to keep his sleeves up. Gordon never saw anyone else do that.

That photo also gives a good impression of just how much wood those old stoves could burn, and did burn, in the cold of the long Alberta winters. As Gordon tells it: *Right from a kid, I helped. Dad would pile wood in long lengths. I was designated to carry the small/light end of the tree. Dad always carried the heavy end. He would hire someone to come with a tractor to saw the wood. This made it a lot easier for Dad, but he still had to do a lot of heavy hauling by hand, then he had to split the wood with his big axe.*

Later in the book, a photo shows Clarence in front of Joe Rousseau's truck, which he sometimes drove. Clarence appears almost in uniform. He wore full-at-the-thigh jodhpurs (a kind of English riding pant) with suspenders and his high lace-up boots. These were, Gordon says, his driving clothes. His look is intense; he stares out from under pursed brows. He doesn't smile.

> *Later, my dad got a Model A [Ford] car. He drove it sparingly. On the very rare occasion Dad would start the car in the wintertime, he never had anti-freeze, so if he was going to stay overnight, he would have to drain the water and warm it up in the morning before putting it back in the car. The car had no heater, so he had to dress warm. One year we went in the car picking saskatoons up on the Third Battle Hill. My sister and I would ride in the rumble seat in the back, which was kind of cool.*

It was his father that Gordon remembers hearing talk, giving him life lessons that are still part of him. He was a hard worker but a loner, and he was away from home much of the time. Gordon's mother, Armande, worked hard too. She seems to have been quieter, teaching by example rather than words. In any event, it is Clarence's phrases that Gordon thinks about. One of them, Gordon recalls, has stayed with him throughout his working life and comes to him when he has a problem or he doesn't quite know what to do: *Where there's a Gill, there's a way… No, where there's a will, there's a way.*

Gordon mentions that a lot, that he reflected on problems always with the attitude that if a Gill was involved, there would be a way to resolve any situation. This was a constant approach for Gordon in his business days.

Clarence also made those jokes out of being poor and having little, like the dinner comment about "rabbit-track soup, all you can eat."

Both Armande and Clarence were hard workers. It was Armande, however, who provided the daily example of hard work and sacrifice. Her teaching came out, not in words, as they did with Clarence, but in the way the family was taught to talk. Gordon still has trouble saying "I"; he thinks it sounds boastful and self-centered. His talk is more about "we" and "ours" and working together. He is a humble man and self-deprecating with a good sense of humour; these qualities he attributes to his mother's family, to the Métis way. Likely, his father's absence for months at a time, out in the bush, made this inevitable.

It is not hard to understand the Métis influence. Even though Clarence was Caucasian, brought up in the dominant settler culture of the West, he was away for months at a time in winter, up on his trapline, and as Gordon remembers life then: *We were so isolated and never had a vehicle until much later but even then, my mother didn't drive. We had to make do with what we had, which wasn't much. My mother worked so hard just to keep us fed and clothed, like, to take care of us.* It makes sense that the Métis way, their adaptation and survival, was the only way they knew.

Talking about his dad, Gordon was quite conscious of a sense of loss, saying, *I never got to meet my dad's parents.*

> *My father was gone trapping from the end of October to basically shortly after breakup, which was in May. My father would come home once or twice through the winter to gather supplies for a day or two and be off again trapping.*

CHAPTER 5:
Armande – Learning to Be White

Armande at Notikewin, 1941

We were half-breeds.

IF GORDON'S NAME suggests a European heritage, his blood mix is about half English-Irish and half Indigenous. He is clear: *We were half-breeds.*

Armande was Gordon Gill's mother and the product of a different time. She did her best to bring Gordon and his sister up as mostly white kids. It was her way to push for a better and easier life for them. For sure, they were to go to school. They didn't wear "Indigenous" clothes, like skins or furs or beadwork. While her mother had made Clarence some moosehide gloves with fancy beaded designs, Armande herself did not do so for her children. She didn't erase their Indigenous blood or the things she learned and passed to them instinctively, like the way they talked, but she did not teach them Cree, nor did she talk in terms of them having other, Indigenous names. Those children, though brought up poor as half-breeds, far from cities or other symbols of civilization, did not know the soul-crushing alcoholism, addiction, despair, and hopeless poverty often reflected by other Indigenous people. Those children of hers have prevailed.

Armande was one of nine children. The two oldest boys died before her father moved the family to the Battle River country. Two older sisters were born at Lac La Nonne and made the wagon trip north.

> *Mom was born on Noel and Justine's homestead on the edge of Notikewin in 1920, the fourth of six girls.*

A photo of Armande when she was about twenty reveals an attractive woman. She, like her mother and grandmother, looks stern and formal in the photos from Gordon's birth year. That gives the wrong impression. *She looks so businesslike,* says Gordon, *but she wasn't. She was so mellow, so friendly. She was easygoing and so nice.*

Armande's high cheekbones and long raven hair complement the determined look of a capable young woman. At 5 feet, 3 inches, she was almost as tall as her husband when wearing the sturdy mid-heeled shoes of the time. No photos are known to exist of Armande in anything but European clothing, dresses, and store shoes.

Gordon's memories of his mother are fond ones, filled with admiration, empathy, and loyalty. He felt that his mother was, in a way, trapped on the farm while her husband was away for weeks and months at a time. She had no vehicle and could not drive one if she'd had one; they didn't use the horses for pulling a carriage or anything like that. Armande was separated from her own parents and sisters, and even 20 kilometres or so might as well have been a hundred. So, it was up to her to keep the place, tend the animals and children, and make do. Not that his mother ever said that she was a prisoner or even complained. But in Gordon's mind, she was like a prisoner. It is Gordon's empathy that gives him that sense of her.

> She couldn't even see her parents that much, even though they were only twelve miles away or so. No one had a car. Noel didn't and we didn't. Mother was always busy. We had no electricity, so she had to wash clothes by hand all the time; just the washing of the clothes all the time was a big job. All Mother had was a washtub and a washboard. She had to twist the wet clothes by hand to wring them out. And she was always baking and canning and gathering berries. Not much spare time in those days.

> I only speak English, and not the greatest at that. My mother spoke Cree, especially when she was with her mother [Justine] and her dad [Noel]. I never learned the language. My mother was embarrassed about the Cree language. Really about anything to do with being Native. That must have rubbed off on me a bit because I never tried to learn Cree or to dress in any of the traditional clothing, even moosehide jackets with fringes and beadwork that became very popular in the North.

> After I turned five, we moved from Notikewin to Hotchkiss, where there were not many Native people. Mother was sort of shy or bashful about the language. Notikewin probably had the most Native people in the area, but outside of Notikewin, the people spoke English. My mom or my granny would translate for Noel. My mother did not want us speaking Cree. She never taught us. That was just the way it was. We didn't think nothing of it.

> Mom never said anything about having lost her language or having to speak English. She didn't say anything bad. She tried to be white.

Gordon chose similar words to describe himself, as being *Métis* and acknowledging that *the Métis had a lot of influence on the development of Western Canada—but we were living on the white man's side of the line.*

However, Gordon doesn't seem to focus on the meaning of Métis very much. He thinks of himself as a half-breed, who is now called a Métis person. He is a member of the Métis Nation, and the bulk of his Indigenous ancestors have French names, but he doesn't think in terms of a descendant of the Red River (Manitoba) Métis, from whom the capital-M Métis name most often derives. For one thing, Gordon's people were farther west than Manitoba at the time of the first Riel action in 1869–1870, and perhaps for another, Gordon is all about the future; for him, the way to be part of it was as a businessman who fit into the business community and its morés.

This is not unusual, even into the seventh decade of the twentieth century and later. One stand-alone line on the "Métis" page in the Canadian Geographic's *Indigenous Peoples Atlas of Canada* is, "Many Métis hid their identity after 1885."

That was the year, Canadian readers may recall, of the second so-called Riel Rebellion. Like the earlier Riel Rebellion of 1870 in Manitoba (both called, importantly, a "resistance" among the Métis), it was a principled stand by Métis and related Indigenous Peoples facing dislocation and the loss of their way of living and land. These reasons, coupled with the disappearance of the buffalo and the inexorable push west by a new population, exacerbated Indigenous and Métis concerns about their land, their homes, and their rights.[19] Ultimately, this resulted in conflict when the Canadian government sent—contrary to Prime Minister John A. Macdonald's promises and negotiated agreement—armed troops to trample on, disperse, and overpower the Métis Nation and extinguish those agreed-upon rights in what Canadian lawyer and writer Jean Teillet calls a "two-and-a-half-year reign of terror."[20]

While Gordon does know that his mother felt embarrassed or perhaps ashamed of her "Indianness," he does not recall hearing any specific talk about it nor feeling any sense of it at home. His sense was more about their poverty and "differentness."

Others, however, recognize this as an enduring legacy of anti-Indian, anti-Métis feeling. The choice of language to describe the Riel resistance, as the Métis would describe their reaction to the inexorable advance of

....

19   Canadian Geographic, "Métis," *Indigenous Peoples Atlas of Canada* (2018), https://indigenouspeoplesatlasofcanada.ca/.

20   Jean Teillet, *The North-West is Our Mother: The Story of Louis Riel's People, The Métis Nation* (Toronto, ON: HarperCollins, 2019).

Canada and its emigrant people into the northwest, a country they called their own—both in 1870 and again, farther west, in 1885—is subtle yet telling. The English Canadians, perhaps because of bigotry, habit, or their place in the world—and likely accentuated by fear and frustration—called the actions of the Métis uprisings or rebellions, and many still do.

The Métis had been, in some ways, the creation of the Hudson's Bay Company, and recognized by them, as a distinct part of the peoples of the Northwest. Often the children of HBC traders, or workers and Indigenous women, and thereafter, the descendants of such children, the Bay had relied on them, as the North West Company and others would later, to make contact with the Indigenous peoples, transport trade goods in and furs out of the country, and man the English company's posts and forts.

The Hudson's Bay Company started its fur trade business based on a Royal Charter (a licence from the British Crown) to trade fur in Rupert's Land. This was the English designation for that part of the Canadian Northwest that drained into Hudson Bay. In the event, the HBC did trade beyond their original grant, beyond the sources of the east-flowing rivers. And the Métis people scattered throughout the Northwest was one result.

"The absorption of the North West Company in 1821 marked the beginning of a half-century of HBC dominance within, and de-facto governance of northern Alberta… [and, quoting Leonard et al, the effect of the decimation of the buffalo and the focus on the fur trade, led to] dependence on non-herd ungulates, especially moose, along with the necessary division of traditionally shared territory into separate trapping areas, [and] caused disintegration of larger tribal society in to smaller band and even family groups…" [21]

This land, or rather the Hudson's Bay Company's rights in it, was sold to Canada in 1870 without consulting the Indigenous people living there (or the Métis). More importantly, it was transferred, supposedly, subject to the rights of those living there.

According to Teillet, in 1869 and leading up to the acquisition of the Red River lands, Prime Minister John A. Macdonald wished to ignore any rights other than those granted specifically to "Indians." He and his government didn't really want to get into the whole business of what a Métis person was. For example, if a child was half Indigenous and half Scottish,

21   Ross, *Teaching in Northern Alberta*, 51

but the child lived with the mother and her "tribe," was that child Indian? What if that child lived as a white man and had more children? Would it matter if those children were of a white mother or not? It could, and did, and does with each passing generation get more complicated. In addition, the Métis themselves evolved into different groups, some becoming part of the distinctive Métis Nation, others either joining their Indigenous relatives or deciding not to, and some, as in Alberta, creating settlements among themselves. Others lived independently, or passed as French Canadians or English, depending on their last name.

In any event, after negotiations with the Red River Métis, including Louis Riel, Macdonald relented and agreed to terms with the Manitoba Métis. However, he did nothing to honour or enforce those now-agreed-upon rights, nor did he stop the scandalous behaviour of the army he sent to Red River to tame the people living there (now southern Manitoba). Their actions—the army was two-thirds Ontario Protestant Orangemen who were anti-French, anti-Catholic, and (conveniently combining the best of both) anti-Métis—resulted in much death, terror, rape, and outright robbery.[22]

The same pressures then occurred with the expansion of Canada westward. (The Canadian Pacific Railway, for example, reached Moosomin on the eastern border of Saskatchewan in 1882). The addition of more settlers from the east, and especially England and the lack of action to recognize and protect the title to the lands they occupied led, in due course, to the 1885 military action by Canada and the resistance, or "rebellion," of the Métis and some Indigenous leaders. How that is relevant to Armande and Gordon's grandparents, specifically, is shown by Clément Chartier's comment. A Métis leader, lawyer, and author, Clément Chartier is quoted in the Canadian Geographic's *Indigenous Peoples Atlas of Canada* as saying,

> We stood up for our rights to be self-determining and to own land. We [the Métis people] were significantly marginalized for seeking our rights.
>
> This was particularly true after 1870 and 1885, the darkest times in Métis history and a dark chapter in Canadian history.[23]

22 See generally, Teillet, *The North-West is Our Mother*; "Métis," *Indigenous Peoples Atlas of Canada.*
23 Clement Chartier, quoted in "Introduction," *Indigenous Peoples Atlas of Canada.*

And especially after 1885,

> …most Métis would become socially, economically, and politically marginalized. In most instances the Métis didn't have title to the land and thus paid no taxes, which precluded their children from obtaining an education. With this marginal existence emerged a myriad of social problems, including poor health, and self-esteem, and poverty.[24]

Archbishop Taché, one of the thought leaders in the old Northwest and a Catholic leader who was nonetheless respected by many Indigenous Peoples, gave advice to the Canadian government to the effect that the Métis "should not be compared with Indians, as they had neither the tastes, habits, nor instincts of the Indian and… were a 'sensitive race' who were easily humiliated with regard to their origin."[25]

The *Indigenous Peoples Atlas of Canada* sums up this feeling:

> This stigma of being labelled "rebels" or "traitors," as well as facing unending racism for being Indigenous, forced many Métis, over several generations, to hide or deny their identity… to escape racism and for their own cultural safety.[26]

This explains to some extent that fear or worry present in Armande— and likely her father, who after all had been a young child at the time of the defeat and hanging of Louis Riel—about being seen to be Indigenous or even Métis. One of the nice things, according to Gordon, about moving to Hay River in 1956, was that the northern community was a good mix of peoples who all got along. This was true for Armande in particular; the differences between whites and Métis and Indigenous Peoples were less meaningful, less contentious. The family fit into the community and was well-respected.

On arriving in the north, Armande, then in her later thirties, started working for wages. First, it was cleaning houses, but then she got on as

24   Canadian Geographic, "Aftermath of 1885," *Indigenous Peoples Atlas of Canada,* https://indigenouspeoplesatlasofcanada.ca/article/aftermath-of-1885/.

25   Gerhard J. Ens and Joe Sawchuk, *From New Peoples to New Nations: Aspects of Metis History and Identity from the Eighteenth to the Twenty-First Centuries* (Toronto, ON: University of Toronto Press, 2016), 152.

26   Chartier, in *Indigenous Peoples Atlas of Canada.*

a chambermaid with the Hay River Hotel when it opened in Old Town, almost on top of the wharf. She stayed working for the hotel owners there and then at the Ptarmigan Inn downtown until she was seventy-six. Gordon says she loved her job.

The hotel manager, Chuck Davidge, says that all the Gills were "top notch"; he remembers Armande very well and with affection. Davidge says:

> When I moved to Hay River in October of 1974 and got to know my neighbours, I really did feel that I was moving into a community. The Gill family were part of the community I got to know, mainly through business, and mainly with Gordon and Treena. It was 1980, when I got into the Ptarmigan Inn, that I started to get to know Mrs. Gill—and it was always Mrs. Gill—you never thought to use her first name. I was young, she was my elder, and I respected that.
>
> It was interesting when Jack Walker and I took over the Ptarmigan Inn in 1980, the previous owners [a prominent brewing family from Calgary] had, I think, at least five to eight rooms in the lower section of the hotel for staff—all brought in from the south. Jack Walker [co-owner of the hotel] started the process of increasing local hires, which I continued. And when you look at Mrs. Gill and her department, she was definitely the team leader—work ethic, quality control—it was her.
>
> I have had nothing but respect for Gordon, Treena, Mrs. Gill, and Mr. Gill. They were great and Mrs. Gill was a great employee. I was proud to work with her, an incredibly hard worker, who ran housekeeping like a tight ship, and worked beyond the call of duty.

Davidge tells of the time an employee came running to his office declaring that: "Mrs. Gill just fell." She was in her seventies. Apparently, she had slipped while wiping down the far side of the shower tub in a room, breaking her arm. After getting medical care, Davidge told Armande to stay home and recuperate, but "four days later she was back running the laundry, with one wing; unbelievable." About Clarence, Davidge called him the "silent partner," always waiting in his truck at day's end, without fail, to pick Mrs. Gill up from work. She was employed by the Hay River and Ptarmigan Hotels for almost forty years.

And, back to Gordon and Treena, great partners in some other business things we did later. When you watched the work ethic that the Gill family members had, you could only want to work as hard.[27]

If Gordon is heroic and a leader, so too was Armande.

She was so nice, so good. She lived a simple life. She liked music and was easy going. She did everything for the family. She worked so hard. She wanted things to be better for us.

....
27   Chuck Davidge, emails and oral interviews with the author.

CHAPTER 6:
A Cruel Life

Clarence with fur pelts

After Dad came back from the war, he set up a second trapline approximately 60 miles west of the Hotchkiss farm, up toward the Chinchaga Hills.

GORDON DESCRIBES A TRAPLINE as a plot of land allocated to a trapper by the provincial fish and game department, where they designate a starting place and mark the four corners.

> *In my dad's case, his trapping licence gave him permission to trap in a space 25 miles wide and about 60 miles long. He had to show his licence when he sold furs.*
>
> *Lucky for Dad, part of his trapping area had a line cut through it from the firefighters going in one time. Dad would go along it and then make trails to where spruce trees were clumped together. There was always lots of game around the spruce trees, especially squirrels, and there was*

less deadfall. He had to cut trails because of the dogs and the sled, so they could get through. This was all virgin territory; it wasn't logged then. In later years, this became a major forest-products area, especially for particleboard and other by-products of the aspen and poplar forests.

Mostly, Dad's trapping was with small steel traps and snares. He got lots and lots of squirrels and weasels. He would cut a notch on a slanted tree, or a big branch, and put the leg-hold trap there, tied to the tree. The squirrel or weasel would run up the tree and trip the tongue on the trap, and the trap would fall, hanging from the tree or branch. The animal would hang there and usually freeze. Those were very small traps, maybe the size of an orange or a grapefruit when folded out. They had a spring, and these two hoops that you separated and held in place with this round tongue. That is what the animal would step on, and it would spring the arms to come up and catch the leg.

Or with weasels and squirrels, he'd use snares, which were loops made out of wire. The snare would catch the prey around the neck, they'd run into it, and it would tighten around their neck. They'd fall off the tree, and it would strangle them quickly. We thought the snares were better. They were lighter than the traps, especially the big traps and they were quicker and nicer. The animal got strangled quickly, which sounds bad, but they didn't get held by a leg and lie there and suffer or try to bite off their own foot.

We'd put three snares in a row up the tree. The squirrels sometimes pushed them aside or missed them, but not usually three of them.

Clarence also trapped lynx and wolves, but not as much. They often followed the trails he made. Again, he used snares more often than traps. For one thing, the traps for the bigger animals were a lot heavier to take into the bush and, in his mind, more dangerous and awkward for him and painfully cruel to the animal. They also damaged the fur more.

The snares for the lynx—sometimes called a bobcat—and wolves were made out of a thin steel cable, maybe the size of the ballpoint pen insert. Clarence set them on a path, twisting the cable in a loop and attaching it to a nearby tree. He covered the edge of the path and the wire with twigs, leaves, and branches and tried to camouflage it and make it look like natural terrain.

> *He added kind of a lock, made out of stronger all-purpose wire, like stove-pipe wire, what we called haywire. It was kind of like those plastic ties, where you pull the plastic through a little box, but you can't pull it back out. The bigger snares had a deal like that.*

Again, the animal would run along a path, put its head through the loop, which closed in tight and, because of the lock, wouldn't spring back. Then Clarence would collect the animals, eventually taking the skin home for sale.

Clarence worked alone, and he was alone a lot. He built his own cabins, his own caches where he could keep meat and furs. He built dog houses and walked the 20 to 25 kilometres a day to check his traps, pushing his long toboggan or helping pull it, keeping the dogs going and fed, working with his hands to free frozen animals from the traps, crouching in the snow while his feet froze, lifting and carrying and skinning them. It was hard work and brutally cold sometimes, and the animals—the bigger animals—were heavy and frozen solid and needed to be thawed to skin.

As a lone trapper, Clarence would be out in the bush for weeks, or even months at a time. In the dead of winter, life was walking to a cabin along the trapline, through the trees and bush and deep snow of an Alberta winter, and later going on to another of his cabins. At each of them, he would die if he didn't get a fire going, maintain the wood supply, and preserve food to eat. It is hard to understand a family man, out in the bush, alone—except out of necessity and personality. His daily life of cold and wind, frozen fingers and toes, frostbitten face, and danger was focused on two main jobs… getting enough to eat and staying warm. Add to that the trudging through deep snow in the cold, where a trip or a slip and fall could be fatal, wondering if a pack of wolves or a cougar was there in the bush, watching and stalking you.

The sun rises late in northern Alberta and sits low on the horizon during the day in winter. It takes its little warmth and light away, leaving dark and frigid nights. One slip of the axe, one trip, one snap back of a trap… it was easy to be maimed or killed. Clarence could have been down on the ground, hurt, the snow covering him, and the dark descending on him, and there would be no help, no one to even know.

> *A lot of lynxes that he caught were in traps that he had set for squirrels; most always they were alive when he got there. He would have to put them down.*

Most of our trapping was with leg traps or snares for squirrels. My dad made thousands of squirrel snares out of brass wire. He'd get rolls of it to twist up into little nooses to catch the running squirrels.

One thing about trapping in those days. Dad never had a snow machine. He used dogs to pull the toboggan. In the bush, we always had toboggans, usually made of two pieces of flat oak for the bottom. It was curled up in the front. The sides were covered in canvas, and there was a set of handles and a frame at the back, and a place to stand. Some toboggans had a brake you could step on, to dig into the snow, to stop the dogs from running, but we didn't on ours. These are different than the toboggans, [komatiks] in the Arctic. They didn't have any trees so they could spread the dogs out on different leads. Ours were always in a row, with the dogs nose-to-tail, except the lead dog of course. It was all one long harness. And they had runners on their sleds, usually made out of frozen fish or bones, or bits of wood, and then covered with mud and iced up.

Gordon remembers going out to the main trapping cabin for the spring hunt with his dad. They would take the horse then, packed with supplies, and they each walked, carrying packs on their backs. It would take them three days. The first two nights would find them bunked down in other trappers' cabins along the way. They were after beaver. The beavers were live trapped in cages, rather than with traps. They were shot, still in the cage.

Dad saw a documentary on TV after we moved to Hay River. It was about how smart beavers were and how hard they worked. He told me he would never have trapped beaver if he had seen that earlier. He said he felt badly about trapping such a strong and smart and courageous animal.

After the family left Hotchkiss when Gordon was fifteen, neither Gordon nor Clarence trapped again but for one or two spring beaver hunts. Soon after, Clarence sold his trapline.

On the use of the traps, Gordon is practical. *It was a cruel business, but it was what we grew up with. It was how we ate, how we survived.*

Clarence didn't trap after moving to Hay River, but for the one or two attempts Gordon mentioned. He didn't hunt either and was mostly content to do his job, spend time with friends, mostly Métis people, and read.

Later in life, when he lived in Hay River, Gordon did go moose hunting.

> *Every year, me and Bill Helmer would head south to near the Alberta border. There is a long thin lake down there, maybe 25 miles long, near the old Kraus cabin, where they had a garden. A creek ran from the north end of the lake for about 5 miles and drained into Hay River. That was a pretty place.*

The two friends would canoe across the river, and because the creek mouth was not easily accessible from the river, they had to portage the canoe and their gear—food, tent, sleeping bags, equipment—to where they could put in the creek. The creek there was only 4 or 5 feet wide in places, but it was deep. There was a lot of grass and open meadows, and they would paddle to the lake.

> *We would go for a week. I really liked the camping, and we would fish. There were a lot of fish in that creek, you could see them if you looked down while you were paddling, and the lake had a lot too. Mostly they were jackfish* [northern pike], *which have terrible bones with little forks in them, but they are really tasty, good eating. You don't want to get them bones stuck in your throat!*
>
> *I liked the fishing and especially trying to get the whisky jacks* [a member of the jay family] *to eat out of my hand.*
>
> *For the moose, we would walk in a big circle and call for them, me at one spot, and Bill at another. Then we'd head back to camp, and in the morning, we would go back and walk the same circle. Seventy percent of the time, we'd find tracks and evidence that a moose had come there.*

Gordon says when he got home, his wife Treena would ask about the moose, supposedly their winter meat supply.

They're still out in the bush, he'd say.

Some of Gordon's friends say he is an embarrassment to the tradition of good Métis hunters. He doesn't care. He liked the outdoors, the birds, and the water. It was enough.

> *I always carried a gun, but you know I don't think I ever shot it, in all those years. I never did shoot a moose. I didn't want to.*

CHAPTER 7:
Noel, Justine, and the Indigenous Ancestors

Granny Justine and Kookum Gray

Noel and Justine were married in 1909 at Lac Ste. Anne.
They moved north to the wilderness in 1916 because he
was afraid the Catholic missionaries would take his
daughters from him and put them in residential school.

HE WANTED GOOD TRAPPING *and his own land. Noel spoke very little English, although the family had a Cree Bible that translated words to English. He tried to learn from that Bible.*

Noel didn't want the church messing with his children. He wanted his own life. None of his children lived "rough" on the street. None begged for change on downtown corners.

At the time, this grand expanse of bush the L'Hirondelles chose was just a part of the mass of land assumed by the Hudson's Bay Company on the authority of the British Crown. The Englishmen had, after all, just sort of moved in. You might say the Hudson's Bay men were like an unwanted but pushy cousin. Except the English had no actual relation to the land except for an ever-increasing occupation of it, initially strictly for business reasons. Later, they came in force, as did the French and Catholics, for those common nineteenth-century impulses of gain, exploration, adventure, and, of course, for their version of "saving" souls.[28]

Lac Ste. Anne is still a sacred site for Indigenous Peoples. It is, perhaps not coincidentally, very close to the starting point of the Alaska and Mackenzie Highways, which will feature later in Gordon's story.

When they arrived in the Battle River country, Noel and Justine moved into a tent with their two daughters until Noel completed the erection of a log house. He started to clear his homestead land with an axe. While there were single men homesteading at the time, Gordon thinks that Noel and Justine were the first family to homestead north of what he always calls the First Battle River (now the Notikewin River).

What history Gordon has of the early days of Noel and Justine is thanks to his mother's sister, Florence Sharp. She has recorded in a local history of the Manning area that:

....

28   There is a whole—and growing—history of the church missions in Canada and their relationship with Indigenous People. See, for example, *The Report of the Truth and Reconciliation Commission of Canada.* The Truth and Reconciliation Commission of Canada (TRC) was created as a result of the *Indian Residential Schools Settlement Agreement* (IRSSA). Also see Milloy's *A National Crime.* For a positive view of the effect of one minister's approach as principal of a residential school, see Paige Raibman, "A New Understanding of Things Indian; George Raley's Negotiation of the Residential School Experience," *BC Studies,* https://ojs.library.ubc.ca/index.php/bcstudies/article/view/1343/1386. See also Nick Sibbeston, *You Will Wear a White Shirt: From the Northern Bush to the Halls of Power* (Douglas & McIntyre, 2015).

In time, Justine and Noel acquired cows, pigs and chickens so they had their own milk, eggs and pork. They also made their own bacon.

Justine and Noel had many sorrows in their time. [In addition to the deaths of their two oldest sons at Lac La Nonne,] Mabel died when she was sixteen years old. Ida died when she was five, and Rachael died when she was nineteen years old after residing in the Calgary Sanitarium [sic] for six years. She had tuberculosis of the bone.[29]

Aunt Florence adds[30]:

Noel used to bring moosehides home from the trapline and Mom [Granny Justine] would tan them and make moccasins. Some were for family and some she would sell to Joe Rousseau or Joe Bissett for resale in the Notikewin stores.[31]

Gordon's memories are of a later time, of course. He says:

I was close with my grandparents. Noel was a real nice man. Justine was a Gray and her family also had L'Hirondelles in it.

Noel was a trapper, but also one of the best farmers around the country. He had one of the most beautiful pieces of land. The land was a quarter section that Noel owned, and probably the nicest quarter section in the area, although there were lots of good ones in the area, but he had beautiful crops and beautiful gardens all the time. They lived by a creek so their garden got lots of water out of that creek. When I was young, they had a teepee up in the yard for use in the summertime. He had sleds for his trapline and a dog team.

His daughter Florence still lives there. In November 2020, Florence turned ninety-five years old.

....

29   Sharp, Florence, writing in a local history of the Manning area, *Saga of the Battle River*, published by the Battle River Historical Society, printed by Inter-Collegiate Press, 1986. Florence passed away just shy of her ninety-sixth birthday, in late October 2021.
30   Sharp, *Saga*, 1986
31   Sharp, *Saga*, 1986.

> *Noel came from the Lac La Nonne area, northwest of Edmonton about
> 40 miles or so, but his people came from eastern Canada. They were
> Iroquois and voyageurs for the North West Company. Once West, the
> Iroquois men and other voyageurs often stayed. They married local
> Cree women and raised their families. It is for this reason that Noel
> and Justine's ancestors, though Iroquois in heritage, assimilated into the
> Cree nation and thus spoke Cree.*
>
> *The Iroquois were ahead of the Natives out here in growing crops and
> gardens and were wonderful farmers for many more years than the
> Natives here. Many of the voyageurs had great farming capabilities.*

Photos of Noel from 1941 show the fifty-eight-year-old Noel to be a
fit, upright-standing serious man with a heavily weathered face, creased
like leather. His cheekbones are high, his lips thin, and his jawline firm and
strong. He looks out from behind heavy glasses with a sense of strength,
determination, and dignity.

About his grandmother Justine, Gordon says:

> *Granny would also tan hides; Dad said one year she tanned fifty moose-
> hides all by hand. It was just like her business, tanning hides. But it's all
> hard work, really hard work. People that would kill moose would bring
> the hides to her because she did such a nice job, smoking and tanning
> the hides. My mom and her sisters helped. They sometimes got paid but
> often just took part of the hide or another hide in trade. They made
> moosehide vests, jackets, moccasins, and gloves. Beautiful work. I have
> my dad's moosehide gloves, which my Granny made him.*

Gordon does not have a really strong sense of oral history involving his
own relatives but that does not seem to detract from his self-identification.
For example, he says:

> *I never knew my great grandparents on Noel's side or any of their other
> relatives. I did hear from the aunties that some of our distant relatives
> fought with Louis Riel. When he was losing, they skedaddled back
> to Alberta! [Laughs.] I identified as Native, then approximately in
> the 1980s we were told we were Métis. Even though Dad was Irish/
> English, my dad's ways were more like a Métis person. When we lived in*

Notikewan, there were a lot of Native people there. Well, we never went around saying we were Indian. It was just our ways were more in line with the Native ways than all the farmers around us; their culture was different. Because my dad was a trapper on top of that.

Justine's parents were Joseph and Josephet [L'Hirondelle] *Gray. He was older, born in 1858. She was born in 1870. I don't know much about them, except that I heard Joseph's father, also named Joseph, had three wives.* [Laughs.] *Not at the same time.*

I just barely remember my great grandparents. Kokum we called her, my mother's granny, and I just barely remember her. She was at Granny's, and she was in her dying days. I do remember seeing Kokum's husband, my great-grandfather Joseph Gray, but he was very sick and died September 8, 1944. I was only three years old.

Noel's parents were Andre and Elise (Delorme), descendants of both Cree and Iroquois peoples. Noel's father was born in 1850 near Lac St. Anne, one of the key Roman Catholic missions in the old Hudson's Bay Company lands. This was far in advance of the Canadian government's formation in 1867[32], before the purchase of the Hudson's Bay Company lands by Canada, even before the NWT was created in 1870. The arrival of "settlers" and the creation of the western provinces were far in the future.

If Gordon and his mother were strong people and leaders focused on bettering their own families' circumstances, then imagine Noel. Not only did he face the difficulties all Métis and Indigenous Peoples faced after the "rebellion" of 1885 and their discrimination and poverty, but he also uprooted his family. He moved them by primitive means hundreds of kilometres into the bush to start fresh, far from home, away from family and

....

32   In what seems like a pretty clear assumption of British ownership of the Northwest, and a lack of consultation with the people living there, Gareth Wilson says of Canada's first Prime Minister John A. Macdonald: "Sir John A. was clear in his purpose for the northwest. In what might be stated as Canada's Manifest Destiny, the Macdonald Government's first Speech from the Throne in 1867 gave as the government's policy and objective 'the colonization of the fertile lands of the Saskatchewan, the Assiniboine and the Red River districts; the development of the mineral wealth which abounds in the region of the North-west; and the extension of commercial intercourse through the British possessions in America from the Atlantic to the Pacific…'" Wilson, *Frontier Farewell*, 33.

friends. He turned his back on his wife's religion and the Catholic church's schooling. He shaped his own destiny with initiative, determination, and independence.

Looking back, Noel was brave and determined. Taking his family from the known to the unknown, from a community of friends and relatives, from the collective to the individual, away from his wife's beloved church was risky—they were still Indigenous and poor. Ironically, Noel's escape and subsequent legacy confirmed, some would say, the national government's early urge to create an "Indian" who was independent, industrious, and self-sufficient. What Noel and Justine lost—or left behind—we'll never know, and what Gordon's generation and others lost is also unknowable. However, this is a family that avoided the blights of alcoholism, broken homes, violence, poverty, and despair. Would they have regardless of Noel's decision to relocate? This, too, is unknowable. It is sad that neither Noel's views about life in 1916 nor his looking-back views late in life were recorded. Perhaps that is one casualty of language, in this case.

And what about Justine?

She followed her husband, giving up more, it seems, in doing what was necessary. In due course, her parents did come North to live.

Noel died at eighty-four in 1967, and Justine at eighty-two almost two years later. They are buried in the Roman Catholic cemetery in Notikewan. Justine's parents are buried there, too. Someone told Gordon that his great grandparents, Justine's parents, are buried across the road in the Protestant part of the cemetery. He doesn't know why that would be, although he was not able to locate the actual graves when he looked at getting new headstones for them.

> *Granny Justine used to make the* [annual religious] *pilgrimage from Notikewan to Lac Ste. Anne Mission when she could. She'd ride the wagon pulled by horses; there were often up to six or seven wagons going together. That was a long way, especially sitting in a wagon.*
>
> *She was very religious.*

CHAPTER 8:
Métis Heritage

Moosehide gloves with beading made by Granny Justine for Clarence

Many Native guys took French names when they were voyageurs. The whites had a hard time pronouncing the Indian names. I don't think they tried very hard anyway. Indians took on all kinds of names that weren't their own, English or French depending on who they were with and what they might call us.

AS A PRELIMINARY and probably too superficial comment, there are English metis (sometimes called half-breeds) and French, and then a further division between French metis and the French Métis, being those descended from the mixed bloods of Red River.

The metis of the fur trade were often the descendants of the Indigenous

Peoples of the land and a French or Scottish employee of one of the fur trade companies. Their parents were usually trappers, traders or transporters of those furs.

The others, those with a capital M, were part of the Red River, Manitoba, settlement whose great glory and vocation was the buffalo hunt. Gordon is metis or maybe Métis. How exactly he is, however, shows the difficulty of being definitive about just *how that word is used.*

In Gordon's case, it is probable that his mother was technically metis, since there were people named Gray in her family tree, apparently from Louisiana originally. However, even that is not clear since Louisiana, and much of the Mississippi River country of the American Midwest, was French or under French-Canadian influence up to and indeed even past the American purchase of the "Louisiana Territory" from the French emperor Napoleon.

But Armande's family were not buffalo hunters. Her family were trappers and voyageurs in the Northwest bush country much earlier than the Red River resistance of 1869–1870. The L'Hirondelle family tree sets them near Lesser Slave Lake, north of Edmonton, in 1850. Gordon's view is that these ancestors were Indigenous Cree, intertwined with the blood of Iroquois and maybe the odd French-Canadian voyageur. It may be they were in Red River earlier, including around the time of the Seven Oaks battle, but there is no record of that.

When you look at the names on the L'Hirondelle family tree, you see a list that goes back to the outreach of memory and research, and the names are of decidedly French derivation . . . names like Delorme, Gladu, Calihoo, Chartrand, and so on. But as Gordon says, Indigenous Peoples often took names that were easier to say to be part of the community. Then it became your family name. And there were various levels of, shall we say, "fatherly involvement" in the creation and upbringing of children of Indigenous women. Who knows for sure?

However, on the other side, Gordon is the descendant of Irish English immigrants with an English name. That Clarence decided to move well into the bush and trap animals for a living is interesting in itself. Was it his solitary nature? His independent streak? Or perhaps just the economics of the Great Depression in his home province of Saskatchewan? In any event, Clarence took on the life of a trapper. In that, he contributed to the first element in the fur trade, the first in the production line of furry goods that became coats, hats, or whatever else was in vogue. But even then, the trade was in decline, becoming marginalized at the edge of the northwestern frontier. So, in that regard, Gordon is at least an English metis, from a long line of French-named Metis or Indigenous Peoples, with some Métis blood as well. It seems.

And he looks more like his mother's people.

The L'Hirondelles (that name shows up in both Noel's and Justine's families; in fact, Noel and Justine share a grandfather) came west as voyageurs—canoe men and trader's helpers—for the North West Company, out of Montreal, the great competitor and ultimately part of the Hudson's Bay Company.

Voyageurs are well known to Canadian school children. Often a combination of French-Canadians and Métis (usually French and Indigenous), they were noted for their strength, their perseverance, and maybe even their singing. It was their role to paddle the big trade canoes west, usually upriver, and cart the canoes and cargo—usually trade goods for the western trade forts—over portages. Sleeping on the ground, rising with the sun, paddling together against the current in all weather, facing starvation and freezing waters, it was not an easy life. Then they would turn around and paddle and portage back with cargoes of fur, outgoing traders, and other officials.

While the Hudson's Bay Company was based on the west coast of that monumental bay accessible from the North Atlantic, the North West Company and its rival, the XY Company, were based in Montreal, on the St. Lawrence River. That journey was much longer; voyageurs were out on the land for extended periods, often paddling far into the northern parts of Manitoba, Saskatchewan, and Alberta, and into the Northwest Territories. Most school kids learn about legendary fur traders and explorers, Radisson and Groseilliers.[33] In English-speaking schools, in the old days, we called them Radishes and Gooseberry. The extent of education, especially as to the fundamental role played by First Nations, Inuit, and Métis people played in Canadian history, is now much more comprehensive.

Radisson and Groseilliers were the first Europeans to explore the upper

33 Des Groseilliers, according to Jean Teillet, *The North-West is Our Mother: The Story of Louis Riel's People, The Métis Nation* (Toronto, ON: HarperCollins, 2019).

part of the Mississippi and Missouri Rivers. Starting in the mid-1600s, they set up trade routes that helped open up the lands around the Great Lakes of the United States and Canada. These Frenchmen, ironically, encouraged the British Crown to grant the Hudson's Bay Company its fur-trading charter. The HBC is still alive, the oldest company in North America.

Radisson and Groseilliers were the models for the dashing, bold, undaunted *coureurs de bois*, the runners, or travelers, of the bush. The canoe is one of the great romantic symbols of Canadian history, and the voyageurs continued their use of the nimble craft in the fur trade on the waterways of the Northwest. Later, the much larger York boats and then flat-bottomed paddlewheel steamboats took over the river traffic while the Métis' Red River carts, and then wagons, ox carts, and the railway did the overland job of supply and delivery. It was the fur trade that really opened up the West to Europeans and led, in due course, to expansion and immigrant settlement.[34]

Jean Teillet, in *The Northwest is Our Mother*, presents a comprehensive and fascinating history of the genesis of the Métis Nation. She says, "the social glue that bound these people together… can be traced directly to the voyageurs—not all the voyageurs but a subset of the voyageurs, the men of the North, who married First Nation women and then 'went free' in the Canadian North-West with their new families."[35] Teillet, a lawyer involved in Métis claims, and herself a grandniece of Louis Riel, outlines the evolution of the name and the culture related to that name. It is now clear that there are different definitions of Métis or metis, and it is also apparent that Métis people are now recognized as a distinct culture. However, for Gordon, his view is that people like him were often just thought of as "breeds," not really white but not really "Indian" either. Even now, controversy over the word Métis creates divisions: Was it good enough to just have some Indian blood? Did one need to be a descendant of French and Indigenous people specifically? Or narrower yet, were Métis only those whose ancestors were the buffalo hunters of Red River? And what of intermarriage? Many Indigenous people lost their rights under the Indian Act because their mothers and grandmothers—even full-blood First Nations—married non-Indians.

....

34   See, for example, Peter C. Newman, *Company of Adventurers*, vol. 1 (Toronto, ON: Penguin Books Canada Ltd., 1985).

35   Teillet, *The Northwest is Our Mother*, .

The term "Métis" has at least two meanings. Without a capital M, it refers to the "mixing" of races, initially between an European man, usually French, Scottish, or Orcadian (islanders from north of Scotland), but also of British derivation, and an Indigenous woman. Contrary to the United States, where "metissage" or "miscegenation" was highly frowned on, in Canada, initially at least, the necessity and value of being connected to the people of the country was easily understood and accepted. The capitalized "Métis" has a more political and cultural meaning, stemming largely out of the issues arising from the resistance, or rebellion, of 1870 in Manitoba, and the later one in 1885, farther west, where the mixed-blood peoples of the West fought to preserve some semblance of land tenure and basic rights in the face of the decimation of the buffalo herds on which they survived and the aggression of Canada in taking over its new purchase. There are multiple histories and studies reflecting the essence of Métis life and the creation of a Métis culture. Thus, say Gerhard Ens and Joe Sawchuk, in their book *From New Peoples to New Nations: Aspects of Métis History and Identity from the Eighteenth to the Twenty-First Centuries*:

> Being a big "M" Métis… relates to a community of people who self-identify as being Métis and recognizes that their ancestors made a political decision to identify as Métis based on shared histories and culture.[36]

They go on to say that mixed blood is not enough to be Métis.

> "If that were the case, virtually all First Nations in Canada and French-Canadians and Acadians would be Métis…"

Suffice to say, for our purposes, that there is no short explanation of what Métis or metis fully means, or even if it is to have the accent aigu over the 'e'. It is, at minimum, a word that encompasses people with a Caucasian ancestor, like Gordon. More to the point, some Métis were brought up in Indigenous families that did not "take Treaty" (that is, identified as Indians under the Indian Act) or who came and went from the Treaty lands, living sometimes on their own and sometimes as part of the collective. Some Métis identified as Red River Métis and lived in communities of other Metis people, and others lived in the mainstream of Canadian

---

36 Ens and Sawchuk, *New Peoples*.

life, not always talkative about their Indigenous ancestors. Some, like the L'Hirondelles, lived in connection with family but on their own.

There is a school of thought that the Métis Nation is limited to those descending from the occupants of the Red River settlement and the struggles for and presumed creation of nationhood that occurred there. The genesis of the nation likely started first with the Battle of Seven Oaks (the Massacre as the English called it or the Victory of the Frog Plain, as the Métis have named the event.)[37] in 1816, followed by what has been called the first Métis land titles case in 1847, and the 1851 battle with the Sioux south of the international border, on the Missouri Coteau. This was followed by the Métis (English and French) opposition to the takeover of the territory by Canada after its purchase of the Hudson's Bay Company lands in 1869/70, or at least resistance until Red River could secure its rights and its status as a province, like Prince Edward Island and British Columbia, which had at that point refused to join Confederation.[38] Gordon has no family history, oral or otherwise, which might shed light on the family's involvement in the Red River resistance or the other steps on the way to Métis nationhood, but the L'Hirondelles and their ancestors are clearly part of the diaspora of Indigenous Peoples descended from the voyageurs and perhaps the buffalo hunters. Gordon's section of the family was in the far northwest well prior to the battles and takeover of Red River in the 1870s and the earlier telltale events of the 1840s and 50s. In some ways, does that make him more metis, even if less Métis?

And is it even relevant in this story? Does it matter that Gordon, whose father descended from the British, might just be called a half-breed—even though he is a member of the Métis Nation? Or can he claim Métis status based on his mother's French-Indigenous genealogy? Would it make any difference? One of Gordon's attributes, as a person, is that he doesn't care all that much about labels. He knows who he is and what is important to him. Moreover, he never had a need to be part of any club but his own and the one he created with Treena. This mixture of 'outsiders' with various Indigenous groups is quite common in the West, and much more acknowledged now than in the not-so-distant past. In Gordon's case, this makes him legally part of the Métis Nation, as defined in Alberta and the Northwest

37 Teillet, *Our Mother*, 55
38 Teillet, *Our Mother*, 55.

Territories. Rather than harbouring embarrassment, rather than hiding his background as many in the West did, Gordon proudly carries his Métis Nation registration card in his wallet.

> *What makes me certain I have Native blood is that I have two chest hairs and no whiskers.*

CHAPTER 9:
Métis Roots Live On

Gordon camping, Whiskey Jack feeding.

I loved to work. I looked forward to getting
going every morning, to get back to work.

WHEN YOU HEAR GORDON TALK, it is not usually about history. He well understands the Indigenous contribution to the evolution of Canada and the political issues that remain. Gordon, however, does not dwell in the past, nor does he complain or see himself as a victim. He understood his people and sought to be supportive of the everyday guy, hiring Indigenous Peoples, and giving them the freedom to do their best.

His focus always seems to have been on the future, on getting another job, getting more work to do, thinking of ways to advance whatever he was trying to do. Sometimes that was personal, for the business, but just as often it was about how to get more work for his employees or find new ways to do the work. Gordon was and is about how to build or try new things, like his venture into video entertainment and online gambling services during the last two decades. Regrets are not something that get aired, except those he has around his mother's hard life. Certainly not regrets about his life or the challenges he faced. Talk with Gordon, and it always is about something happening, something someone did or was doing at work. Gordon loved work and loved to work.

He is proud of his heritage now, but not into politics or causes. His talk is not of injustice or residential schools (except in his special case, thankful for the one he attended). He is not a victim. Perhaps he was one of the lucky ones. For one thing, humour touches all of his conversations.

For another, Gordon was blessed with grandparents who were independent and self-sufficient. And his own mother seemed to focus on raising her children to do the best they could in the world in which they found themselves. Whether Armande's effort to have her family assimilate into the local white culture (be brought to the "white side," in Gordon's words) was a good idea, who can say? That Gordon seems at peace with the world, both when he had money and when he did not, and happy with the life he has led, seems pretty special, in a world where not many, no matter what background, heritage, or culture, can say that.

Gordon has not maintained the family's ties to its Indigenous past— moose meat, tanning hides, beadwork, trapping, and speaking Cree—but he appreciates these things and values the things he has and the life on the land that he experiences from time to time. Gordon often has a laugh at something in a self-deprecatory way, making fun of himself. He has a gentle humour, one which he thinks of as separate and different from the humour of whites and of "full bloods" or Treaty people. He at least feels a distinct difference, a Métis difference.

If you look at the photos of the family in the early days, from the 1940s, their clothes are those of the white society: a man's suit, a white shirt and tie, and big Coke-bottle-lensed glasses for Noel, and city dresses and mid-high heels for Granny and Justine and Armande. Gordon and Mildred are dressed in clothes that would fit in any English home. Yet, they all thought of themselves, in their inner beings, as Native or half-breed. Gordon himself points to his quiet sense of humour and soft, self-effacing way of talking, and his sense of the collective "we," not "I" when describing himself. He is a proud man, but not one interested in seeking or hogging the limelight. He also says he inherited his calmness, his lack of worry, from the L'Hirondelle side of the family.

Gordon's niece Marvelle says:

> Thinking about Gordon being taught to never use I or me; this is something that runs through all of us in the family. I feel that the Native history has been lost partially because of the shame of being Native that was instilled in so many. It does take a community to build a village. Modern times has separated us from WE to I.
>
> I do believe being métis we were raised not to boast or talk about our accomplishments. I'm not sure why, maybe it has to do with a tribe mentality where everyone worked together, and it was a combined contribution and not just one person that made the world go around back in those days.[39]

There are other aspects to what Gordon calls his Native heritage, like his diabetes and his rare blood type, A Rh negative, which Gill calls his "Indian blood." He doesn't think that kind of blood was found in blood banks in the old days. Gordon admits that he knows nothing of the technical issue, only that he heard of this—Indian blood—when he was younger.

According to a feature article in *Maclean's* from 1955, it is not the Rh negative that was the issue for some Indigenous mothers but rather the absence of a specific protein/molecule antigen (not one of the five

....
39   Interview with the author.

common ones) that gave them their rare blood type, which could be very dangerous—if not fatal—when mixed with a different kind of blood from the father. *Maclean's* writer Norman Depoe put it thusly:

> Red Cross doctors last year came across twenty-one unknown possessors of the rare blood type …. All are métis living near Edmonton, and all are closely related. The long chain of heredity that produced the unusual blood stretches back to the chance migration of a single Iroquois brave around 1800 from a village near Montreal to the west. This, plus the other accidents of history and fate, led to a unique mingling of Iroquois, Cree, French and Scottish blood which in the twenty-one cases so far discovered completely lacks two of the mysterious, heredity-determined Rh antigens found in the blood of nearly everyone else in the world.[40]

And there is the issue of religion.

When Gordon was asked if he was brought up in the church, he laughed and said:

> *Ha ha, this is almost like a joke. When I was born, I was baptized Catholic. It wasn't until about grade six. A priest and a minister would come to the school on a Friday to teach us religion. Every Friday. So, from grade six to seven, I was going every Friday to this hour of religion with the Catholic priest. Then my dad heard about that, and he was Protestant. He said, "No damn way you're going to that class again. You're going to the United minister." So, then I went to the United teachings then in Notikewin. Once we went to Manning for school, there were no more religious classes. We lived in the bush and had no transportation, so we didn't go to church. If my granny would have had any say, we would have been going to church. She was a devout Catholic.*

> *But for me, actually, I ended up being very confused about religion. I never did go to a church or service. I always wondered who God was because there were all these different religions with different gods. I'm thinking someday I'll come up with my own. [Laughs.] I eventually*

40 Norman Depoe, "What You Don't Know About Your Blood," *Maclean's* (November 26,1955)https://archive.macleans.ca/article/1955/11/26/what-you-dont-know-about-your-blood.

did. I came to the conclusion that Water is my God. The reason for that is the earth we are on, Water is everywhere. It forms a huge percent of our body. No matter what you look at there is water in it. Even steel has water in it. Wood, trees, everything has water in it. Also, it is indestructible. You burn it, it turns to steam and vaporizes and forms droplets and rains somewhere else. So, water is the only thing that I can think of where God/Water is everywhere. Water is in the voids of space. It's in abundance in our planetary system. Then I kind of find out later that water is smart. Different experiments have been done with water and water is smart. I'm figuring and come to the conclusion, God is Water.

So, is it just coincidence that Gordon grew up between two of Canada's greatest rivers and that his working life, through pure happenstance, started on a small tug working the Mackenzie River? Later, as a ship's engineer, Gordon spent much of his younger years chugging across lakes, up and down major rivers, out into the Arctic Ocean, and into Alaska. His work on the water and then later building craft for use on the water meant he had the lives of many men in his hands. Mistakes were potentially life-altering or worse. His feeling for water and its connection to God and his life's work raise spiritual questions that we cannot begin to answer.

One aspect of his life view that we can suggest is that of his personal relations with others. Gordon's humour is ever-present, as is his sense of respect for others. And while he denies the religious affiliation of his grandmother or his father's people, he does believe in—as we see by what he practises more than what he preaches—doing unto others as you would have them do unto you. The Golden Rule.

Back in those days, people did call us Indians, and we were surrounded by Polish, German, and Ukrainians; we did not mind being called Indians. It was all in fun, most of the time, and we would call them names back too, but people that were half Native and half white, were called half-breeds. It was not until years later that I started hearing the word Métis. Although it may have been used but I never heard it. It was always half-breeds. Then the Métis status come in and it sounded a lot better.

CHAPTER 10:
Fleeing Residential School

Birchbark canoe, Crazy Horse Monument Museum, Black Hills, SD. Author's photo

"We instill in them [Indigenous children] a pronounced distaste for Native life so that they will be humiliated when reminded of their origin". Bishop Vital Grandin.

SEVEN YEARS *before* Noel took his family to the North Country, departmental reports from Indian Affairs documented the failure of residential schools, the alarming death rate of Indian children, and the ongoing deplorable conditions of the buildings themselves. Noel would be unlikely to have known of these (and other earlier and equally damning) reports. He would, however, have heard about children going to school and not coming back.[41] He bundled up his surviving family into a wagon and drove them north, pulled by a team of horses, to avoid the Roman Catholic residential school, an act that says much about Noel. It is so sad that his story was not taken down, his words not recorded.

Noel's grandson Gordon attended first an Indian Day School, (later changed to Federal Day School in Hay River) but lived at home, and then later attended the Yellowknife Residential School, Akaitcho Hall. This chapter sets out some history of residential schools to add context to the life and times of Gordon Gill in the NWT, and his own personal experience in such a school.[42]

After the defeat of Riel's forces and his hanging in 1885, there was less patience or sympathy, which had not been particularly prevalent before, in white and governmental circles (usually the same thing) for the plight of the Indigenous Peoples. Residential schools continued, but budgets were not raised and were certainly not adequate for the mandate given.

Times were not good for Indigenous people, and they had not been for some time. The fear in settler circles after the 1885 uprising continued for years, and that consciousness continued for generations.[43] Worse, the old ways were no longer available, especially in the southern parts of the prairie provinces of Manitoba, Saskatchewan, and Alberta.

As Garrett Wilson writes in his wonderful history of the West after 1870, it was a case of farewell to the frontier, almost literally. In the ten years after Riel's first effort at preserving the rights of his countrymen, the West had changed forever. The burning question for the government of Canada was how to ensure that the Indigenous residents of the frontier changed with it. The situation facing the government was untenable, as it was for the residents of the great land. There was a push for settlement of the apparently vast and open land, one that could populate the lands multiple times over, and provide the growth and development the country seemed to want. The peoples of the plains were not seen, then, as having "ownership" of any particular parts of it, although large territories were seen to be controlled

....

41   *A National Crime*, 92.

42   Gordon and Mildred attended the local provincially mandated public schools while living in northern Alberta. For an exploration of Métis schooling, generally, in that area, see Ross, *Teaching in Northern Alberta*, 131-132.

43   See Garrett Wilson, *Frontier Farewell: The 1870s and the End of the Old West* (Regina, SK: University of Regina Press, 2007).

by one or other often warring tribes.

With the sudden and disastrous demise of the buffalo (the source of all that Indigenous life required) and other wild game, the earnest desire by the populated and voting part of Canada wasn't a relatively empty, massive, and "unused" third of the continent, but rather the assimilation of the Indigenous Peoples, including the Métis buffalo hunters, into "good, tame, and Christian Indians." [44] Especially after the Riel scare, what else could be done? And wasn't it so much more desirable, for everyone's sake?

So, it is not of much surprise that the government sought a solution that would supposedly help the Indigenous population get prepared for its future as part of the Canadian nation. The government sought the help of churches, and the churches sought the help of the government, and *voilà*, much of Indian and later Métis policy—including residential schools— was born.

In his long and detailed history of the residential school system in Canada, which historian John S. Milloy has titled *A National Crime*, and what the *Literary Review of Canada* calls "One of the 100 most important Canadian books ever written," Milloy provides a "powerful indictment of the racist and colonial policies that inspired and sustained them." Milloy himself says, with notable restraint, "The history of the federal school system is long and complex."[45] He examines the foundation of the schools and the supposed need for Indigenous children to be brought there and to stay there (in a residence) and concludes:

> The federal policy has been since Confederation and what it would remain for many decades... a policy of assimilation, a policy designed to move aboriginal communities from their "savage" state to that of "civilization" and thus to make in Canada but one community—a non-Aboriginal one...[46]

To this end, the Department of Indian Affairs stated in 1890 (shortly after Noel's birth) that:

> ...it would be "highly desirable," if practicable "to obtain entire [complete] possession of all Indian children after... seven or eight

44   Milloy, *National Crime*, xxxviii

45   Milloy, *National Crime*, xxxviii.

46   Milloy, *National Crime*, 1.

and keep them at school… until they have had a *thorough* course of instruction."[47]

The effect was "marginalized Aboriginal communities stripped of… self-government, and denied… self-determination," and the result "sorrowful" and "tragic." As early as 1944, a joint committee of the Senate and House of Commons of Canada concluded, that the government's goal "had clearly fallen short," and "showed no sign of imminent success. By every indicator… Aboriginal people, far from being assimilated, were still separate and second-class citizens, [with] … a single unifying threat—growing Aboriginal poverty."[48]

Even earlier, in 1907, Dr. P. H. Bryce of the Department of Indian Affairs went against the wishes of his superiors to report on the residential schools. Over and over, he and other doctors both before and after him chastised the department for its "criminal disregard for… the welfare of the Indian wards of the nation," who were led into a "trail of disease and death."[49] The result of the Bryce objections was not surprising. "The federal government of the day stonewalled him by cutting his research funding, barring him from speaking at medical conferences and eventually pushing him out of his job." However, in the summer of 2022, the Canadian government erected a plaque to honour the printing of the Bryce report. The location chosen was the address of the printer at 61 Sparks St, in Ottawa, James Hope and Sons. Coincidentally, James Hope was the great-grandfather, and one of the 'Sons' the maternal grandfather of Christophe John Hope Brodeur, who features in these pages as photographer, adviser and publisher/editor of the Hay River Hub newspaper.[50]

Malloy's examples of the findings of various medical inspections from the 1890s forward show a charade of caring amid the dark reality of tuberculosis, serious overcrowding, underfunding, physical and psychological distress, including open wounds, malnutrition, filth, poor housing, and depression. Manual labour requirements and physical punishment and restriction were additional impediments to children's health.[51]

47   Milloy, *National Crime*, 7.
48   Milloy, *National Crime*, 9.
49   Milloy, *National Crime*, 97.
50   https://www.cbc.ca/news/politics/peter-bryce-plaque-ottawa-national-truth-reconciliation-1.6599608
51   Milloy, "Part 2: The Reality at Work, 1879 to 1946," *National Crime*.

There were other prominent voices against the idea of residential schools at the time. For example, Alfred Fitzpatrick, the founder of Frontier College, a literacy organization founded in 1899 to teach reading and writing in work and logging camps, railway construction sites, and the like, had this to say:

> Instead of breaking up the Indian's home and taking his dear ones to a school, leave his children at home. Let our missionary teachers… take their women folk and pitch their tents beside the Indian's camp and teach the whole Indian community… Equally important is a desire to share the Indian's knowledge, to learn his language and his work.
>
> Do not take the boy and girl away from home… to a community school. Such a breaking of family ties demoralizes those who leave home and those who remain behind.

Fitzpatrick criticized the exploitation of the Indigenous Peoples and the taking of so much of their land and resources. His words continue:

> The hand, head and heart of the Indian, as of the white man, must all alike be educated.[52]

Professor James Morrison of St. Mary's University in Halifax compares Fitzpatrick and his contemporary, the Reverend George Raley, who was also opposed to residential schools but worked within the system.[53]

> The Rev. George Raley is an interesting example of someone "kicking against the pricks"… in Government and the church as Alfred Fitzpatrick did as well. Certainly, some interesting parallels with Fitzpatrick—both Protestant missionaries, born in the 1860s and starting their careers in the 1890s, very active 1914 to 1930s, both drawing on the new discourses of Social Gospel values in terms of changing the society around them, and both respecting Indigenous knowledge—quite unusual and ahead of their time.[54]

52 Chapter 7 from the unpublished manuscript *Schools and Other Penitentiaries* by Alfred Fitzpatrick, c.1933, National Archives of Canada,--File: "Schools and Other Penitentiaries" MG28, I 124 Volume 161 courtesy, Professor James Morrison, St. Mary's University, Halifax, NS.
53 Email to the author, October 2021.
54 Email to the author, October 2021.

But alas, neither the concept of residential schools nor their actual operation changed as a result of this opposition.

The world of Indigenous related literature is extensive now, and growing daily it seems. This is true also of Métis history and in particular Métis education. There is much of importance in that history, many complaints, and multitudes of interpretation, personal experience, and academic study. The Métis story (and the Indigenous one as well) is awash in prejudice, poverty, abuse, discrimination, and a lack of formal education. Focusing on Gordon's story doesn't mean the history of other Métis people should be ignored or discounted. As he often says, himself, the stars aligned for him.[55]

Gordon did go to a public school in a primarily settler district, not a residential school or even, a so-called "Indian Day School" except when the Gill's arrived in Hay River. While his school career was not an overwhelming success, still, Gordon was good in math, and perhaps more importantly, he knew mechanics and welding was his goal. Which of these, and other elements, made the difference in Gordon's life? Whichever combination of stars and fate and parenting and environment and genetics made up this quite unique man, one sentiment seems clear: Thank goodness Gordon was not sent to residential school until he was old enough to take care of himself.

And this is but one story among thousands. There are still many more Indigenous stories to be told.

....

55　See for example "Teaching in Northern Alberta Communities; The Importance of Place, Past and Present" by Campbell A. Ross, Instructor Emeritus, Grande Prairie Regional College.

CHAPTER 11:
Métis Script; Métis Adaptation

Birchbark baskets, photo courtesy Chris Brodeur.

I basically identify with the Native and Métis.

WE USUALLY CONSIDERED *ourselves Natives. But Métis was not well known at that time. We figured we should be Treaty but what happened was our grandparents took script, Justine and Noel. Taking script disqualified us from being status, like Treaty. Kind of strange how Native blood can run through your veins, but you still cannot identify as Treaty.*

My grandparents did not want to take script, but it was more or less forced on them. The government basically wanted to breed the Native out of us.

Canada's Métis policy was a splendid success if you were a speculator or one of the country's chartered banks. How, you might ask, did chartered banks end up, in northwest Saskatchewan, with 99 percent of the Métis script, more properly called "scrip," and thus the land destined to provide a home for them?

If the Indians had received the rights of Treaty and the whites did not need or merit them, then what should the government of Canada do with the Métis? The people of Red River had been there in one form or another for millennia. Their descendants had lived there, taken up recognizable title to their land, and adopted a system of governance and land tenure, along with skills and a way of life. This was true of the Saskatchewan Métis as well, and their other relatives spread throughout the great northwest of Canada. After the execution of Ontario Orangeman Thomas Scott, the subsequent action by the people of Red River was, to them, a resistance against a type of invader. Jean Teillet makes a very convincing argument that the Métis were simply trying to preserve the rights they had earned and won. For the majority of English Canada, the Indigenous Peoples of the west were rising up against the lawful authority of the government. Canada, as purchasers of the land rights, and as the inheritor of British sovereignty, surely had the right to take the land and lay out the rules for its occupation and use, or so the thinking went. Thus, action to prevent or delay that was rebellion. Whichever is the proper word, resistance or rebellion, all Métis—involved in the resistance or not—were suspect.

Is it such a surprise that the settlers and those bringing commerce to the land that the settlers were entering wanted their government to take control of such land? If nothing else—since some Indigenous right to the land was even then assumed—something had to be done to allow the railways access to the great western lands. And given the influx of whites and agitation for proper recognition of their place and rights in the West, and Prime Minister John A. Macdonald's stated policy of "colonizing the fertile lands of the Saskatchewan,"[56] it is no wonder that relations got off to a bad start. As Campbell Ross reports, "Canadian expansionists sought to use the instruments of federal power to bring northern Alberta [and northern Canada generally] into the national vs fur trade sectoral economy." Whatever the reason, the arrogance of the government and white society, built on their sense of superiority and Eurocentrism, was the cause of much pain and misunderstanding in Canada, not unlike the scene in the United

....
56   Wilson, *Frontier Farewell*, 33.

States, Australia, New Zealand, and South Africa.

As for Métis policy, this too started early, under Prime Minister Macdonald, with the acknowledgement by the federal government that Métis rights would need to be extinguished too. The method was developed of issuing "scrip," or sometimes "script," in payment for any land or other claims that a Métis person might have.

"Scrip was issued to those adults and children who could document that they were of Indian-European ancestry and who had been born in British or Canadian territory."

Jean Teillet argues persuasively that Macdonald agreed to recognize Métis rights and property as established by their usage in Red River but that he refused to enforce the agreement he made when he sent armed troops of largely anti-French, anti-Catholic, and—what a surprise—anti-Métis Orangemen to "peacefully" and ceremonially take over what became Manitoba. He then reneged, according to Teillet, in a manner both cynical and purely political.

The scrip system was set up and operated in the full knowledge and often connivance between government agents and speculators, Teillet says, so that no Métis would ever actually get title to land that had been promised them. Her version, convincingly, is a searing indictment of the Canadian political parties at the time, both Conservative and Liberal, and of their co-conspirators, the banks, and the speculators.[57]

Métis scrip was "literally provisional certificates entitling the bearer to a certain amount of federally owned and surveyed land in ... the North-West Territories." Land scrip (for 160 acres of land) or money scrip ($160 cash to be used to buy land), later increased, was granted to the Métis people of the northwest to compensate for the extinction of their rights and any claim to "Indian" title or the rights of "Indians" under any of the treaties negotiated in western Canada with them.

> "Actually, there were two Aboriginal cultures whose future was being forecast here in 1899-1900, represented by two commissions, the Treaty Commission and the Half-Breed Commission. What few protections were to be made available through Treaty #8 to Aboriginals who took treaty ...were not to be available to ...the Metis".

----

57   Teillet, *Our Mother.*

> "[T]he Commissioners did not care whether an individual signed treaty or took scrip. There was no blood test. Choosing between being Indian or Metis was not a big deal for the commissioners or the signators…The main concern of the commissioners was extinction of title and that would occur through adhesion to either document."

And why did the Métis agree? Campbell Ross suggests that:

> "…improvident focus on the immediate cash advantage played a key role. In 1899, 1,234 scrip notes were issued, of which only 48 were for land."

However, there were a lot of factors at stake for the Métis looking to take scrip. Ross himself says that while some Métis in northern Alberta were there already as descendants of the historic fur trade people,

> "…others were essentially economic refugees from further east and south, moving on as railroad and settlement pressed upon their cobbled together lifestyle… Metis had moved to new locations when they became displaced elsewhere. Northern Alberta proved to be the place from which there remained no further exit".[58]

This suggests that taking the money might also have been smarter, and more conducive to moving on. Further, the Métis in the later years may have heard of the swindles involving land scrip in Manitoba and Saskatchewan, they may well have been reluctant to trust the government's assurance of unlimited rights to fish and hunt (as proved wise), and they were right to be uncertain about the nature and location of the land to be given.

Noel was likely in the Lac Ste. Anne area when the Half-breed commission came through.

There is some question of how the scrip business was dealt with in the L'Hirondelle family. It appears that Noel's brother took scrip, and it may be that it was assumed Noel did too. In Canada, if you were not identified and accepted as a member of a particular tribe, as recognized under the Indian Act, you could not be included in the Treaty, and if you didn't prove your Métis status, then you didn't get scrip. So, it is possible that Noel, and

58　Ross, *Teaching in Northern Alberta*, 51-56

others, simply fell through the cracks. If they were away and didn't get registered, they simply had no status and thus no payments or benefits from the government. They were, in that case, also free from the regulations governing their kin. Many others simply took whatever cash they could get and moved further away from the new communities being established by the newcomers. A quick look at the list of L'Hirondelles who took scrip in 1885 shows that most took cash, and only a very few took land.[59]

A search of Gail Morin's list[60] of those who were eligible for scrip as a result of being Métis and able to show descendance from the Red River settlement or other western settlements between 1870 and 1885 does reveal large numbers of L'Hirondelles, but not Noel or Justine. There were claimants with similar names to various ancestors, but so many names in the Gill family tree are duplicates or so common that it is hard to draw conclusions. For example, Joseph and Josephet(te), were common names at the time.

The difficulty lay, according to Ens and Sawchuk, in the inability to properly define what ancestry should be classed as Indian or Métis for the government and land tenure purposes. "Consequently, persons of mixed ancestry could choose either Indian Treaty or Métis scrip and, in many cases, they took both. This haphazard policy regarding the choice between Treaty and scrip and the ability to move back and forth between the two statuses… ushered in a new era," one that "defined and counted identities in an all-or-nothing manner."[61]

The unfortunate outcome, and a long-simmering issue in the status of Métis people and the wealth of some of the immigrants to the Northwest, was set out in a speech by Prime Minister John A. Macdonald in 1885:

> …this grant of scrip and land to those poor people [the Métis] was a curse and not a blessing. The scrip was bought up; the lands were bought up by white speculators and the consequences are apparent.[62]

Archbishop Tache recommended granting nonnegotiable scrip. This was not accepted. The result, according to the Canadian Geographic's

59 Morin, *Northwest Scrip.*
60 Morin, *Northwest Scrip.*
61 Ens and Sawchuk, *From New Peoples*, 189–191.
62 Quoted by Ens and Sawchuk, *From New Peoples*, note 77, 561.

Indigenous Peoples Atlas of Canada, was that land speculators bought scrip from Métis at very low prices and sold it to the main Canadian banks.

> Out of 14,489 issued, land speculators ended up obtaining 12,560 money scrips. They also managed to leave the Métis with only one percent of the 138,320 acres of land scrip issued in north-west Saskatchewan.[63]

It appears that Noel and Justine either chose or were directed to Métis status themselves, perhaps by their own parents' decisions about their status. They chose to not identify or even stay with the large Indigenous communities at St. Albert or at nearby Lac Ste. Anne or Lac La Nonne, where they had been born, but rather strike off on their own.

Thus, they fit the comment by Ens and Sawchuk that although:

> "Metissage was nearly universal in the fur trade, the biracial descendants of the fur company servants did not automatically assume a Métis identity; indeed many… were assimilated among the [Indigenous] bands of the northwest… and, affirming the random nature of the scrip system, "Sometimes, some family members took treaty while others took scrip. This occurred among First Nations people too as many took scrip and became Métis. This meant that even within one family, some family members could become status Indians and others, Métis."[64]

This happened in the L'Hirondelle family, according to Gordon's oral history. Some uncles were Treaty; others joined a recognized Métis community, like at St. Albert, northwest of Edmonton, and still others carried on as individuals outside of either community. Families living with white fathers, were more often raised and schooled in white communities. The possible combinations of upbringing for Indigenous children were multi-fold, and the possible or even likely outcomes even more so. What-might-have-beens are spread all over the map.

In Gordon's story, we see that Gordon and Mildred were both Indigenous, perhaps Métis, through their mother's family, and "half-breeds" as a result of their white father. They went to regular small-town schools,

....
63   Quoted by Ens and Sawchuk, *From New Peoples*, note 77, 561.
64   Ens and Sawchuk, "Chapter 8," *From New Peoples*.

not residential ones. They lived at home. What impact Clarence's English name and his race had on these decisions are speculative only. Gordon's uncles on his mother's side were Métis as well, albeit with English-type names, like Sharp and Hodgson. Gordon does not recall anyone from the Notikewin areas going to residential school and it appears from the Campbell Ross work referred to in the bibliography that this was common in areas of, for example, northern Alberta, where there was a public school nearby. However, Hay River had a day school, which by definition does not contain a residence.

So was the treatment and the outcome for many Indigenous children in Canada just a matter of luck and location? Was the difference racially based, in the sense that Gill and Sharp didn't sound Indigenous? Was Armande's reluctance to reveal too much of her Indigenous side a positive, after all? And what about language? Gordon and Mildred spoke English only, thanks to Armande. It will never be known what has been gained and what has been lost by Armande adapting her life, perhaps a result of her parents steering her that way too.

Gordon chose, or had chosen for him, the white way. His grandparents started down that path, and Armande cut the trail wider in order to survive and make the world easier for her children. These adaptations—in language, dress, approach, customs, names, and culture—with a Caucasian husband, in the Gill family at least, led to the complete loss of the Cree language, just as their ancestors gave up their Iroquoian words. Many peoples have struggled with the value of adaptation versus the determination not to give up one's historic, in this case, Indigenous language and culture. How different would life have been if the Gills didn't have that inclination and social pressure to adapt, or if Clarence, the English speaker, was not around?

It is so hard to say what should have been, let alone what might have been.

As it is, much of the Métis life continues with Gordon. He spent as much time as he could in the forest, making and trying out moose callers, attracting birds. He loves nature. He likes to laugh and doesn't like to brag or play big. He is reluctant to even talk about his life, without much prodding and tugging. He has a passion for birchbark, for its look and smell, for the lovely fires it makes, for the uses it can be put to, like the funnel shaped moose calls he has made (including a supersize one he called his "Texas Moose Caller"), canoes,[65] baskets, and for the taste of the slow-dripping birch syrup.

It seems ironic, given his upbringing, that Gordon concludes here by saying: *I ended up being one of the early members of the Hay River Métis Sunrise Association.*

....

65   "The primary mode of transportation for the Northwest Company was the birchbark canoe. First developed by the aboriginal people of the eastern woodlands, these lightweight, durable craft varied in size depending upon their use. The 7.5-metre (25-foot) *canot du nord* was used to transport heavy loads of goods and furs. The canoes were made of wood and birchbark sewn together with spruce roots and sealed with rendered pitch. They were easy to repair and carry. Although the canoes were light and their French-Canadian and Scottish crews experienced, the lengthy journey from Montreal to the fur country was exhausting." — Interpretive sign; Rocky Mountain House NHP, Rocky Mountain House, Alberta.

CHAPTER 12:
Lionel – Hope for the Future

Lionel Gagnier, courtesy of Joe and Lionel Gagnier, Jr.

I got hope that there was more out in the world from Lionel
Gagnier, Uncle Lionel. He lived with my aunt Adeline, and
they had a boy, Joe Gagnier, my cousin.
Lionel convinced Dad to go to Hay River to find work.
So, he did.

THE STORIES ABOUT Lionel Gagnier abound "North of 60." [Meaning
north of the 60th parallel of latitude, the southern border of NWT]. A long-
time resident of Hay River, Joy Stewart, is quoted in Eileen Collin's oral
history of Hay River.[66]

Stewart, whose father was often Gagnier's business partner, called him

---

66   Eileen Collins (ed.), *I've Been Here Ever Since… An Informal Oral History of Hay River*
(Hay River, AB: Tourism Advisory Committee of the Town of Hay River, June 1999).

a "giant of a man." She said he was actually called "The Paul Bunyan of the North."[67]

Collins's history [68] tells many stories of Gagnier's exploits. One story has Lionel helping a motorist with a flat tire and no jack by lifting the car by its bumper. Another had Lionel going out onto the big lake when an airplane "got hung up on the ice."[69] He just pushed the plane free manually, by himself, out of whatever was hanging it up.

One winter on a very cold and bitter day, Ms. Stewart reported:

> [t]hey were putting some pilings in for Shell or the hotel. They had a crew of men working. All day long you'd hear that bang, bang, bang. One piling just got started so it was extremely long, and it slipped. [Gordon explains that sometimes the steel piling would get an ice film that would make it too slippery for the chain around the piling to hold]. The piling slipped. There were two workers underneath. They would, surely as I'm sitting here, be dead. Lionel saw it. He stepped in and he took the force of that piling coming down at that speed, caught it and threw it over… He did save the lives of those two workers. I don't think Lionel's back was ever the same after that.[70]

Gordon agrees that steel pipe, ice, chains, and cold weather made for a very dangerous combination.

According to an article published in the local newspaper[71] just before Lionel's death, Lionel had two passions, work and adventure. He was born in Bourget, Ontario, a tiny French farming community near Ottawa on November 13, 1913 . Lionel tried farming, working in the gold mines in Timmins and Sudbury. And then Lionel heard about opportunities out west. Like many other young men of the time, Lionel heeded the call, riding the rails to Edmonton. Actually intending to go to South America with a couple of friends, he said " the truth was, we were broke and had to go to work in Yellowknife". The big pay at the Yellowknife gold mines, two

67   Collins, *Ever Since*, 149-151
68   Collins, *Ever Since*.
69   Collins, *Ever Since*.
70   Stewart, in Collins, *Ever Since*.
71   Hay River Hub, from the collection of the Gagnier family, circa 1986-7, actual date unknown.

and a half times what he was earning in the northern Ontario mines plus room and board, "seemed like riches". Lionel didn't learn to speak English until into his 28th year.

The gold mine at Thompson Landing paid well, but the isolation made the mining settlement grim. He left, swearing not to return, but he did. Later, Lionel made his way to Hay River in 1947. That first winter he cut wood to make ends meet. But with the construction of the Mackenzie Highway, Lionel saw a future in the north. In 1955, self-taught, he started a construction company and five years later teamed up with long-time partner Don Stewart, Sr. Together they established successful companies like Igloo Building Supplies, Gagnier-Stewart Construction and Igloo Theatres.

Gagnier sold his interest in the businesses in 1980 but continued, like Gordon, to work. A devout Catholic, Lionel volunteered to help build the Roman Catholic church in Paulatuk, in the high Arctic. The Hub writer Kirsty Jackson reported that Mr. Gagnier "volunteered for the project because he likes to see buildings finished". After that, he "found himself constructing an Anglican church and rectory in Aklavik, an [sic] rectory in Fort McPherson and a church in Inuvik. …They just asked for my help. That's how it got started".

The article foreshadows Gordon's own life. It seems that Gordon has adopted his mentor's words as well as his deeds. The Hub quoted Lionel using phrases that Gordon would use in describing his own life, such as "Working, that's what I like the most" and "I have to work". Lionel "enjoyed showing the product of his labour", the reporter said.

Gordon worked for Lionel during the school year. Gordon's job then was to run a steamer, which warmed the ground so Lionel could, in the dead of winter, keep going, driving piles for the base of the Hay River Hotel then under construction. Gordon himself did the same kind of work with his cranes in later years. It was just another way in which Gordon followed a man who was, in many ways, his mentor and idol. Lionel, in his time, like Gordon later, was part of the Hay River business community, and although Gordon was not the social lion of his time, he too worked well with others, invested, built, and tried to make things happen.

In Lionel's case, he was a recognized part of a group of Hay River Old Town "founding" families; names like Stewart, Dean, Miron, Carter, Lefebvre, Steiner, Porritt, Kostiuk, Godwin, Gaetz, and others are still recognized in street names around town. These were among the many who arrived shortly after World War II and built the businesses and fisheries of the area during the late 1940s and 1950s. It was Lionel Gagnier who urged Clarence to come to town for work in 1956. Lionel was also one of the main builders of New Town Hay River after the major flood of 1963, when the townspeople were encouraged to move to the mainland from the river island the town had previously occupied.

Lionel looked out for people, which you could say about Gordon Gill too. In addition to the job for Clarence, his sort of brother-in-law for a time, Lionel arranged for a job for Armande at the Hay River Hotel when it was opened by his friends, the well-connected Calgary brewers named Cross. Gordon himself started working on the tugs in 1956, again thanks to Lionel, at least in part. It was Lionel who got the Department of Public Works (DPW) job for Clarence, who parlayed a contact there into a summer job for Gordon on the MV *Malta*. Despite the fear he felt in the big storm that summer, Gordon was connected to barges and tugs and gold dredges, and thus northern rivers, for the rest of his working life. He offers: *Somehow, working on the tugboats fit me. The welding and mechanics and problem solving. It was all good. And there weren't that many places to spend money.* Gordon admired Lionel, saying:

> *Lionel was a devout Catholic and an exceptionally good-looking man. His wife Christine was very good-looking, very distinguished and unusual looking. She had been Lionel's best friend's wife. The best friend died. Lionel went down to give his condolences and found the partner of his life… Christine and Lionel could really put on a feast.*
>
> *Lionel would come to Granny's for Christmas, and he always seemed sort of prosperous and that's the kind of guy I wanted to be. I looked up to him because he had money. Lionel would tell us different stories of what he was doing up in Hay River. He was a really hard worker, and really strong. He did a fair bit of logging, contracting, Cat work. He did all kinds of stuff, so I looked up to him.*
>
> *It wasn't the money. I never worked just for money, and now that I have some money, it doesn't matter. It hasn't changed me. I am still a meat-and-potatoes kind of guy. I still like Spam and baloney. I think*

what motivated me was the chance to do something, to have maybe the security and not always feel poor. The first summer in Hay River, after I came off the dredge, I had a bank account and money in the bank. It felt good. Maybe it was the security.

CHAPTER 13:
Going North

NWT Archives/ Bobby Porritt fonds/N-1987-016-0844.

When my dad went up to Hay River in the spring of 1956, he wrote a couple letters back to us and said how much work and stuff there was in Hay River and what he was doing. In the spring of 1956, my dad got me a job with DPW where he was working. That came as a total surprise. That's how we came to move to the Northwest Territories.

THAT IS WHERE Gordon began to earn his reputation for honesty, and hard work.

Clarence had hired on with the Department of Public Works, a department of the federal government, which, in those days, was responsible for Canada's territories, then the Yukon and the Northwest Territories. The department was based in this southernmost NWT town. The territory was not a province, being rather an area governed directly by the federal government from Ottawa. Thus, the federal Department of Public Works played a huge role in the North. As one of the main departments of government there, DPW was responsible for much of the infrastructure of daily life. One such role was owning, and operating water borne digging machines, dredges, that cleared navigation channels, removed obstacles from the rivers and lakes, and generally maintained harbours.

The MV *Malta* was a Public Works tugboat which moved a dredge, in this case Dredge 251, and related barges to its positioning points where the dredge would clear channels, excavate passageways, dig out rocks, and attend to other related marine transport support work.

Gordon's first task was to get to the harbour in Hay River to meet up with the tug.

However, going north required a bus trip over the long, undulating, graveled Mackenzie Highway. The road was closed in by trees all the way north, and there was nothing to see; it was often rutted and bumpy like a washboard or washed-out where fast-running rivers and streams forced their way across. It was always dusty and the trees, though noticeably shortening on the route to Great Slave Lake, would hold the dust in place. Driving the road in the dust was always risky, even twenty-five years later. Most years saw horrific, dreadful fatal accidents caused by the lack of visibility; often as big transport trucks billowed up the fine silt into clouds that would not dissipate. Passing another vehicle, either approaching or following, was often like playing Russian roulette.

This was the only road to the North, and it was rugged. And like its namesake river, it was both a travel route and the method of communication in the North in those days. Just like the paddle-wheelers and the tugs and barges that would stop along the river, so the bus would stop at the side of the road or where a number of dwellings or a tiny bit of a community was gathered, like Keg River or Indian Cabins near the NWT border. Both the road and the river were essential for the delivery of supplies and people. Even now, between Manning and High Level and from there to anywhere, it is mostly a long, lonely line through the trees.

Built by American soldiers during the Second World War, the road was meant to be kind of a sister road to the Alaska Highway. They both start as Highway 43, about 70 kilometres west of Edmonton, at a 90-degree angle to the northern Yellowhead route of the Trans-Canada Highway. The Alaska and Mackenzie Highways follow the same route until they split at Valleyview, Alberta. The Alaska road heads west to Grande Prairie and into northeastern BC and then the Yukon and Alaska. The Mackenzie Highway leads straight north to the south shore of Great Slave Lake via Peace River.

The northern sections of both roads were built after the Japanese attack on Pearl Harbor in 1941. The Americans joined the Allies in World War II and immediately set out to protect Alaska and the West Coast from Japanese invasion. The roads north, as well as infrastructure route for airplanes, were purpose-built for access to the Norman Wells oilfields and for the supply of defence material in the case of Japanese incursions via the North. Aid to Russia, like the Northwest Staging Route, also followed the northern routes. US soldiers and equipment, with some Canadian help, built air strips, roads, and the Canol (Canadian Oil) pipeline from Norman Wells to the Yukon.

For Gordon Gill in 1956, that highway to that job, no matter how bad, meant a way out, a way off the bush farm and the narrow confines of life there. But that way out required a very long and uncertain hitchhike or a bus ticket on the northbound Greyhound.

> *My dad sent a letter with the Greyhound bus driver, who dropped it off at our driveway. He put the letter on the driveway with a rock on top of it and the envelope had the money in it for me to get a bus ticket to go to Hay River. I remember the letter saying that I was going to go work on the dredge; I didn't even know what a dredge was, but I soon found out. I was fifteen years old at that time.*
>
> *Prior to that, a kid came from Hay River and went to school in Manning for one year. He had stories about Hay River, and how much he liked it, and his dad and him were moving to different parts of the country. So, I got a little information about Hay River from him.*

The bus driver's delivery was enough to allow Gordon to buy a ticket for the 560-kilometre trip to Hay River. No depot existed there, not even a roadside café or gas station. Both the money delivery and the road were examples of the real North in those days.

> *I went out to the highway to wait for the bus. You just stood at the side of the road and waited. The bus didn't come when it was supposed to. That wasn't unusual. It was a rough road, and there were lots of washouts and other problems. But I had made up my mind. I was going to stay on that highway, waiting for the bus to take me to Hay River*

if I had to stay there all night, and I think I did. I think I waited for eight hours.

I wasn't going to miss that bus. I was never going to come back to that Hotchkiss country. I knew that life on the boat was going to change my life, which it did because then I would have good money. Kids in Hay River didn't have the kind of money I had.

The money in the envelope was just enough to get the bus ticket, and I needed to take a lunch. At that time, there was only one place to eat on the whole highway and that was at High Level. There was a café there—just the one café to my knowledge. It was on the Greyhound bus that I met Joe McBryan. "Buffalo Joe" was on the same bus, going to join his parents in Hay River.[72] The bus ride took a long time because there were washouts and everything on the road in those days. It was a long trip.

It was a terrible road even twelve years later. Long-time Northerner Jake Ootes describes his journey north in 1968. Speaking of the still largely unpaved section of the Mackenzie Highway north of High Level, Alberta, Ootes said:

We hit construction at High Level, Alberta, the main extension of the Mackenzie Highway, littered with giant potholes, thousands of curves and many miles of mud and gumbo. The driving was treacherous and occasionally downright dangerous. As we were only able to drive at thirty to forty miles per hour, the drive from Edmonton to Yellowknife, a stretch of eight hundred miles, took three days.[73]

Gordon arrived in a place he had never been, Hay River, in the middle of the night, at age 15. No one was there to meet him. It was 3:30 a.m.

Joe McBryan's parents picked him up, but I didn't know where Dad was. Anyway, he had to be to work early in the morning. I seen a light on at a building. It was almost like a fishing caboose, so I went and

---

72   Joe McBryan later became the focus of the TV show *Ice Pilots* about his life flying DC-3s in the North.

73   Jake Ootes, *Umingmak: Stuart Hodgson and the Birth of the Modern Arctic* (Vancouver, BC: Tidewater Press, 2020).

knocked on the door, and sure enough, this bachelor lived in there, and I told him who I was. He had met my dad talking with Lionel. This guy and Lionel knew each other, so he said, "Well, why don't you just hang here with me. I'm going to be hauling gravel in a few hours." So, I stayed with him for a few hours and talked with him; he didn't speak very good English, but we made out fine. In the morning, he pointed me out to where Lionel was, so I went and met up with Lionel, and Lionel took me to the dredge.

Lionel used to hire me too when I was a kid in Hay River whenever there was spare work and his partner, Rudy Steiner, did too. They were partners in certain projects. I always had work. Eventually, in the early 1970s, our old town of Hotchkiss turned around economically; it did pretty good because the oil exploration, the logging, and that kind of stuff made life better for people there. But it was nothing like what I ended up doing in Hay River and being involved in the marine industry. I was so lucky to get to go to Hay River and to get a good start on my career. It was a good town, and the marine industry for the whole North was getting more and more important.

CHAPTER 14:
Hay River

Hay River, NWT, Old Town, Great Slave Lake with ice.

Mother and Mildred came later. That was to Hay River, and in September 1956, I continued school at the Federal Day School there. It was called the Indian Day School then.

HAY RIVER IS A SMALL TOWN by southern standards. The population has never reached 4,000 people. It is the largest town and the second-largest community in the NWT (after Yellowknife, the capital city). The Mackenzie Highway, the Great Slave Lake Railway, and the Hay River all meet in the silty delta on the flat southwest shore of Great Slave Lake. It is literally the end of the road for each of those routes.

Hay River is a town of islands and river channels with a flat, treed main-land that stretches to the horizon. It has the only "Indian Reserve" in the NWT[74] and a beautiful sand beach. The river that gives the town its name

....
74   Salt River Indian Reserve near Fort Smith also has territory in the NWT.

runs 700 kilometres in the extreme northwest of Alberta with a bit of a detour into northeast British Columbia before emptying into Great Slave Lake. In its last 130 kilometres or so, north of the 60th parallel, it drops over the "Hay River Escarpment,"[75] first at the 32-metre (109-foot) Alexandra Falls and then at the smaller 14-metre (50-foot) stair-like Louise Falls. The river carves a deep, abrupt canyon in this otherwise (but for the sharply dropping escarpment) incredibly flat and homogenous land of mostly smaller evergreens.

This is, for most Canadians, a largely unknown town in an oft ignored and far-off territory. It is called the "Hub of the North" by the local chamber of commerce because it is a major inland seaport and the North's centre of transportation. Everything at one point had to go north or come south through that hub. Spokes went in all directions and by various means. Early on, the first peoples travelled the land by canoe, on foot, or by dog team and sled. Later, Cat-trains, trucks, and rail joined the snow machines, steamboats, and then diesel tugs and other ships. The highway and the railway were major spokes, as were river and lake traffic and aviation. Then there is the road west to the largely Indigenous community of Fort Simpson (and up the Liard Valley to BC). It branches north at Fort Providence, across the Mackenzie River to Yellowknife and again at Simpson to follow the big river down toward Fort Wrigley. To the east, a branch crosses the Hay River to the Indian Reserve turnoff, the site of the former lead-zinc mine at Pine Point, the mostly Indigenous village of Fort Resolution, and the old government town, formerly the capital of the Northwest Territories, Fort Smith.

Gordon arrived in his mid-teens and made a life and a successful career from this base. Until he and his wife Treena departed for the south almost forty years later, it was in Hay River and on the banks of that river and on the lakes and rivers north of there that Gordon found his life's work and his balance, which allowed him to thrive and grow. There, Gordon was able to apply his training in welding, mechanics, and ship repair; learn his trades; establish his companies; provide employment; and build his

75   Gordon said, *A geologist told me once that the escarpment runs from Fort Simpson to the State of Maine on the east coast. There are places where it can't be seen for miles, then it comes up again, dipping and diving across the continent. Like, it was the front edge of the polar ice, or something like that.*

reputation—all related to the work on these northern waterways. He started by working the tugs and then repairing them and the barges they towed or pushed. He built ferry boats and oil-drilling platforms, tugs for exploration and transportation, gold dredges, housing barges, and vessels for offshore cartage and drilling. His work was the manifestation of what kept the industry running.

And it was important for the town and the North. It is hard to say which had the greater impact—Gordon on Hay River or Hay River on Gordon. But it was there that Gordon made or seized opportunity.

There are few places like Hay River anywhere else in Canada where you can find, in one spot, an Indigenous fish camp and reserve, year-round big-lake fishing centre, marine port, transportation hub, business and tourism centre, and the base for mineral exploration.

Initially, the mouth of the Hay was the site of a seasonal fish camp for generations of so-called Slavey Indians, which is a derogatory name now replaced with the more proper word "Dene," which means "The People." Although initially used for trading as early as 1837, the local history informs that in 1892, Chief Shatla decided to make the northeast bank of the river a permanent place for his people. That brought the Anglican mission and then the Catholics and the Hudson's Bay Company and the Northwest Mounted Police, and so the village became a place for trading and missionary work.[76]

After the discovery of gold in Yellowknife in the 1930s and silver-pitchblende at Cameron Bay on Great Bear Lake, the ancient trail north from Peace River was developed into first a rough track for Cat-trains in the late 1930s, and then a rugged "highway." After World War II, there was an influx of new residents, usually younger people who pursued the main economic drivers of the time: commercial fishing, construction, and transportation from the ever-increasing marine traffic going north to the communities and out into the Arctic. The latter was pushed along during World War II by the need for secure shipping of the uranium and silver from Great Bear Lake and the oil fields at Norman Wells, and after 1960 by expanded oil and mineral exploration. The opening of the Pine Point lead-zinc mine and the completion of the Great Slave Lake Railway in 1964 added to the

....

76 Collins, "Introduction," *Ever Since.*

town's importance, as did the Northern Transportation Co. Ltd.'s decision to phase out the transportation system's historic southern route from Waterways/Fort McMurray north around a tough portage at Fort Smith.

The Collins Hay River history book is an informal oral telling of the Hay River story published in 1999.[77] It brings to life the old days and the struggle to make a life in a place with more fish and game than people. There are stories of the people, the economy—with its basic labour and construction work—the housing (more poor shacks than houses), and only a few steadfast businesses. Old-time residents lament the loss of the fun and community events, and the trust and reliance that came with isolation and hard work to bind the community together.

The old-timers talk about the wonder of pavement seemingly inching north, little by little every year up the highway. Their memories include long, dangerous, dust-encircled driving journeys, being pulled out of the mud by big trucks, or having to take the ditch to avoid those same trucks. Often, the stories are of the true danger of driving empty roads for hundreds of kilometres in minus forty degrees or being towed through mud and quagmire by Caterpillar tractors, losing bumpers and mufflers along the way. Usually, they are about blindly passing in the dust. Sometimes they are about death.

Of course, progress and advancement have taken place in the North, just as elsewhere once remote and alone. People at the end of the various routes from civilization are happy to have regular phone lines now, TV, email, GPS, cell phones, and the internet. No more reliance on a radio phone, where the operator connected you with another operator in Peace River so you could connect with real land lines, and not having to say "over" at the end of each sentence.

Modern communications, of course, have changed the community. However, in Gordon's time, especially in the '50s, '60s, and '70s, this was part of the real North, largely unknown to southerners. It perhaps didn't have the romance and glory of the ice covered Arctic, but it was, and still is, remote, self-reliant, and basic. In Canada, places like this are often there for a purpose—government, resources, a dam, a mill, or a mine. It is still that way but without so much gravel, dust, high prices, and isolation. Gordon's

....

77 Collins, "Introduction," *Ever Since.*

life in those days, whether staking claims, or away on a river boat, was devoid of phones, radios, television, newspapers, magazines or any of the other forms of communication which modern society has come to expect. The only relay was the ship to shore radio used for reporting position or in the case of emergency.

For Gordon, the opening of the North, whether in terms of jet engines, better roads, or telecommunications, did have an effect on his business. Presumably those effects were both positive and negative.

Opening up the "near north" also brought some changes in attitude. Things have become more like "in the south"—sad in some nostalgic ways but happier no doubt for most residents. People don't automatically stop when they see a car pulled over to the side of the highway. Neighbours don't just drop in for tea without an invitation. Northerners don't always remind newcomers that propane freezes at cold temperatures and to put a light bulb in a can and cover the tank with snow if you don't want your furnace to quit in the night. The parties and the beach times were wild and fun. Everybody knew and often relied on everybody else. These are the kinds of things that Gordon grew up with and contributed to as a long-time resident. And there was a freedom, for better or worse, to try and fail, or to succeed spectacularly, build without permits or the heavy red tape of the big cities to the south, and make deals based on a handshake. In some ways, memories of the northern ways sound like country-music songs.

Satellite-assisted technology is wonderful of course, and brings the near and far north into sync with southern Canada. However, these changes also bring time constraints, rules, administrations, bureaucracies, taxation, zoning and planning laws, and expectations. There are banks, and all the usual shops, and the offices of southern lawyers and accountants, and other north-reaching endeavours. Now, of course, houses are modular or in newer, nicely landscaped, modern subdivisions. There are beautiful larger homes along the river. It is quite cosmopolitan.

Going (nearly gone) is reliance on neighbours and men out on traplines or living in a shack and enjoying the freedom of the frontier.

Some things change for the worse. Greater accessibility by car, for example, or by short plane rides to Yellowknife, means that the air service is nothing like it used to be. The old stand-alone, fully equipped (by the Pentecostal Mission) hospital is now a nursing home, and the local health centre faces ongoing budget cuts and downsizing. There is only a part-time doctor now; in 1975, there were three or four of them. Likewise with lawyers. The town is down to a part-time lawyer who restricts his practice and only does that out of a sense of duty to the area.

Gordon shares in this lament for times past. As he says:

> We used to have great times at the beaches in Hay River as well, when we were kids. There are miles of broad sand beaches. Everybody would try to learn a song and we'd have between five or six of us. We would be able to sing five or six songs right through and it was fun. People would have a guitar or just sit around a little fire and sing without a guitar. I remember I used to have a little mandolin and we had a lot of fun with that on the beach.

> There was so much driftwood. We built shelters from the wood spread all over the beach and huge bonfires. We could swim at the mouth of the river and on really hot days in the lake, but man, the water was so cold. Summers were sunny and hot, and the sun stayed up until close to midnight.

> And the town was pretty casual then too. Especially in Old Town. It was a place where you could pull a shack onto a piece of empty property and be allowed to stay for the winter, or where newcomers might find accommodation sharing the upstairs of a house until they got their own. It was a place you could find, if you wanted to, a tiny furnished one-bedroom shack for rent that worked just fine for your summer job working in the office or maybe the popcorn[78] yard at government-owned Northern Transportation Company Limited [NTCL].

In the early days after the highway arrived and southerners started arriving, homes were made out of almost anything. They were usually tiny, maybe two rooms, with outhouses, or an old caboose used for ice fishing, with bunkbeds added "made to measure" to take up the least amount of

---

78   Called the popcorn yard since it was where the small freight, the light stuff, was strapped to wood pallets and stacked by small forklifts, rushing around from warehouse to storage spot to barge ramps like so many wasps, and as contrasted with the Heavy Load Yard, or Island D, where the trains and huge forklifts and cranes did the barge loading.

room. One house didn't need decorating. Every second board was printed, "W. H. Menzies Fish Company." In the 1970s boom, the choice of a place to live was, literally, between one apartment to rent, one mobile home for sale, and one regular house on the market.

The Collins book records similar regrets: the loss of house parties, visits, crafts, and sports that accompanied the coming of TV, the "southernization" of the place. Gordon was, of course, happy about the TV, at least in the short run. It was, he remembers, *In Hay River when I seen my first TV. They brought in canned TV.*[79]

Many of the old-timers talk about the sense of isolation, where the planes were few and far between and the road often impassable, and when the people concentrated first in the Indian Village and then, after the war, across the river in the Old Town, and how crossing the river—easily paddled in summer or skated in winter—was more common because people were friends with everyone, on either side of the river. But, of course, who doesn't want a movie theatre, better restaurants, and more than one liquor store where you don't have to complete a form with your order and hand it to the government clerk behind the counter to fill for you? It is easy to complain about Walmart coming to small towns if you live in a big city (not that Hay River has a Walmart).

One story illustrates the old Hay River. Jane Godwin, who with her husband had the grocery store in West Channel (and later in New Town), "carried" the Pope family of six by supplying groceries one summer. John was out on the lake, salvaging a barge that had run aground. When he came back in, job completed, he was paid $3,000. "That was a lot of money. I [John's wife, Mary] went with him to Jane's and we handed it to Jane. She said, 'I don't know what I can do about this.' John said: 'Well, you keep it … You trusted me, and I can trust you.' That was the thing. You could do that in those days."[80] Jane Godwin became an unofficial type of banker.

History as recorded in a place like Hay River perhaps sends another message. The streets in town, it seems, are designated to honour the history of the Hay River businessmen, most of whom were white and imported from the south. They were thought to be industrious, hard-working, visionary, and community-minded but mostly white and mostly male, names

---

79   Recorded on tape and physically delivered to town by air.
80   Mary Pope, quoted in Collins, *Ever Since,* 131.

like Stewart, Gagnier, Miron, McBryan, Wright, and Gaetz. There is one main commercial street named Courtoreille, but that recognizes a fishing family from Alberta who arrived in 1949. There are a couple of prominent Indigenous names, too, including Camsell and Sibbeston, but otherwise, Indigenous history seems to be missing.

It does raise the question of what names are remembered and honoured and why. There are presumably other legacies of those whose father's father's father fished the lake or the river and raised their families and maintained their culture, and who are honoured in their own ways. But perhaps those people are not on town council, and were not "builders" in the southern, Anglo-Saxon Protestant way. It is not Gordon's way to consider, much less worry about, this kind of thing. Perhaps it is ironic; in Gordon's mind, he fit in. He was, after all, a businessman. And Hay River was a town of good people.

> *It was a total mixture of people. I never felt any prejudice over being Métis. I never felt a moment's discrimination.* [Unlike in Manning, where, according to Gordon,] *they were nice people but there was kind of an invisible line between whites and others.*

The span of these years is the span of Gordon Gill's life in the town. He has seen the decline of fishing and has played his own role in the marine transport business through its rise, boom times, and decline.

Whoever you were, and wherever you came from, the northern petroleum rush of the 1970s and 80s was such a boom, and an exciting time.

One of the main business activities in Hay River was the transshipment of freight and fuel from the docks and storage yards sheltered near the mouth of the river to communities along the Mackenzie and the Arctic coast. There have been a number of tug and barge companies throughout the years, but the primary one was the Canadian government's crown corporation, Northern Transportation Company Limited.[81]

As North of 56, reported in 2012,

> Northern Transportation Company Limited (NTCL) is the prime transportation company for delivering goods down the Mackenzie River and coastal Arctic communities.

---

81 To get a sense of the rivers and captains of the NTCL system, see *NTCL – 75 Years* at https://youtu.be/fPMPA5pVM9k and *NTCL – River Men, River Boats* at https://youtu.be/VwRjDRC6gJE.

NTCL has been in business for more than 75 years. It operates a fleet of fourteen vessels, varying in size from 1,500 to 7,200 horsepower. The vessels pull or push barges that bring the goods to Northern communities. Using a versatile fleet of Arctic Class II ice breaking tugs, specially designed shallow draft Home Trade tugs and a large fleet of dry cargo and dual-purpose cargo and fuel-carrying barges, NTCL delivers to 22 Northern communities.

NTCL is headquartered and operates its traditional tug and barge service from the Port of Hay River, NT, on the south shore of Great Slave Lake. It has a supply of 1,500 containers. It costs $4,243 to ship a 20 [foot] container from Hay River to Inuvik, according to the Company's posted rate sheet.[82]

In a recent interview, Cameron Clement, the former president of Northern Transportation Company Limited, remembered the town from his early years, when he was there as a young man in his twenties:

The early '70s was a magical time in Hay River. It was such a boom time. Trucks were coming and going 24 hours a day, freight piled in, and forklifts buzzed around like so many wasps.

Hay River was great in the summer. The town was so welcoming; in early May, a huge influx of people from all over arrived. Some had jobs and some just showed up. We hired them all and such a rag-tag group of hippies, farm boys, draft dodgers, and students it was. In some ways, the bonds created a sense of excitement. Most of us were young, in our early twenties. It was like our war, like what our parents felt about World War Two.[83]

NT would move 250 men (and some women—usually cooks) through the Hay River camps and onto the boats, or to camps farther north, in a short time. It was such a hive of activity.

We were our own summer community, part of the town but separate too. Even the phrases came back to me now: "mug up" at night,

---

82   Norman Eady, "NTCL: The Waterway to the North," *North of 56* (July 2, 2012) https://northof56.com/infrastructure/article/ntcl-the-waterway-to-the-north.

83   Cameron Clement, interview with the author.

going across the dusty street to the "zoo" (as the bar at the Hay River Hotel was called), cash advance days to look forward to. It was special.[84]

The days of May and June—when the sun fills the sky and melts the ice enough to allow tugs to move—are bright and fresh in the "near north". The days are warm and long, the sun won't stop shining, so you need blackout curtains, and the land warms by the day and by the hour. The air has such a pure quality, and the natural world expands, the warmth, and the work change rapidly, opening the sky and the feelings of the place.

In the boom years, kids would arrive from the south by bus or car and find a shack to share, and a job, or they'd get hired in the south by NTCL and be delivered by the Eldorado Aviation DC-3s and -4s to the various camps and agencies, and steered to the commissary for bedding and assignment to a bunkhouse. The communities of the northern river system, and those of the whole western Arctic, were supplied and serviced through this harbour. The docks and wharves, the trucking yards, the terminals—all were like little anthills of activities. People came from all over, even overseas, to play their part in the Mackenzie River trade, the oil fields, and the shaping of Canada's future. Meeting new people, exploring, learning your job, working and playing hard, buzzing like wasps, scurrying like ants, all in the frenzied atmosphere to get freight moved, was as Clement said, magical.

And then it was pretty much all over.

The oil activity ceased, shut down by the federal government to reflect bigger issues of the economy, the environment, and Indigenous concerns, not unlike the present day. The traffic stopped, except for some small action, and when the world changed, so did the role, or at least the reality and pace of a northern seaport, rushing to supply the Arctic with drill pipe and exploration equipment.

And it remains quite a magical place; it is still the end of the road north, literally and figuratively, stopping at the edge of Great Slave Lake. You can drive back down the highway 50 kilometres or so to Enterprise and locate the branch roads to Yellowknife, Fort Smith, and Fort Simpson. You can get "out" to Edmonton or Fort Nelson, and on to other busier highways,

84   Clement, interview.

even the Alaska Highway, but whichever way you go, it is still a mass of trees, water and wilderness, a country filled with lots of nature, an occasional community, and not much else.

It is home still to Indigenous Peoples, pioneers, explorers, and adventurers, of good and industrious people, and of stories of the old days, when people had to save each other's lives—and did, like it was routine.

The surprising thing is the number of people who moved North "for just a year" or "just for the experience," and whose children are now the leaders and parents of new leaders coming along.

Hay River, the Hub of the North, is a small community, still on the frontier—as much as there is a frontier, with satellites and internet—an interesting town with a unique history. There are at least five separate parts to it (Indian village, reserve, Old Town, West Channel, and New Town) and arguably more because of the sprawl south along the river and down into some of the river flats south of town. Half of the people living there identify as Indigenous or Métis, but by northern standards it is thought of as primarily a white town and, by some Northerners, more of a northern Alberta town, joined as it is by landscape, geography, and road to that jurisdiction. It was known for fishing and shipping for much of its life. As both of those old-time industries declined, the town continued as a service town. Perhaps it still has to find its own future, or at least a new future.

For sure, it has had a good past.

As Gordon was quoted saying in the Collins history (1999), after he and Treena moved south:

> "I really miss the North. I miss the long summer days and the work and the people. If there was work—shipbuilding and crane work there—I'd be back … It is a good town."

CHAPTER 15:
The Flood, Fishing, and "Old Town"

1963 flood Hay River NWT Archives/Bobby Porritt fonds /N-1987-016-0172.

Treena's [Gordon's future wife, Treena Gudmundson]
family was living in the Carter Fisheries office at
the time of the big flood in 1963. The flood-watch
people woke her and her family in the middle of the
night to get them out before the flood really hit.

THE RIVER'S WATER, *backed up by huge ice jams that couldn't get
into Great Slave Lake, eventually rose to the ceiling of the Gudmundson
place and the mixture of water and wind and ice pushed the house 400
feet or so down the road and up against Weis' Grocery Store. It was
so cold that Treena's dad found the couch frozen to the ceiling, and*

> *other furniture frozen in place like going down steps, where the flood*
> *water receded.*

This natural disaster caused the relocation of the Hay River townsite from low-lying Vale Island (facing the lake at the mouth of the river) across the West Channel of the Hay River to the mainland. This created, in effect, a long and narrow stretch of buildings and infrastructure for about 8 kilometres south along the river.

Local minister Ivan Gaetz described the town as it was caught in one of the worst floods in its history:

> During the late days of April 1963, the Hay River was receiving spring
> runoff in northern British Columbia and Alberta. However, the Great
> Slave Lake ice was solid with all its winter strength. The breakup on
> the river was edging further north and on a Tuesday morning disaster
> struck. Muddy water and ice flowed freely over the town properties in
> an effort to spill out onto the lake which normally breaks up enough
> to receive the force of the high water.… Homes, outhouses, garages,
> and other buildings floated down the streets and were scattered
> randomly throughout the town. The Pentecostal Chapel floated into
> Pope's yard, across the street and the Legion Hall took up position in
> the churchyard—an interesting switch of locations.[85]

More than one storyteller talked of finding his boat on top of someone's car when the flood started to recede. A friend of Gordon's, Julien Lefebvre, spoke of how, when the flood waters receded, both his dad's car and his brother's had boats sitting on top of them.[86] Another resident, Ken Hunt, recalled that he jumped from barge to barge because of the water. The barges were tied up in the snye (a dead-end piece of water where NT stored boats and barges). "The water was so high, they went in [to town] with a kicker [a motor on the back of an open boat]… they went right over a car in the water… and they broke the windshield with the bottom end of the kicker."[87]

Gordon, then twenty-one, and his dad went to check on the damage to their own house. They were able to canoe right up and into the front door.

The flood, which changed the town (albeit not quite as much as

....
85   Ivan Gaetz, in Collins, *Ever Since*, 57–58.
86   Collins, *Ever Since*, 93.
87   Collins, *Ever Since*, 73.

the government hoped and expected, since people continue to live on the island now called "Old Town"), was one side of a two-sided coin. The good-sized river from the south gave the town its harbour, life, and purpose—Indigenous, business, fishing, and location. On the other hand, a river that breaks up earlier than the frozen inland sea into which it flows is a disaster waiting to happen. Each year, the flow of ice jams and cracks and rises, blocking the water flowing from Alberta. The residents look on nervously, since in no place in or near the town are the banks high enough above the water, but it is also a pretty river, winding north and giving rise to fishing, boating, and the lifeblood of the town, its good natural harbour that's enhanced from time to time by the type of silt-removing dredge that Gordon worked on in his first year in the north.

The Hay River's flow winds through silt and sand, creating islands and protected anchorages for boats and barges and the docks and wharves and ship-repair facilities that serviced the entire North of 60 river fleet. Then it empties into the Great Slave Lake. The second-largest lake in the vast Northwest Territories, it is also the deepest lake in North America with a depth of 614 metres.

Vale Island is the largest island in the Hay's delta. It was where the settler town was originally located; the missions were across the river, in the "Indian Village." After the monster flood, the federal government decided to build a new town on the mainland. There's a distinction made every so often in these pages between Old Town (Vale Island) and New Town, where everyone was supposed to move. The former is resurrecting itself in terms of residences and has always hosted the fishing, transport, and floatplane businesses. It was old, and the houses were often more ramshackle, home to hippies, Métis, back-to-the-landers, and others who perhaps were more rebellious. New Town holds the industrial section, the newer schools and health centre, downtown offices, and town and government departments.[88]

88 In a height of irony, as this work was being finalized for publication, the Hay River again backed up, bringing what has now been described as "unprecedented" water levels and flooding, worse than the 1963 flood and probably the worst in recorded history. Chunks of ice larger than trucks lay strewn on golf course fairways, lawns, and pushed up against fences... in the New Town and even further upriver. See, for example:https://edmontonjournal.com/pmn/news-pmn/canada-news-pmn/residents-forced-to-flee-n-w-t-town-due-to-heavy-flooding-from-river/wcm/e7cee8b3-4857-46c5-9eac-629be3bc2a5b, and https://ca.news.yahoo.com/weeks-flood-hay-river-homesteaders-152250700.html

Being on the shore of a huge lake that drains into one of the biggest rivers in North America, a mere 65 kilometres away, Hay River was an obvious base for the fishing and transport industry. Historically, commercial fishing was very important and was almost a business and culture unto itself. Gordon explains:

> *Treena's family lived with the other fishing families in West Channel. It's a separate part of town where one of the two channels of the Hay River flows into the big lake. It's away from the town proper, the Indian Village, and the dock areas. It was the community where most of the fishermen lived and where the fish companies were located.*

Fishing was always an element of life in Hay River. The Indigenous Peoples fished the area for generations and then settled at the mouth of the river. But after the Second World War, and specifically after the construction of the highway from Grimshaw north, the town experienced a rush of people coming to fish the lake.

> A surer but localized new industry was commercial fishing, inaugurated on Great Slave Lake after the war... and the largest operator on Lake Athabasca immediately moved equipment from that lake and began fishing the large, relatively untouched new supply source... A winter fishery for lake trout and whitefish was started in 1947–48 at the western end of the lake, handy for shipping whole fresh fish by refrigerated trucks from Hay River over the Mackenzie Highway to the railhead at Grimshaw or direct to Edmonton. The fishery achieved a peak nine-million-pound catch (10 percent of Canada's freshwater total) in 1949–50... It employed some 500 men... [and] gave Hay River a considerable boost by creating local employment and business in fish processing, boat outfitting and repairing, trucking and other activities.[89]

One of the prominent fishing families was that of George Carter. Gordon speaks fondly of them. When Treena's family—already fishermen from the Icelandic areas around Gimli, Manitoba—arrived in Hay River, George Carter put them up in an office he had by the dock. Gestur Gudmundson, Treena's dad, sold all his fish to Carter. The fisheries company also owned,

....

89 Zaslow, *Northwest Expansion*, 323.

itself, the *Diana H*, which operated as a fishing boat on Great Slave.

Carter's son Merlyn flew fishermen and their families and thousands and thousands of pounds of fish back and forth to the fishing station at Moraine Point, and elsewhere on the big lake. He operated an air-charter company from the dock area in Hay River and flew Gordon out to exploration sites from time to time. Merlyn also had a tourist fishing camp at Nonacho Lake, east of Great Slave, where he was tragically killed by a bear on a routine maintenance trip. Now, the aviation industry in Hay River and all air travel to or from the town are based at the Merlyn Carter Airport. The runway stretches almost from the lake near West Channel across flat Vale Island to very near the highway coming north onto the island.

At one point, Vale Island boasted at least five fish companies, mostly in West Channel. These included, according to Ron (Badgie) Courtoreille, "Alaska Fisheries, Gateways, Kutcher & Trefiak, and Carters. Then in wintertime you'd have Bulmer, Clark. Later on, Bushman's. I recall Inland… There were two fish companies in the town proper [now Old Town] Menzies and McGinnis."[90]

This was a large industry for the town—there were up to nine fish companies buying and shipping fish—in the forties and fifties, and it continued, although marketing of the fish was taken over by the federal government's Freshwater Fish Marketing Corporation. The industry declined through the late 1960s and thereafter.

The wharves were busy in West Channel when fishing was good. Now, there is little evidence of the hurly-burly of fish boats and nets, fish boxes, and the private fish-packing companies.

At the other wharves, in Old Town, significant construction was undertaken after the acquisition of Yellowknife Transportation in the 1960s when NT focused its primary shipping out of Hay River rather than Waterways/ Fort McMurray on the Athabasca River.

Earlier, from the later 1800s, northern missions, Hudson's Bay stores, the North-West Mounted Police (NWMP, the predecessor of the Royal Canadian Mounted Police), and occasional trappers and traders were supplied by freight canoes and wooden scows, then paddlewheel steamboats, and eventually steel tugs, which pushed barges down the Athabasca River

90 Ron (Badgie) Courtoreille in Collins, *Ever Since*, 28. Some remember seven or eight companies, more in winter.

and out onto Lake Athabasca or down the Slave River to Great Slave Lake and across to Yellowknife and the Mackenzie, and even occasionally up the Peace River. Initially, this southern route was based at Athabasca Landing, about 145 kilometres north of Edmonton, and the closest spot between that city and the Athabasca. Freight wagons were a constant feature of the old Athabasca Landing Trail, which used to push north from Edmonton. There was great excitement when Athabasca Landing was reached by its own railway.

However, the relentless push of history sought efficiency, and rails soon reached a new northern terminus near Fort McMurray (and another went to Peace River). This all but doomed Athabasca Landing in favour of the new transshipment point at Waterways. That route, now shortened, was prominent, especially when uranium and gold mines started to dot the shores of Lake Athabasca. Of course, the northern trade—supplies and people north, furs and people south—remained important, especially with Fort Smith as the government centre for the Northwest Territories. The old fur-trade fort was expanding as the idea of a closer government took hold. The problem was that Fort Smith, then accessible only by way of the Slave River flowing north out of the confluence of the Athabasca and Peace Rivers and sitting on the border between Alberta and the NWT, was also the site of extensive and treacherous rapids. All shipping north of that town or coming south required a 24-kilometre portage and all the manhandling and equipment such an endeavour involved.

Thus, as the Mackenzie Highway was developed and improved, and especially when the Pine Point (Great Slave Lake) Railway was finished in 1964, the rerouting of freight to the Hay River area became self-evident. For one thing, the western approach saved the time and expense of the arduous portage between Fort Fitzgerald and Fort Smith. For another, it avoided a much longer and thus more dangerous trip across Great Slave, and finally, the chance of being iced in (or out) was much greater with the farther distance to the Slave River, thus shortening the shipping season.

Accordingly, Hay River's role as the main transshipment point for the Mackenzie and Arctic communities and later the Alaska oil fields was heightened significantly. The increasing pressure to supply expanding oil, gas, and other exploration equipment for work in the far reaches of the Arctic, and southern goods and groceries to formerly unreachable Arctic communities, made for boom times from the mid-1960s through to the late 1980s. The federal government's National Energy Program[91] and the crash in oil prices in the mid-1980s then took their toll on the town. Its industries and suppliers, like the large local hardware stores, joined the decline of the northern transport tug and barge system.

The magnitude of the former shipping base and its related supply, fabrication, and repair businesses, like Gordon Gill's Northern Arc Shipbuilders Limited—and the end of that magnitude—is most easily seen at the ship works at the north end of the Hay River harbour. There, rows of derelict, boarded-up tugboats, supply boats, other vessels, and barges are left to rust on the big-timbered slipways, surrounded by weeds, chain-link fences, and piles of other rusting, useless equipment. How long the "good" tugs will last, or whether they get moved north to, say, Fort Simpson, or Tuktoyaktuk remains to be seen.

With fishing and river boats out on a huge, deep, white-capped lake, facing wind, ice, and waves breaking around them, desperate times are not uncommon. Imagine floating and being pushed by the wind and waves, your engine dead, at 24 kilometres per hour and trying to figure out where you'd hit land, or if you would. Help was often as near or as far as getting help from another vessel.

In one story in the Collins book, a major fishing boat was already towing another disabled boat in a storm, having trouble, but turned about to gather in a flooded fishing boat with six men aboard. The bigger boat towed both together into the sheltered delta of the Slave River, out of the big wind and waves. There, among a number of tugs also waiting out the storm, the fishermen were welcomed aboard for hot coffee, a meal, and a chance to get their clothes dried.[92] Meanwhile, a couple of the men took the engine apart, cleaned it, drained all the water, and got it going again.

Another time, a fishing vessel was half sunk and floundering. A larger boat (likely a competitor) dragged it into the river's mouth and beached it on a sand bar so it could be pumped out. It seems routine in the

91   See Taylor C. Noakes, "The National Energy Program," *The Canadian Encyclopedia* https://www.thecanadianencyclopedia.ca/en/article/national-energy-program) February 7, 2006; July 24, 2020) for detailed information on the federal government's various activities to encourage oil-and-gas exploration, reduce prices, increase taxation supply grants for Canadian ownership, and related topics.
92   Fred Dimion, in Collins, *Ever Since*, 46.

telling—pump it out, repair anything needed, and get moving again—but imagine the courage and strength needed to go out onto that huge deep lake again.[93]

> *My ambition, like, my dream, was to be like Lionel, to get out of Hotchkiss, to have lots of work and be able to put a few pennies in my pocket. I didn't plan it, but later, like how it unfolded in the end, Treena and I would say that our life was like a dream come true.*

93   Fred Dimion, in Collins, *Ever Since,* 46.

CHAPTER 16:
Starting on the River

YT Expeditor, at Hay River harbour, NWT.

My dad got me a job on DPW's Dredge 251 in Hay River.

DAD HAD BEEN WORKING *for DPW right at the dredge. That's how he got me the job when he got talking to the dredge master. The dredge master had asked if he had a son and my dad said he did. The dredge master said, "we need a bull cook/deck hand,"[94] and that's how I got that job. My dad worked for DPW too, but he only worked near where I was for couple of days. Then he was sent to Hay River and Enterprise. I never seen my dad until the fall of the year. Dad worked more or less as a labourer; he did a little bit of everything, carpentry and shoveling whatever had to be shoveled. He was also a truck driver. Dad was never on the tugboats—he was onshore—so I was by myself on the dredge.*

In the North, especially, due to the sandy and earthen nature of the soil, the strong river currents quickly move huge amounts of silt into piles

....

94 A bull cook was an all-around grunt, cook's helper, messman, and cleaner.

and bars, filling river mouths and channels, shifting the directional flow of the river, and generally meddling with any kind of navigation. Dredge work involved creating channels or removing impediments to boat traffic. Then there was all the marking and signage work and the replacing of marker buoys, docks, ramps, and the like. This was federal jurisdiction, navigable waters, and so the Department of Public Works (Canada) and the Canadian Coast Guard each had quite a large base of operations in Hay River. It was their collective task to keep the rivers and lakes marked and clear for transport. It is hard to describe, now, how essential the marine supply service was to the North in those days. Often, if the sealift didn't get through, the people didn't eat except for whatever they could find in the bush or out on the sea ice.

Various approaches were used to assist the tug and barge traffic; it was a constant job. Two of the most common approaches to clearing channels for shipping were shovel dredges and suction dredges.

The suction type relied on big pumps to suck the river silt through huge pipes or hoses to be deposited either on shore or on barges and scows for dumping later. The other kind consisted of a shovel or excavator set on the dredge, which dug out the silt or, in some cases, rock and gravel and, swiveling, deposited the rubble onto a vessel, likely a flat-bottomed scow or barge. Later the scow would be emptied, the digger scooping the debris onto an out-of-the-way area. Gordon's new home and workspace was a shovel dredge; or rather, the rooms and kitchen built onto the barge that accompanied the dredge to its work sites. Freddie Frip was the dredge master, and Ernie Sibbeston and Nick Kostiuk were deckhands.

Gordon didn't know a thing about the job he was to do. But, as always, he was a friendly and willing worker.

The dredge pulled out of Hay River and set up in Wrigley Harbour on the west end of Great Slave Lake, where the lake narrows to commence its run to the Arctic. The dredge's job was to dig out part of an island to make a tie-up place for the boats and tugs coming off or getting ready to go out onto the grand expanse of the big lake. This is the start of the Mackenzie River, the start of a fast and powerful river as it gets squeezed out of Great Slave Lake like toothpaste out of a tube.

Gordon hung in there all summer and worked hard. He wasn't that far away from his dad, but he was only fifteen and didn't see him or his mother or sister until the fall, when Mildred and Armande moved north.

He recalls:

> *We weren't that far away. Wrigley Harbour was only 35 to 40 miles away, but there was no way of getting there unless you went by boat or a floatplane. I started school a little bit late 'cause I was on the dredge. All the guys on the dredge were so nice it was unbelievable, and everybody just couldn't teach me enough. The engineers, the captain [Syd Marian], they had me steering the boat and doing all kinds of stuff and running the engine. Mind you, I had to clean the bilges, but these guys just couldn't teach me enough; they were so happy to show somebody.*
>
> *I couldn't get over how nice the people were that made the work there so nice. And I was the bull cook (like a kitchen helper), and everybody could have made a lot more mess if they wanted to, but because they knew I was doing the cleaning and stuff and mopping the floors, they were all so darn neat and tidy about things and accommodating to not make my job harder. Because when I had spare time, I was out there helping them and making their job easier, and they were helping me, and it worked out really good.*
>
> *So, between helping the cook, washing the dishes by hand, and peeling all the potatoes and carrots, anything that had to be peeled, I had to do it, whether it was turnips, potatoes, or carrots. Then on top of that, I had to do all the dishes, mop the floors because we stayed on a barge that had rooms on it. So, I mopped the hallways, each room, and in the kitchen. I was cleaning every day, and then I had to look after the generator, and if there was any spare time, I had to go and be deckhand on the dredge. So, they kept me hopping.*
>
> *I think every day I started at seven in the morning. I believe our cook started at six in the morning. The cook did all the breakfast cooking, and I did all the washing. I was paid $1.50 an hour at this job. So, it was a 25-cent raise from what Norman was paying me on the farm. Although we worked extra hours in those times, there was no overtime pay. Especially for deckhands, we weren't paid overtime. It was just straight time, but I made quite a bit more working on the dredge than*

on the farm. On the farm, you couldn't work in the fields because of rain days and things. With Norman, it was mainly just a month in the spring that I worked for him, then nothing until fall. When I worked for Norman, I helped him in the spring with seeding and then I helped him in the fall with harvest.

Basically, I was the kid, the lowest guy on the totem pole, but they seemed to like me.

I worked on that dredge on the Mackenzie River for those two summers. Then it missed the next year while it was retrofitted. That dredge, it sank the next year in the Sans Sault Rapids below Norman Wells.

The Sans Sault Rapids is a rough section in the Mackenzie River. Gordon calls it "wicked" and says that there was no fixing the dredge that time. In fact, Gordon thinks it was destroyed in the rapids and that DPW never did find it. Below the rapids is a section of the Mackenzie known to the river men as the Ramparts,[95] where the cliffs rise perpendicularly above the big river. They are upriver from Fort Good Hope [now called K'ahsho Got'ine in the South Slavey (Dene) language].

And whether Gordon noticed or not, this was a land where the Indigenous Peoples and Métis people like himself were in the majority. They were the people of the land and the water, skilled, important, and visible.

. . . .

95   Ts'ud'e Niline Tueyata in Dene. One of the significant changes throughout the entire north of Canada is the change of names of many communities, lakes, rivers, and other geographic points to the local or original names after two and a half centuries of English and French naming and mapmaking.

CHAPTER 17:
Crossing the Lake

MV Malta

He should have gone back to the protected area.
It was his decision to make. He was the captain.

AT THE END of Gordon's second summer on *Dredge 251*, it was time to
return home for the school term. It almost didn't happen.

> *It was the very fall of the year 1957. We were preparing to leave Wrigley
> Harbour and head out across Great Slave toward Hay River. The
> season was ending. The MV* Malta *made up the tow, with* Dredge 251,
> *two mud scows, and the house barge. We got started, the tow strung out
> behind the tug. Out by the lake outer buoy, which marked the exit from
> the Mackenzie, the wind started.*
>
> *The tugboat captain didn't like the look of the weather and wanted to
> turn around. In hindsight, he should have done that, gone back into the
> protected area of Wrigley Harbour. That's where all the boats anchored
> if they were windbound.*

> *The dredge master insisted that the tow go on, out across Great Slave to Hay River. The captain was easy goin', and tried to get along, but he didn't want to go out on that big lake. The dredge master was always more aggressive. "I'm running this goddamn show and we're going." The captain should have pushed back, but he didn't. Maybe he thought he could make the crossing. I don't know.*

> *The wind was starting to blow pretty good. It soon got to the point that there was no way to turn around. We were out on the open water. There weren't any islands or anything to shelter behind. If we did try to turn back, the waves would hit us broadside. There wasn't much side height on that little tugboat. Captain said that the tug would most likely capsize in the waves if he was to try. The only option was to keep going eastward.*

> *The storm was coming out of the northeast, the huge east arm, the waves rising up from the far stretches of the deepest lake in North America. It was near 2,000 feet deep, the distance phenomenal, a clear sweep of over a hundred miles. That really slowed us down, running into the wind like that. Hours later, we were only halfway home. There was hardly any movement forward, just up and down and rolling in the waves.*

Gordon could feel and hear the relentless *womp, womp, womp* of the MV *Malta*'s flared bow as it pounded down on the denser fall water of Great Slave Lake. A pointed bow with sharper sides would have sliced through the waves, but the flatter, splayed-out bow caught the surging waters, rising then pounding downward, hard, over and over and over again. The boat would shudder each time. The noise was unbearable. Gordon's stomach was tensed for so long it ached.

The tension on the tow was getting horendous. Every slam of the boat was met by resistance from the barges stretched out behind, the waves pushing them back against the heavy cables connected to the vessel in front.

> *We lost the houseboat a couple of hours later. Then the cables pulling the two mud scows snapped one after another and they broke free too. They all washed up later at Point La Roch, about halfway to Hay River from the Mackenzie. At least then we started to make progress, with three dragging barges gone.*

Many hours of being thrown around by the waves, and thinking we were going to die, we got within a mile of the Hay River outer buoy. Dredge 251 sank.

All you could see was the tips of the three spuds—you know, those long pipes forty to sixty feet long that sit at the corner of the dredge. They lower them to anchor the dredge in place when it is working. They get raised up when the dredge is being moved. Well, that's all you could see on the whole lake, and only once in a while; mostly, they were hidden by the waves.

The Malta was still connected by cable to the dredge. Oh my God.

One of the deckhands cut the tow cable with an axe and the Malta was able to navigate into the Hay River shipyard. What an ordeal.

Two days after the storm subsided, the salvage began. The lake was like a mirror. It was so calm; you could see the curvature of earth and three spuds poking maybe four feet out of the water. The lake was starting to ice up, so we just made it. The house barge and the two mud scows were no worse for wear. That dredge was a different story.

John Pope and some other divers went into the freezing water and sealed off the compartments in the dredge. They bolted all the manholes in the hull, then pumped out the water, and the dredge refloated itself to the surface. Once it was in dry dock, it had to have a complete refit and overhaul that took all the next season. That storm was a dandy. We all thought at times that we wouldn't make it. We had our life jackets on. Thank God we made it.

When we got back to Hay River, DPW fired the dredge master immediately.

Here is another example of Gordon's perseverance. Or maybe he just didn't know any better. You know the boat crews are a superstitious lot, and you know that whenever they would meet up, whether in town or while tied up at a dock or bound together sitting out the wind, talk would always turn to what had happened to each other, how their ships handled things, all the usual talk.

First, Gordon was away from home, from family for the summer. He was young and feeling his way, just sixteen when the *Malta* almost went down in a storm. He watched the dredge, and the houseboat and scows go down. And then his dredge sank in the rapids later. And he would have heard about the *Clearwater* too. From the summer before.

The *Clearwater* was a Northern Transportation Company Limited tug that sank in 40 metres of water during a storm on Lake Athabasca. That was in 1956. All hands were lost. Built in 1943, this 24.4-metre-long (80-foot-long) vessel had only an 81.3-centimetre (2-foot-and-8-inch) draft. It was later salvaged by NT and rebuilt for service on the Mackenzie River under a new name, the *Horn River*. That tug made a stop in the Fort Smith Bell Rock Camp in the summer of 1969 to pick up a new cook and to assist with the launching of the new tugs being built there. Even then, it was still talked about as a death ship. The crew, perhaps like mariners elsewhere, were quite superstitious. One thing everyone on that boat learned was never to put a can of anything upside down. The crew was careful to ensure those loading groceries were aware of their own strict rules.

Getting a cook to serve on her was a tall chore until the chubby, dirty-aproned but jolly and friendly Art Robinson took the job that summer. In 2013, *Horn River* was up on the big timber dry dock at the NT shipyards in Hay River. It sat there until at least 2019, awaiting the scrap heap.

Gordon was just sixteen. Two sinkings in his two years in the north, one which he saw up-close and personal. And then "his" dredge sank again the next year. You have to wonder if he would go back on the boats again. But with the perseverance and determination he became known for, he did go back, not only to work on the ships, but to explore the whole of the river system and out into the Arctic, and then, in due course, to repair and fabricate tugs, barges, drilling platforms, and a vehicle ferry for others to work on. In those times, these vessels were the lifeblood of northern business and subsistence.

> It wasn't till I got a job with Yellowknife Transportation after being at Akaitcho and outside that I went back on the tugboats. By that time, all was forgotten.

Armande as a young woman, 1941.

Gordon and Mildred at the Hotchkiss farm.

The tug Malta, barge, house barge and dredge.
NWT Archives/NWT Archives/Federal Department of Public Works:
Yellowknife Sewer and Water Project./N-1998-019-0083/

Gordon playing guitar aboard Dredge 251 House barge.

The Radium King, built in 1937, former flagship of the NTCL fleet.
NWT Archives/Henry Busse fonds/N-1979-052-0616/

Gordon and Treena's wedding ... a day late.

Hay River Old Town in the 1963 flood.
NWT Archives/Bobby Porritt fonds/N-1987-016-0166_142

Gestur's Fish Boat.

Radium Franklin on the Bear River,
NWT Archives/Bruce Hunter Fonds/N-1981-002-0022.

NT Tugs, the Snye, Hay River, Spring 1970, author's photo.

Dry Dock, Tuk harbour, Beaufort Sea.

Gestur's snow cat, Great Slave Lake

Gestur's snow cat and caboose

Alexandra Falls from the Hay River Gorge,
NWT Archives/Bobby Porritt ©Postcards/ N-1987-016-0768_141

One of the "new" NTCL tugboats, circa 1969/70.
NWT Archives/Fred North/ N-2011-005-0216_141

Tug and "Tow"; NWT Archives/Felix Labat fonds / N-2004-027-0576

NT Tower Tug Matt Berry east Great Slave Lake;
NWT Archives/Rene Fumoleau/N-1995-002-10365

Gordon and Treena

Lionel Gagnier, photo courtesty
Joe and Lionel Gagnier, Jr.

Lionel Gagnier as a young man,
as Gordon first remembers him.
Photo courtesy Joe and Lionel
Gagner, Jr.

Gordon, Treena, Brian and Trent, 1998.

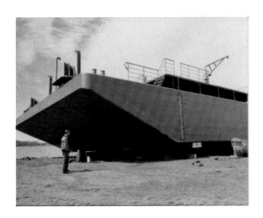

Barge under construction, Northern Arc Shipbuilders' yard, Hay River, NWT

Canmar barge before launch, with Lindberg tug in the background,
West Channel, Hay River, NWT.

Yard boat Kakisa moving Tower Tug Kelly Ovayuak, Hay River harbour, courtesy of MTS.

MTS Tower Tug Edgar Kotokak , courtesy of MTS.

MTS Tug and barge on the Arctic coast, courtesy of MTS.

MTS Tug Nunatpuk at Hay River, courtesy of David MacDonald.

Canadian Coast Guard Vessel Eckalo, the Snye, Hay River harbour, 2022,
courtesy of David MacDonald.

Town of Hay River, looking north to Great Slave Lake,
courtesy Hay River Chamber of Commerce.

Northern Crane Service Mobile Crane, courtesy Bob Van England.

Gordon and Leo Davis, checking out new Leibherr Crane.

CHAPTER 18:
Akaitcho Hall –
Gordon's Residential School

Gordon at Akaitcho Hall Residential School.

I did not want to go to school.

I ATTENDED *Sir John Franklin Vocational School in Yellowknife. I was enrolled in mechanics and welding in 1960–1962. That was all I ever wanted to be. Akaitcho Hall, where I lived, was really good. It was like the military; you had to make your bed just right. They taught discipline, hard work (every day there were chores), and to get along with people.*

Some would say that those were qualities Gordon had from his parents and grandparents already.

That school and Yellowknife's main street were both named after the most famous British explorer ever to seek the Northwest Passage. This quest, by Sir John Franklin and others, was to locate a northern sea route from Europe to the riches of China. At a time when the European nations were desperate for a shorter route to the magnificently different wealth of the Orient, the romance and adventure, and the glory and wealth of being the great discoverer of such a route were aptly described by the popular Canadian historian and writer Pierre Berton in his book on the subject, *The Arctic Grail.*[96]

A grail is a chalice or treasure of unique value, much like the Holy Grail sought by the Crusaders. A trade route to China and the Far East, with its spices, silks, and other exotic products, which avoided the long and treacherous sea route around the tip of South America and across the Pacific Ocean, or the easterly journey around Africa, was surely a grail worth pursuing. The sea trade, after all, was the basis of the wealth and empire of the relatively small countries of Europe who sought them—the British, Portuguese, Spaniards, Dutch, and others.

Unfortunately for Franklin and his crew, their chosen east-to-west route through Canada's Arctic Archipelago was, after they turned west at the top of Baffin Island, subject to treacherous ice and long months of frozen darkness. Not even halfway through to the Bering Sea north of Alaska, the pack ice encircled the expedition's three small ships, holding them there, trapped in the slow-moving ice, for two deadly winters. Franklin and all his men perished. Despite repeated and lengthy searches, little trace could be found of the crews' final resting place or the cause of their untimely deaths. And although Inuit oral history is clear that the ships being frozen in the ice over two winters was common knowledge, for whatever reason, the British who followed found hardly any evidence of the desperate efforts of some of the sailors to walk to safety, which, not surprisingly, failed. Perhaps the survivors didn't ask or trust the local people or didn't think to do so.

Whichever is the case, the mystery has only been solved over the last thirty years or so. The various expeditions and searches, now with detailed

....
96   Pierre Berton, *The Arctic Grail* (McClelland and Stewart, 1988).

anthropologic technology and modern testing equipment, make for a wonderful exploration and an intriguing account of this famous story of the far north. There are a series of very interesting books detailing the history and results of the search by Owen Beattie and John Geiger, but the starting point is the excellent *Frozen in Time: The Fate of the Franklin Expedition*.[97] Beattie's alma mater, Simon Fraser University, recognized Beattie by saying, "He gained international attention in 1984 for his investigation into the lost expedition of Sir John Franklin, which had left England in 1845 searching for the Northwest Passage."[98]

However, naming a vocational school, which was designed to teach Indigenous children (and others) how to cope with the modern world, after Franklin seems ironic. Franklin was, it turns out, a pretty much failed English explorer. In one expedition north of Yellowknife, he had to be taken care of and in fact saved by the Copper "Indian" leader Akaitcho, for whom the residence at the Sir John Franklin School is named. In another attempt to explore the Arctic, Franklin was rescued by a seriously competent Scottish fellow, Sir John Rae. There is no suggestion that the students thought in these terms, but surely there is some lesson for educators and politicians in all this.

Here is what Gordon has to say about his time at his version of residential school.

> *While I was at school in Yellowknife, I stayed in Akaitcho Hall. That was a residence for kids while they went to school. It is named after a famous Copper Indian, who was chief of the Yellowknives Dene Nation; Chief Akaitcho acted as interpreter, guide, hunter, and saviour for Sir John Franklin on Franklin's earlier land explorations.*
>
> *I was about nineteen years old when I went there. We had to fly there. There was no other means, no roads built in those days. I think we flew there in a single Otter plane.*

There is significant pain and much controversy in Canada about the role of and motivation for church-run, government-sponsored residential

97   Owen Beattie and John Geiger, *Frozen in Time: The Fate of the Franklin Expedition* (Greystone Books, 1987).

98   Simon Fraser University, "Owen Beattie | Almuni | Department of Archaeology," https://www.sfu.ca/archaeology/engagement/our-alumni/alum-beattie.html.

schools. Ample evidence of the traumatic effects that residential schools had on young Indigenous children is presented in the news almost daily. Many as young as five years old were snatched away, without warning or explanation, from parents living in the bush or in small settlements. Many died. Virtually everyone was affected, and many were physically or sexually abused. Children were punished for speaking the only language they knew. They were forced to shed their own clothes and take on white clothing, and their hair was cut short. This alone was a traumatic experience for Indigenous Peoples for whom hair and hair length is extremely important[99]. The people who experienced this often felt abandoned and stripped of all self-knowledge and self-respect. They were taught that their parents were stupid, and their culture was useless and savage. They were told they were heathens. Self-esteem was something they would not hear about, let alone know in their lifetimes. It was a tragedy.[100]

Here is what one of the leaders of the Roman Catholic Church in Canada, Bishop (later Venerable) Vital Grandin, is quoted as saying about the purpose and effect of residential schools in this country:

> We instill in them [Indigenous children] a pronounced distaste for Native life so that they will be humiliated when reminded of their origin. When they graduate from one of our institutions, the children have lost everything Native except their blood.[101]

This same bishop was an adviser to Indigenous leaders in the negotiations with the federal government, reporting that those leaders wanted schools.[102] That may have been true, but it does seem an awful conflict of interest.

The Roman Catholic and other churches acted as agents of the government and of God, apparently, operating mission schools and the connected residences. It was they who cut the children's hair and their ties to their Indigenous communities, banished their languages and cultures, denied them their own clothes and customs, and, most of all, their families and sense of belonging—of being worthwhile. Terrible results followed for a

....

99   There is wording in Dee Brown's seminal work, *Bury My Heart at Wounded Knee,* that acknowledges that one of the signs of strength and power was the length of one's hair.
100 See in detail, Milloy, *National Crime.*
101 Ryan Thorpe, "Genocide on the Prairies," *Winnipeg Free Press,* June 4, 2021, https://www.winnipegfreepress.com/local/genocide-on-the-prairies-574563652.html.
102 Milloy, *National Crime,* 54.

whole population and for many generations.[103]

Even in the late 1960s, the churches, with the active assistance of the police and social workers—few that there were in the North—were "scooping" children, often from under the noses of their parents. A tugboat would dock, or an airplane would fly in and the Mounties—the supreme agent of government authority in those days—grabbed and took the children with no explanation, no translation, nothing. Often, those children died, their parents unaware that their children were buried in graves, sometimes unmarked, mostly untended and some only now being discovered. (There are reports concurrent with the writing of this that point to numerous unmarked graves being located by ground-searching radar in Kamloops and at Cowessess First Nation, for instance).

Parents, not notified, were left wondering why the government had stolen their children and not returned them.

One quite common justification for the use of residential schools was that the government of Canada had an obligation to protect the Indigenous Peoples from the rapid transition facing them.

This is reflected in the memoirs of Prime Ministerial Secretary Gordon Robertson.

In the 1950s and 1960s, he was a very senior advisor to the Prime Minister of Canada. From November 1953, and later during John Diefenbaker's years as Prime Minister, Robertson served as Deputy Minister of Northern Affairs and Northern Development and, as a result, was the head of government in NWT—that is, the Commissioner of the NWT.

As such, Robertson was involved in the takeover by the government of the church-run residential schools in the NWT, although church-run residences and hostels continued. Robertson said that the huge risk facing the people of the North was the widely scattered nature of such peoples, only some of whom were living in or spending much time in actual communities. The risk of not having the centralized or residential school system was that Indigenous children would either have no education at all or a much delayed one, and thus "a lifetime of no source of livelihood other than hunting and trapping." [104]

....

103 Sibbeston, *Wear a White Shirt*; Milloy, *National Crime*, 54.
104 Gordon Robertson, *The Memoirs of a Very Civil Servant: Mackenzie King to Pierre Trudeau* (Toronto, ON: University of Toronto Press, 2001), 175.

In a more drastic post, Robertson reported that in 1950 there were but seven students enrolled in high school in the entire Northwest Territories. Robertson justified the use of residential schools as the choice between an education, necessary in the changing world, and no education. He quoted with approval Diamond Jenness, a noted northern scientist and advisor who in 1962 set out clearly that the only other choice than Indigenous education was a dehumanizing journey into welfare dependency.[105]

Robertson's fear was that, in effect, an uneducated and unsophisticated people faced the onslaught of the Industrial and Technological Age, and thus something had to be done by the government. That something was residential and vocational training, usually away from the person's home community.

That concern was also expressed by a member of the then "advisory" NWT Territorial Council. Lyle Trimble is quoted as saying:

> It is unthinkable to me that this nation [Canada] feels no shame that our vast territory is home to people who have no clothing save what they make from the creatures they catch, who starve to death if the caribou change their migration route, who cannot reach a hospital if they break a limb, who cannot communicate with each other except by word of mouth at a chance meeting on the tundra [or in the bush] and who have no understanding of, nor role in, this country or this century. Yet such and worse is the case… everywhere one looks there is deprivation of the worst kind. The people are just emerging from the Ice Age. They are totally unequipped to deal with a wage economy and the abuses of the white man.
>
> The Eskimos [Inuit] have sixteen words for snow but not one for government—they know nothing of it.[106]

Trimble was speaking of the Inuit of the Arctic, but much was the same in the "near north" as well. The system of government imposed on the land was not congruent with the needs or the practices of those that lived there. "White" towns—like Yellowknife, Inuvik, and Hay River—were fine and more modern, albeit still much behind the southern cities and towns of the

....
105 Robertson, *Memoirs*, 117–118.
106 Ootes, *Umingmak*, 59.

country, and they attracted and worked for the incoming non-indigenous people. But that left the unseen Indigenous Peoples who had moved to town, or been moved there, struggling to cope and exist in that framework.

"And," it has also been observed, "often 'put' in places that didn't make sense in terms of flooding, potable water, access to traditional lands … and a myriad of other problems."[107] In other villages and communities, there were few jobs or opportunities, a system of government unknown to the people, and no real ability to maintain a land-based life. That same friend averred: "No real path to success … their previous lives taken from them and the way forward so obfuscated and unknown that 'success,' whether in their terms or those of the white, patriarchal, settler society that imposed itself upon them, was virtually unknown."[108]

In Hay River, for example, in the 1970s, half the town's population was Indigenous, but they seemed to be unseen and unconsidered by the remainder of the population (except for the court docket in the local papers or walking the streets, sometimes intoxicated). Gordon, as a respected member of the business community, did not face that same feeling.

There is a sense, in some ways, that what happened to Gordon was an assimilation in its own right, albeit with a more loving and gentle approach by his mother's people. And it had a happier result. And his own experience in residential school, by his own admission, was not the same as the common NWT experience.

Gordon was, he says, *luckily older when I went to residential school, nineteen or twenty.* He went for a shorter time, and, perhaps most importantly, he went because he wanted to. He spoke English, and he was bigger than the little kids scooped by the church and RCMP against their will. Also, maybe fortunately for Gordon, Akaitcho Hall was non-denominational; it was not a "church school" or part of a mission.

Gordon also had the example of his independent-minded white father and Indigenous grandfather, who had left the influence of the church and moved away so it could not take his own daughters. Clarence's attitude wasn't agreeable to religion nor "brainwashing" as he called it. By then, independence had rubbed off on Gordon. He wasn't religious, either, and he wasn't prone to being pushed into what to believe.

107 Laura Matheson, editor and writer, email to the author.
108 Matheson, email.

That comes through in this bit of oral history, about going to school:

> *Prior to me leaving Hay River, the school people in Hay River suggested to the Yellowknife school administrators that they try and persuade me to take grade twelve. When I did go to Yellowknife, the school did that, but I said, no if I had to finish grade twelve, then I'll just go back to Hay River. So, Yellowknife said no, no, no, you can go into the mechanics and welding course, and that's what I wanted. I found out it was the Hay River School that wanted to persuade me to take grade twelve so then it kind of made sense. But I wanted to take the trades, and that was all there was to it.*

The school in Yellowknife was Gordon's pathway to a world he was happy to join.

Gordon's comment, more than once: *I really liked going to the residential school in Yellowknife. It taught me discipline. It was one of the best things I ever did.*

It was where he started his vocational training and set the stage for his working life, his marriage, his family, and his business success. It was, for him, a positive experience. He knows it was not for most.

In fairness, would any school have done the same for him?

The Gordon Gill story is not of pain and dislocation, or the loss of one's place in the world, but rather of him finding his place, first in the frontier, and second in his work, of quietly going forward in the face of racism or, perhaps more correctly, of accepting it when it happened, and accepting the good in people when it didn't.

What was different in Gordon or his upbringing that allowed him to move forward as he did? It may have had more to do with his age and situation, and his positive personality, mixed with the example of the personal traits of his parents and grandparents. Regardless, taking up residence at Akaitcho Hall didn't seem, from his perspective, to cause him harm.

Akaitcho Hall, according to the National Centre for Truth and Reconciliation website, was:

> …opened in Yellowknife, NWT in 1958. The residence was operated by the federal government without church involvement and, for much of its history, had a large non-Aboriginal population.

Inspectors' reports show that the hostel's laundry facilities and janitorial storage were inadequate, and that office and counselling spaces were non-existent. Akaitcho Hall was transferred to the Northwest Territories government in 1969, which operated it until 1994.

The residence is gone now. It used to sit on a large lot beside the Sir John Franklin High School, just east of the main downtown area, up the hill from Yellowknife Bay. For a comparison of this residential school to others (and some were pretty horrific), see the Milloy book, *A National Crime*, referred to in the notes and source list.

Gordon remembers, some sixty years later, that *Akaitcho Hall was pretty impressive, at least to me. It was a residence for us students who were there in Yellowknife to go to school.*

The main structure was long and rectangular with a high ceiling. This structure sat on a full basement, which held a large laundry room with large washing machines, dryers, and steam irons. There was also storage, offices, and at one end of the basement, the main entrance. There was a second entrance at the same end, opposite side on the upper level that was used by the students coming and going to the school that was only maybe 200 feet away.

The upper main structure was where the dining room, the kitchen and more storage was located. On the inside was a long hallway where you could enter the dining room, the kitchen, the girls' dorm, or the boys' dorm. Because the whole place was built on a rock pile, you had to climb the stairs to get to the dorms. At the top, on the boys' side, there was a common room where we would gather to listen to orders coming from the supervisor, or just hang out with others. I was never in the girls' dorm, so I can only speak about the boys' side.

Each room housed two people. Beds were stacked, and there was a desk and closet for each of us.

There was one common washroom for all the boys. It had showers.

I thought the whole building was top-notch. It had a new smell, and it was clean, everywhere all the time. The place had a warm and friendly atmosphere. So it doesn't sound as though it was like you hear about other residential schools.

There was absolutely no tolerance for alcohol. If caught, you would be on the next plane home. There were restrictions to going downtown, so most everybody stayed close to the residence. There was always something to do. There was always a lot of gym activity, for example.

There was a curfew time to be indoors, and at a certain time, the lights had to be out. If your chores were done on Sunday, you could go to church. You didn't have to. That was one difference.

We also had movies there somewhere; you could go if your record [behaviour] *was clean, and the chores done. A very high percentage of the students were there to learn. What a great group.*

For context, one writer who is part of a group challenging eugenics,[109] Paula Larsson is quoted, at *Eugenics Archives*, as saying that Akaitcho was a non-denominational day school and residence built by the federal government in 1958 as part of its program of Indigenous education in the North, and that "many students report positive experiences at this school, including Nunavut MP Nancy Karetak-Lindell. Akaitcho Hall was the last residential school to close, in 1996." The Eugenics Archives, as the website says, "reflects the collaboration of scholars, survivors, students, and community partners in challenging eugenics."[110]

Interestingly, there is a bit of battling truths, or websites, at least. The Truth and Reconciliation Centre says Akaitcho was primarily non-Indigenous; however, the Eugenics Archives website (funded in part by a department of the federal government) claims the opposite.

Gordon's memory of the boys in the school around 1960 or 1961 suggests, at least for that time and place, a difference from the National Centre for Truth and Reconciliation view.

Of the sixty-seven boys in his class (boys or young men close to

....

109 Definitionally, the approach to improving the gene pool of humankind by selective breeding, among other approaches and more generally, discrimination on the basis of race or other generalizing factors.

110 E. Dyck, "Canada | Around the World," *Eugenics Archives* (2013, September 14), https:// eugenicsarchive.ca/discover/world.

the end of their schooling there), Gordon counts forty-nine of them as "Native/Métis."

Interestingly, Gordon recalls their class photo, where all of the boys are wearing collared shirts and ties, and many have suit jackets. There is no Indigenous dress or long hair, which was presumably unremarkable in its attempt at homogeneity in those days.

Further, Gordon indicates that despite forty-nine of the group being of Indigenous descent, all of the names are English. And, with a couple of exceptions, they are all smiling. Gordon does not draw any conclusions from any of these facts. He repeats his feeling that the stars aligned for him and that his experiences are not necessarily anyone else's.

This brought up the old quotation of "walking in another's moccasins," to which Gordon replied, *"Yeah, and if you do walk a mile in a man's moccasins, you are a mile away and you have his moccasins."*

CHAPTER 19:
The Crash on Suicide Corner

Gordon (in white t-shirt) and others at Akaticho Hall.

The first few months in Yellowknife, a guy, his name was
Bob Grant, he was a police officer; he had a nickname,
something like Little Hairpin. He got along with the young
people and would come to the school, and we did not
really realize what he was doing—he was recruiting.

FAR IN THE FUTURE was Gordon's role as a leader in the northern marine
industry and later the formation of Northern Arc Shipbuilders and
Northern Crane Services. It might have included the RCMP instead. Such
is the way of life and plans.

Grant would talk to this guy, Bill Elliot and myself and a number of others and got us convinced that we would fit good into the RCMP. So, I thought, well, here goes my mechanics and welding, but you know it is somewhat different and a chance to travel Canada anyway. So, I carried on in the mechanics anyway, but I passed the medical for the police academy. Everything was just moving ahead slowly at a snail speed.

The RCMP—more formally, the Royal Canadian Mounted Police—are the Mounties. It is a federal police force, so it polices the territories, but it also functions in some places as the local police and in place of a provincial police force. Established in 1873 by Sir John A. Macdonald after exaggerated reports of the potential for "Indian degradation" and unexaggerated but real concerns about the prevalence of American whisky traders "preying on the Blackfoot Indians" the North-West Mounted Police, as they were then called, were rushed west on an arduous trek to put Fort Whoop-Up and other such places out of business.[111] The Americans were indeed taking advantage of Indigenous peoples north of the 49th parallel, bringing rotgut so-called whisky up the Whoop-Up Trail from the head of navigation on the Missouri River at Fort Benton in Montana Territory and taking anything and everything the local Blackfoot owned home with them. The massacre of a group of very intoxicated Assiniboine people by American wolf hunters, in the Cypress Hills, provided further motivation for the Canadian government to act.

Since then, the Mounties have had a long and involved history of policing in Indigenous communities.

Based on the Irish forces of the British government and wearing the British symbolic redcoats, the force was set up initially and continues to be almost military in its centralized training at "Depot" in Regina, Saskatchewan. Its famous red serge uniforms, with blue pants sporting a yellow stripe down the sides, and the flat-brimmed Stetson hat with the pointed top, is well known as a symbol of Canada.

Gordon thought seriously about joining the RCMP. However, another of the serious accidents in his life affected these plans. He explains:

After getting out of school for the summer, I was working at Con Mine in Yellowknife [Consolidated Mining and Smelting (Cominco)]. *I was just outside the bank and met these fellas that I knew from Akaitcho Hall. They*

111 Wilson, *Frontier Farewell*, 23–24

did not go to the school, but they had girlfriends that stayed at Akaitcho Hall, and these guys would come to our dances and things and that's how I got to know them. I was standing on the street corner and these fellas pulled up and said to hop in, we are going to the airport for a ride. In those days, there were only a few places to go to—the old town, the mines, or the airport. These were the only roads in Yellowknife at the time. So I thought, well I'd go, and once I got into the car, I could tell they had been drinking.

By the time I realized they were drinking, we had already gone past the Con Mine turnoff. So, I thought, well I guess I'll go for the ride. I remember going out to the airport and we turned, then we were on our way back, and there is a place on the road called Suicide Corner because of all the accidents that happened there. I was sitting in the back seat. We were headed toward that Suicide Corner, and that is when everything kind of blanked out; I do not remember the accident or any part of it. I was twenty years old.

*The car hit the cribbing that was circled around the telephone poles; the cribbing around the poles was filled with rocks to hold the telephone/ power poles up [*different from areas with soil where the poles are sunk in the ground!*]. When the car hit the cribbing, the whole top of the car wrapped around the pole and then fell back down. That is when the driver was trapped in there, and the steering wheel went into his legs and stomach. The other guy in the passenger's seat, Frank Oswald, he was pinned in there. I was in the back seat, and the only way out of there was a little wee window in the back of the car, and I crawled out of it, and I guess I left the scene of the accident.*

While they were taking the other two people out, a nurse who happened to see us at the airport, she said, "I seen that car when it left the airport, and it had three people in it. How come there are only two people now?" So then the police started to search for me and found me about three quarters of a mile away, lying in the ditch. I do not remember any part of the accident or after and basically came to about two weeks later in the Yellowknife Hospital.

I had broken fingers, every part of my body was bruised, the skin from the front of my ears and face had all the little pinholes from the imprint of the upholstery; on the ceiling of the car, there was vinyl with pinholes in it. Blood squirted out my face from the pinholes in the upholstery. When the top of the car wrapped around the pole, my face slammed up against the upholstery and then the power pole. Blood came out every little pinhole that my face hit, from my ears forward. My nose was flattened, and I had skull fractures from my eye socket to my teeth. More skull fractures above my eye also. I am lucky to be alive.

My memory was slow, so slow for a long time. My memory came back fairly good, but my thinking was slow, and the same with speaking, and it took a bit of time to heal. My speech took a while to come back also. I think the brain trauma has affected me even today.

I have a tough time reading, and to tell you the truth, I have never read a book in my life. I started a Zane Grey book years ago, and when I read, I'd forget and have to read the same page all over again the next night. The book stayed on the night table about a year and a half, then Treena finally took it and put it away. I finally asked her, "Where did you put my book?" Treena made a good joke out of it.

The biggest single thing that changed the direction of my life was the accident. I was continuing to do my mechanics and welding courses, but had I been able to go into the RCMP, that would have taken me in another total direction. The RCMP training did not happen because in the accident my trigger finger on my right hand was severely broken and stuck out sideways for a long time, for about three years. Both knuckles were broken on my trigger finger; even now my index finger is pointing the wrong way. So that ended my RCMP career. Simple as that, that was the reason they told me anyway, but I could have had brain damage. They never told me that, and the trigger finger was enough that I couldn't get in. So, I just carried on working at Con Mine and carried on with welding and mechanics while staying at Akaitcho Hall. Then I went to Norman Wells, about halfway up the Mackenzie River, for the summer of 1962 and worked for Aklavik Contractors on the new airport from May until September. I was a mechanic's helper at the new airport being built.

I spent two years in Yellowknife.

CHAPTER 20:
After Akaitcho Hall

YT Expeditor; NWT Archives/Ben Hall Collection/N-2013-015-0159.

After I left Akaitcho Hall, that's when my life began.

AFTER AKAITCHO HALL, *it was basically schooling in Calgary and Edmonton. I took mechanics and welding at the Southern Alberta Institute of Technology* [SAIT] *in Calgary for three years and then to NAIT* [Northern Alberta Institute of Technology] *in Edmonton for another.*

Because I was from the Northwest Territories, they kind of had a special program that went on for six months; they treated everyone from the NWT like they were from the bush and that we didn't know anything about mechanics. Although I had the same vocational training from Yellowknife as the rest of the class, when I went to Calgary, I had to start all over again, so I took the six-month course in heavy-duty diesel mechanics. I really liked it, and it covered a lot of stuff that we had taken in Yellowknife, but at the same time, it was more advanced.

Gordon recalls that the course material and the education was just as good in Yellowknife as it was in Calgary. It was just that the SAIT instructors assumed the Northerners didn't know anything, that they were just "dumber." The interesting thing is, that for all his problems reading and learning, Gordon got top marks in his courses. Was he just focused and determined, after fifteen years of wanting this schooling, or had he found his niche?

And then what I did, I enrolled in welding night school at the same time during those six months in Calgary. I ended up getting a welding ticket out of those classes. I was in Calgary for six months, and then I would go back to Hay River. Then the second and third year in Calgary, I was there for two months, taking the first year of heavy-duty diesel mechanics. I took some night courses in bookkeeping while I was in Calgary also. I was even able to help Treena for a little bit [when she was doing the books for the company], but then she left me in the dust after she got started on the books. But the course taught just enough so I had a basic understanding in the business end of it. I was never sorry that I took the course. The following year I started my apprenticeship in Calgary.

I think I finished that course in May or something like that. When I finished my course, I went back up to Hay River in the spring. Then the following year, I took my schooling in Edmonton at NAIT; it was also heavy-duty diesel mechanics. I think it was a three-year apprenticeship program. But I was four years into it because I had to do that six-month thing before. I was never sorry that I took that six-month course before. So that was kind of the end of my schooling, and I got my Red Seal. So now that made it so I could be a mechanic anywhere in Canada.

Gordon got summers off, which he needed to make money to continue his schooling. During the SAIT and NAIT years, Gordon worked summer jobs, first for Yellowknife Transportation, another tug and barge company in Hay River, then on a survey crew.

That was also about when I got my nickname, Black Bear. The reason was that one summer, I worked on a survey crew between Pine Point and Hay River. I was a line cutter. I think I was about twenty-one years old, but not quite sure. I had an axe and a machete; basically, I cut brush for the whole summer. I never wore a shirt because we were always hot in the bush. When I did finish and come out, I was so, so brown from being shirtless all summer that Bill Helmer and Max Morgan started calling me Black Bear. That name kind of hung on me. Some people still call me that to this day.

CHAPTER 21:
Treena

Treena after Bryan's birth.

Treena was born October 24, 1945, and christened Treena Kristbjorg Gudmundson.

TREENA'S FAMILY ARRIVED in Hay River in 1962. Her dad was already involved in fishing at that time. Gordon explains how that came about and a bit about the fishing industry itself:

> *Some Natives from Kakisa* [an Indigenous community west of Hay River] *and others from Saskatchewan and some Icelandic people from Manitoba fished Great Slave Lake; that was both in winter and summer. It was a big industry at the time.*

> *My wife's dad, Gestur Gudmundson, was a fisherman for many years. He moved his wife Lara and their children, Treena and Derek, north to Hay River in 1962 from Riverton, Manitoba.*

It almost didn't happen.

In the spring of 1962, Gestur finished up his winter fishing on Great Slave Lake and travelled back home to Riverton. When he arrived, he told Lara and Treena to prepare to move to Hay River after the summer fishing season was over, to be ready to move in early September. This gave them months to get packed and ready. They told everyone they knew, relatives and friends, they would be moving away in the fall.

When Gestur was finished with the summer fishing, he was to go back to Riverton, pack his belongings and away they would all move to Hay River. Well, when Gestur got home, he had chickened out. He just wasn't prepared for such a major change, after all. He announced to Lara and Treena that he was calling off the move. Well, there was no way that Lara and Treena and Derek, Treena's younger brother, were going to accept that decision after all the people they had told they were leaving. After Lara and Treena got finished with Gestur, the move was back on. They did get to Hay River in time for Treena and Derek to start school in their new home, and Gestur was happy afterwards with the decision to move north.

Gordon's niece describes the Gudmundsons as a close family as follows:

Lorene was Treena's older sister of three years, and her brother Derek came along nine years after Treena. Treena loved spending time with her sister Lorene and her husband George. Lorene and George lived in Prince Rupert, so get-togethers were few and far between and treasured. Lorene was a great big sister to Treena and gave her advice from time to time. I do remember Treena passing along some of her advice and this too would have a slant of humour in it. Lorene and George had two children, Debbie and Jeff.

Treena's sister passed away much too young, and Treena was very lonely without her. Treena inherently picked up the role of being Debbie's auntie/mother. Gordon and Treena and Debbie would go during the summer to Treena's hometown of Gimli, Manitoba to visit relatives there. Debbie would also once or twice a year visit in Edmonton with Gordon and Treena.

Derek was Treena's younger brother, and he grew up in Hay River.

> Derek was great with his nephews Bryan and Trent. Derek played guitar well and could sing CCR [Creedence Clearwater Revival] songs well also. Treena admired Derek for how great he was with his nephews.[112]

There was a large contingent of Icelanders in Hay River, almost all of whom, in that generation, were there as fishermen. Local Indigenous Peoples and a lot of immigrants from the Canadian prairies, including mixed-blood people, fished the lake as well. Many stayed, the Gudmundsons among them.

> *Treena was also very proud to be a pure Icelander, to have "pure Icelandic blood," which was quite different from me!*

Gordon and Treena met when he was back in Hay River for his Christmas break in December of 1962. That was the beginning of their relationship.

Gordon's niece, Marvelle, describes Treena as "very blond and very attractive," about 5 feet, 6 inches in height. "When Treena was in her teens, she was a very slim lady and she once showed me her wedding dress and no word of a lie, I could have put my fingers around her waist, and they would have almost touched."[113]

Gordon and Treena were quite a contrast, at least physically; she was quite thin and blond, Gordon was reasonably tall, stocky—a big presence—and dark, dark-skinned and dark-haired, a big man, although quiet and gentle. They were married on October 12, 1964. That wasn't the date they planned.

It was like other northern things, at the mercy of the weather and the boats. The wedding was scheduled for October 10. The only problem was that the groom was still out on Great Slave. He was the engineer on Yellowknife Transportation's *Arctic Lady*, trying to get back across the lake to get to their home harbour from Yellowknife. One good thing, the captain of the *Arctic Lady* was Earl Harcourt, who was also a part owner of the company, so people were paying attention to where the boat might be.

Treena would go to the Yellowknife Transportation office in the morning to see if there was news about the ship. In the absence of cell phones, and with spotty radio service, all the office could tell her was that

112 Email from Marvelle Kobbert to the author.
113 Marvelle Kobbert, email to the author.

the boat was late, and they weren't sure when it would arrive. However, Treena was assured they were all right. Eventually, this proved correct, and Gordon arrived back in Hay River, not in time for the wedding, but in time for a hastily rescheduled ceremony. People living on the lake knew to expect the unexpected and to adapt. They did.

Gordon and Treena had two sons, Bryan and Trent. Gordon's niece, Marvelle Kobbert, describes her memories:

> Treena often spoke about raising their two boys back in those days and hand-washing diapers and clothes; it was a challenge to keep up with everything, but she did. Treena's love for her boys was never ending and same for her grandchildren. Treena's humour runs all through her boys and grandchildren; they have definitely inherited the ability to make people laugh. What a great tool to have, the gift of laughter! Treena and Gordon were the perfect pair and worked side-by-side in business. From the time Gordon decided he wanted to go on his own and not travel so much, they were a team.[114]

Gordon remembers his sons begging to come along with him to work. He'd tell them that they would have to stay in the truck, and it was probably going to be pretty boring, but they would want to come anyway. They would want to help him pump gas into a generator or do other odd jobs, but pretty soon, they would be asleep in the cab of the truck.

He was happy in his marriage. He describes how Treena was a partner in life and business and that she supported him in his desire to do well. When asked about his happiest times, Gordon answered, *When I first met Treena. How good we got along when we got married. How saving she was and that helped me save.*

Treena was, Gordon says, a perfectionist. She was so good and precise in doing the books for the company that she was repeatedly praised and listened to by Gill's long-time accountants, Barry Ashton and Jonathan Smethurst. If there was a major decision, any decision, really, affecting the business or any question about the finances, "You'd better check with Treena," was often Ashton's response.

Treena handled the house, the office, and their boys so Gordon could work, and work more. He never resented the work; in fact, he felt it was

114 Mildred Kobbert, email to the author.

its own reward. Gordon says he looked forward to going to work every day, but he acknowledges that he "missed out"—with friends and with his kids, going camping or whatever—because of how much he worked and travelled and how much he was away, on the tugs or working overtime, or travelling for work.

> *Treena was a real worker. I remember especially 1982 when Northern Arc built all those Loram barges, and the* MT Gordon Gill *tug and the* Abraham Francis, *a ferry for the Peel River way up north. We were always busy, mostly with repairs, but that year, we were building all kinds of things.*
>
> *Treena looked after everything at home plus all the bookkeeping and the finances at work.*

Jonathan Smethurst remembers well his first involvement with Gordon and Treena. Having arrived in Hay River from England via Toronto, he was a young accountant in the offices of Fraser, Matthews, and Company (later Ashton Chartered Accountants). "I moved to Hay River in about October 1982. Barry Ashton assigned me to do the year end for Arctic Offshore, which Gordon and Don Tetrault and others had established for the Beaufort Sea work."[115]

His memory is that he presented the financial statements, as accountants do, for the annual general meeting of Arctic Offshore in November of 1982. "That would have been my first involvement with Gordon Gill. I later did the year-end for his company, Northern Arc Shipbuilders. I am surprised Barry had me, a newcomer, do that work, which was so important to the firm. Gordon and Don were the first clients I was sent out to serve. That was the start of a forty-year relationship with Gordon and Treena."[116]

Jonathan felt the need to make it clear how essential Treena was to the initial survival of Gordon Gill's company and to its ultimate success.

> As far as I know, Treena's knowledge of bookkeeping was entirely self-taught. I believe her background was as an operator at the telephone exchange. Up to the mid '80s, like most small businesses at that time, the records were entirely hand written. There were

115 Jonathan Smethurst, telephone interview with the author and follow up emails.
116 Smethurst, interview with author.

no in-house computers. I think I may have started her off with the in-house computer system (Accpac) in the early '80s, but she took this on and expanded the system to a full payroll/accounts payable/accounts receivable computer system, including training the accounting staff in Edmonton (for payroll, accounts receivable, accounts payable, bank reconciliation).

Treena was entirely responsible for the whole financial record system of Northern Arc. She kept a close tab on everything: payroll (with fifty-plus employees in the summer), job costing (essential so that the company could properly invoice work), payment of expenses, billing out to customers, collection of receivables, monitoring the bank balance etc. Yes, she had one or two ladies to help her, but her workload must have been tremendous. This was on top of running a household and raising a family.

I have read, and agree, that the first million dollars is always the hardest part in any company's development. Treena would have had an essential role in this. Her attention to detail and insistence on doing everything "right" was remarkable. It was not all easy going for Gordon and Treena Gill and Northern Arc. There were many times when, although on paper the company was profitable, managing the cash position was extremely difficult.

It was fun times; I worked as Northern Arc's external accountant for almost twenty years, before I became the full-time chief financial officer of Northern Crane. Treena continued to be responsible for the whole accounting system until I joined as CFO in July 1999 (and after that continued to work in the accounting).

The Gills were great; they never complained, always paid accounts without quibbling, and were very loyal. They always listened politely and carefully. They may not have agreed with me all the time, but then their whole life was on the line with the success or failure of their company.[117]

Gordon talks about Treena a bit, in terms of what she did:

117 Smethurst, interview with author.

Treena did crafts and knitting. When we moved to Edmonton, she took many art courses; drawing and painting, which she loved. I think she was very good at her art. One time we went to Newfoundland for a week so she could take a painting course. We had more staff then and she wasn't having to do the day-to-day bookkeeping.

At work, people called me the Godfather. There was no paper with me, no writing or letters from me. Everything was verbal, by word of mouth. I relied on the lawyers and accountants and such to do the proper writing. Treena used to read me letters and other documents.

Gordon is obviously very proud of Treena. He mentions her sense of humour, her intelligence, her support, and her other good qualities.

However, Treena passed away from cancer in 2020, and Gordon finds it difficult to talk about her in any more personal terms. He misses her immensely. He is clear that they were partners in every way, and that he relied on her. To what extent Treena's influence and example changed Gordon isn't clear, but both her example and support likely played a large role in who he eventually became.

Gordon's niece, Marvelle, helps out, saying this about Treena:

Treena's parents were of Icelandic heritage. What I remember of them is Gestur was a commercial fisherman on the Great Slave Lake and Lara was a fantastic cook. Lara had multiple sclerosis and was in a wheelchair all the years I remember her.

Despite being in a wheelchair Lara could bake squares and goodies that would make any young girls eyes grow wide. From my memory, Gestur is where the humour that Treena inherited came from, possibly along with cousins and relatives she grew up with in Gimli, Manitoba. I do remember Lara laughing and maybe she also had quite a sense of humour because boy, oh boy, Treena was so quick on the draw with comebacks and jokes and old comical songs from when she was growing up.

Clarence Gill, who would end up being Treena's father-in-law, prided himself on not laughing and being a serious sort of guy. Well, that all went out the window when Gordon brought his girlfriend (Treena) to meet his parents. Clarence started laughing from then forward.

Treena could put a smile on anyone's face, make you spit your coffee across the room with a quick joke, sympathize with you, and you would come out feeling better. Her quick joke or saying would pull your spirits back upright.

In Hay River, Treena was friends with Gidget Dean; well, those two were a pair to be reckoned with. Gidget and Treena's humour ran parallel and had the friends at parties and get-togethers practically rolling on the floor. I was probably pre-teen when I saw them together and they made me laugh but because I was young, I think they censored their jokes and actions until the younger ones had left.

Gordon and Treena were an ideal match. Gordon is very quick-witted also, like Treena, so the pair were great together. Treena was not a person to talk about herself, but she did pride herself in doing the books for all of Gordon's and her endeavours. She had only taken a short correspondence course in bookkeeping but kept extremely accurate books; an accountant had asked her where she had taken her schooling in accounting, and she told him about the correspondence course. The accountant couldn't believe that was all she had taken and told her she was a natural. Treena was a strong lady and told it how it was. Through my eyes and ears, she was a cut-through-the-bullshit kind of lady, she took challenges head on! [118]

Marvelle later said:

She excelled. Treena's and Gordon's house is filled with her artwork, but she was like any artist—her own worst critic. I think she was very talented. I have one of her pieces, which I treasure.

Treena also crocheted; she made afghans for everyone in her family and extended families. She made all sorts of things by crocheting, sewing bags together for her granddaughter Kristen's homemade

---

118 Marvelle Kobbert, email to the author.

jewelry. She was very artistic and had a knack and an eye for decorating her homes, which were always so beautiful!

Gordon and Treena also had a gold dredging barge on the Liard River. Treena loved it out there in the deep nature and on the river. She talked fondly of that venture.

Treena's love for her family ran deep. She and her Gudmundson family endured losses of young and old loved ones. Treena's strength through the losses never faltered, but don't let her strength fool you because if Treena loved you, you knew it! Treena's love for Gordon was immense, and her commitment to their relationship and lasting marriage vows were taken seriously.

Treena once mentioned to Gordon a quote of her dad's, Gestur's. He told her when it came to the commitment of marriage, even or especially if you've had disagreements, at the end of each day ALWAYS go to bed together each night. Her dad's advice could have been foundational in the continuation of Treena's and Gordon's commitment to each other in every venture they embraced. Living in the beginning of an era where divorce is so easily decided upon, the advice of Treena's father could possibly have been one fundamental key to their success in life. Building and growing companies takes team players and Treena and Gordon supported and encouraged each other throughout their many ventures. Telling about Treena could take a book all on its own with her many talents, ventures, and morals. She was incredibly strong, strong-willed, focused, and did the work and learning necessary to get the job done with quality. Yin and yang would express how well-rounded Treena was; she knew how to focus and learn what she needed to, to do all the books to start and grow their business ventures, and she had the humour and grace to let loose and enjoy life, and the compassion and caring for her family and friends.

Both Treena and Gordon endured many obstacles in life. They have risen above and worked through them and didn't let them slow them down. If there's a will there's a way. Oh, if there's a Gill, there's a way![119]

Gordon and Treena were full partners in their businesses and in life. He is proud of what she did and what she was and happy about how well she supported him.

And, it seems, Gordon too responded and adapted, with humour, hard work, and a strength of character of his own, one which was supported by both his Métis upbringing and by Treena's unwavering support.

It was so good how willing Treena was to go along with my ambitions.

119 Marvelle Kobbert, email to the author.

CHAPTER 22:
Staking Claims

Gordon gold mining near Lillooet, BC..

It was exciting times! Here I was staking moose pasture claims and selling them for $8,000 a piece as soon as I staked them.

HISTORIC EVENTS—at least in the context of Northwest Canada and industry—seemed like destiny in Gordon's time. The rush to stake mining claims in the North was no different.

Pine Point is a point of land jutting out of the south shore of Great Slave Lake about 90 kilometres east of Hay River. It was also the name given to a lead-zinc mine established by Cominco in the early 1960s that led to, among other things, the construction of the Great Slave Lake Railroad. It also set off a "gold rush," or at least a lead-zinc rush. Although that doesn't have the romantic sense of a gold rush, it was still an important economic step in the development of the North.

Promoters and middlemen arrived, ready to buy claims from anyone who had staked even close to the Cominco property. Mining companies, some brand-new with no mine and really no other assets, bought up claims as fast as they could. Think of the excitement—this company, which didn't exist two weeks ago, now had mining claims "adjacent to the giant lead-zinc holdings of Consolidated Mining and Smelting!" Or whatever other hype came in handy.

Promoters from the south took rooms in the Hay River Hotel, and hung out in the bar, waiting for the claimstakers to come in to sell. It was the centre of excitement and enthusiasm, and there was much chatter. Everyone wanted in on it! Gordon was part of this mid-1960s rush. *$8,000 a piece as soon as I staked them.*

Staking claims should not be confused with prospecting—where the goal is to find minerals or precious metals and stones. This was more like figuring out where the last claim was marked off as being claimed, grabbing the next one and the next one after that, and registering them.

Gordon was working with Northern Transportation Company Limited in 1964. That company had taken over Yellowknife Transportation and got Gordon in the deal. But things slow down considerably in those waterways in the winter, and Gordon had not yet taken up full-time work doing repairs over the winter.

Gold fever had taken over the North. Except, in this case, it was lead and zinc fever. So, taking time off from NT in the winter of 1964–1965, Gordon took a crash course in how to stake claims. Then, he and his partner, Pierre Simpson, from Fort Chipewyan in northeast Alberta, went out into the bush near where Consolidated Mining Company had staked a major lead-zinc property before the Pine Point mine opened, "freelancing" as claimstakers. They were out to make some money, and they weren't alone. Gordon was twenty-three years old.

They were a good team, Pierre and Gordon. Pierre was, in Gordon's words, a "real Native"; he was strong and used to the bush and a good worker. Gordon's kind of guy.

I met Pierre when we both worked at YT. I picked him because he was a real bushman. He didn't know anything about staking claims, but he knew how to live in the bush a lot better than I did. Thank God I had him. He was excellent in the bush.

Pierre could carry huge packs weighing 500 pounds on his back, held in place by just a tump line [a strap from the pack around his forehead]. He was the champion of the Hay River Winter Carnival for many years. Pierre would carry weights like this for a certain distance, say 100 yards in a race. The veins in his neck stuck out like bicycle tubes.

Canadian historian Morris Zaslow writes about the Pine Point Rush (named after a point of land covered with pines, not surprisingly, on the south shore of Great Slave Lake): "All promising ground surrounding Cominco's holdings [at Pine Point] was staked, more than 24,000 claims involving over eighty companies in 1964–65 alone."[120]

All the staking activity and the speculators, well, it made for interesting times. Everyone was talking about mines and claims and making money! Gordon and Treena, too, got caught up in the penny stock market. They were investors! Gordon was pretty excited by all this.

You knew it was a boom; even the barber was giving buy-and-sell advice.

This was the start of an involvement with mining, gold dredging, and staking prospectors throughout his life.

Because I got this experience with mining claims at Pine Point, I was hired to stake claims on the Tree River up along the Arctic coast. It was good pay—$500 a day in cash, paid if I worked or didn't. Like on the way to Coppermine, we had to wait in Yellowknife until the weather cleared and they could fly us in. But they paid us anyway.

There was big money floating around. There was plenty of excitement in those days.

We stayed in the village of Coppermine [now Kugluktuk, Nunavut] and every day, a bush plane flew us out to the Tree River. It was kind of funny to call it that. There were no trees anywhere in that part of the Arctic.

---

120 Zaslow, *Northward Expansion*, 346.

> *This was 60 or 80 miles east of Coppermine. We weren't prospectors. We just took up claims based on what the map said wasn't claimed. Every day the plane waited for us to finish, then flew us back to Coppermine.*

When Gordon left for the Tree River job, he and Treena had $250,000 worth of penny stocks. It was a crazy time! All he did in Coppermine and Tree River was work.

There were no phones, no radio, no TV, no newspapers, no communication at all. He didn't hear of the crash in mining stocks. When Gordon returned to Hay River a month later, their quarter-million in stock was down to $10,000. It was all they had left of their mining investments.

Gordon just smiles now; he says he didn't worry about it. This seems particularly surprising. Wouldn't he have been devastated? Apparently not.

> *I remember taking it pretty good; it was all penny stocks. I forget what the stocks cost me, but most of the penny stock we had completely disappeared when the market crashed.*
>
> *I think this was in 1965/66 and the Pine Point hype died down as quick as it flew up.*
>
> *Not only had I been in the Arctic when it all happened, back then when I was buying and selling stocks at the Royal Bank, it was all done by mail. (Snail mail, we called it back then.) Treena and I both thought it was too good to be true. For a short period of time, we were rich, on paper. The birds were all in the bush. (Laughs).*

This is just one more example of how, time and again faced with some serious accident, change in circumstance or misfortune, Gordon fought back, calmly, with resilience, and an ability to adapt.

Gordon bought a new Oldsmobile 88 with the money that was left.

> *The motor was a big one, 455 cubic inches.[121] Even driving at 60 miles per hour you could step on the gas and spray gravel. It was a big hit around town.*

----

121 A lot of CCs or litres.

CHAPTER 23:
The Northern Transportation Route

Unidentified man at Port Radium, Great Bear Lake with bags of pitchblende
concentrate ready for transport on NTCL barge, 1939.
NWT Archives/ Richard Finnie fonds/N-1979-063-0081.

NT went all over the north, from Fort MacMurray to
the uranium mines on Lake Athabasca, from Fort
Smith to the high Arctic, and from Fort Norman on
the Mackenzie all the way across Great Bear Lake.

THE MARINE INDUSTRY that was so crucial to Gordon's future was the
lifeblood of Hay River and the North as a whole. As a minister of the

Government of the Northwest Territories (GNWT) said in a statement to
the assembly:

> Mr. Speaker, the Hay River Harbour is the NWT's marine gateway,
> providing services to residents and businesses up and down the
> Mackenzie River and into the High Arctic. The port's strategic loca-
> tion, with connections to CN Rail's Meander subdivision and the
> public highway system, positions it as the portal between the Arctic
> coast and southern Canada. From there, marine resupply operations
> are undertaken for communities and industries, contributing to low-
> ering the costs of living and doing business in the territory.
>
> The harbour is also important to the NWT's commercial fishing
> industry on Great Slave Lake, which has the potential to help
> diversify the NWT economy and increase locally produced food.
> Canadian Coast Guard operations, RCMP, and other federal agen-
> cies also make use of the port, providing important aids to naviga-
> tion and marine safety.[122]

Hay River Harbour is sheltered from the direct onslaught of the Great
Slave wind and waves. A Canadian Coast Guard station, with its own vessels
playing a critical safety and enforcement role, is an added component to
the waterfront. And the government owned Northern Transportation
was based there, taking barge tows to communities, and exploration sites
all over the Arctic in answer to the demands of the North. The harbour
is also only 64 kilometres by lake travel from the head of the Mackenzie,
the big river that is almost literally (for boats and supplies) "the Highway
of the North." Moreover, the road and, in due course, the rail line from
Edmonton via Peace River to the docklands at the harbour, relegated the
formerly important ports of Waterways and Fort Smith to history just as
they had done for Athabasca. Moving freight via Hay River avoided the
rapids, the delays, and the expense of portages, plus the long lake crossing that had bedeviled northern transportation from the beginning. Like
everything else, transportation evolved to those methods and places where
it could be more efficient, easier, and less costly.

122 Government of Northwest Territories, "Wally Schumann: Hay River Harbour
Restoration," *Ministers' Statements and Speeches* (February 9, 2017), https://www.gov.
nt.ca/newsroom/news/wally-schumann-hay-river-harbour-restoration.

Until 1967, the town and the rest of the NWT were run entirely from Ottawa, with some small regional officers scattered throughout the North. Of significant importance to Hay River, the Mackenzie River communities, and the northern coastline (and, in due course, to Gordon), were the federal government facilities, especially docks and wharves, serving the Hay River (and other) harbours.

All that infrastructure (plus furnished homes for teachers and social workers, and the various government buildings, among other facilities) was the responsibility of the federal Department of Public Works. Their operations in Hay River were quite large and in later years, these evolved to include a fleet of dredges, tugs, barges, scows and other boats, which along with the local Canadian Coast Guard ships and aids to navigation and safety, were crucial for the Mackenzie River transportation and extended supply route. (This function has continued, although now devolved to the government of the NWT.)

While transport in the North was initially by canoe, eventually and inevitably, roads and railways supplanted these. Thus, when Gordon and his family arrived in Hay River, much of the supplies needed by those in the camps, trading posts, and missions of the North travelled by the 1948 road, the Mackenzie Highway, to Hay River. The goods and equipment were then reloaded onto barges and shipped via the Mackenzie, Canada's longest river, to docks and communities down river and out along the Arctic coast. Later, when the Great Slave Lake Railway was completed to Hay River's harbour in 1964 (helped along by the need for a rail line to the new lead-zinc mine at Pine Point), fuel and other cargo were an even bigger commodity, and heavier freight could be moved north and south, spurring development.

On the big lakes—Athabasca, Great Slave, and Great Bear—and in the open sea of the Arctic, tugboats towed long, narrow barges strung out behind them on hard wire cables. They looked like a group of ducklings trying to keep up with their mother.

On the rivers, those same barges would be arranged in a "tow", that is, manoeuvred into place by large cables, and positioned together in front and alongside the tug. An "anchor" barge was attached to the bow of the tug with steel cables, and the rest of the barges were connected to each other by heavy ropes.

This made for a more compact and more controllable "push." Cameron

Clement's comment on this approach was that "when a river tow was roped together, the tug and barges became one unit, so as to successfully navigate around bends in the river."[123]

The barges were, after the war, mostly flat-deck steel vessels, some with wooden structures to keep cargo dry. Some were refrigerated ("reefer barges"), while others were bulk tankers or reinforced for heavy loads.

The tugs themselves were, from the late '30s on, made of steel. However, Gordon acted as the engineer on reputedly the last wooden lake vessel, the *Arctic Lady*.

The northern transportation route, first from Alberta, and latterly from Hay River, has been the lifeline of the North, connecting communities and the people. It has a long history, even before the founding of NT. Initially, a function of supplying missions and traders like Réveillon Frères and the Hudson's Bay Company, the transporters in due course supplied trappers, communities, mines, and miners, the petroleum industry, the military, and the US-Canadian Distant Early Warning (DEW) Line sites, which were built during the Cold War to monitor potential over-the-pole airborne threats from the then Soviet Union.

And worrisome to some now is the old story. Will history repeat itself, now that there is an all-season road to Inuvik near the Arctic Ocean, an extension which has now reached Tuktoyaktuk on the Arctic coast? Will that prove an easier and cheaper location to service the upper river and Arctic communities? Necessity rules; the real purpose of making NT a Crown Corporation was to control the delivery of pitchblende for uranium. Gordon was involved in that too.

> *I never did the Great Bear Lake Run but I did work as the engineer on the* Watson Lake, *hauling ore down Great Bear River.*

....
123 Clement, email to the author, 2022.

CHAPTER 24:
Northern Transportation Company Limited (NTCL) – A Brief History

Radium Gilbert and barge with ore, Great Bear Lake;
NWT Archives/ Edmonton Air Museum Committee Collection/N-1979-003: 0337.

After Yellowknife Transportation was bought by
Northern Transportation Company Limited, I carried
on with Northern Transportation basically for eight
more years before I went into business on my own.

NORTHERN TRANSPORTATION COMPANY LIMITED is one of the Northwest Territories' oldest companies. Initially, one of a number of small transport companies in Alberta, Northern Waterways Limited, sold its minimal marine assets to White Eagle Mines, which had a mine on the east shore of Great Bear Lake. They changed the name to Northern Transportation Company Limited and commenced using the tugs and barges to serve the Great Bear Lake mine.

Two years later, in 1936, Eldorado Gold Mines Limited purchased the company for its own mine in the same area and also supplied services as a general shipping company. At the time, the transportation needs in the North were primarily handled by the Hudson's Bay Company, with a number of wooden steam wheelers and barges.

Soon, the age of steel tugs arrived. In 1937, the *Radium King* and the *Radium Queen* started operation, the *King* on the north side of the Fort Smith portage and the *Queen* on the south run. (The *King* had a crew of ten and, different from other tugs in the North, it had space for ten passengers).

While the Depression raised concerns about the future of the Northern Transportation predecessors, the Second World War and specifically the construction of the oil pipeline, road, and telegraph from Norman Wells to the Pacific coast provided a lot of freight to move.

Then, in 1944, the federal government took over Eldorado, which controlled a large amount of the mining of radium and uranium in Canada, and its transport subsidiary. After the war, the re-energized NT took over Hudson's Bay's transport arm and, later, Yellowknife Transportation. Both Eldorado and NT, along with Eldorado Aviation, operated as crown corporations until 1985, at which time the federal government transferred the company to the Inuit, as part of their land claims settlement. The Inuvialuit from the western Arctic and Nunasi Corporation from the east each took fifty percent ownership and the norther.

NTCL became part of the NorTerra Group of Companies. In 2014, Nunasi Corporation sold its half interest to the Inuvialuit.[124]

The Eldorado Mine (radium, uranium, and silver) has a complicated history. New interest in radium and uranium in the latter half of the Second

124 "Nunasi Corp. Sells its Half of Norterra to the Inuvialuit," *Nunatsiaq News* (April 1, 2014), https://nunatsiaq.com/stories/article/65674nunasi_corp-_sells_stake_in_norterra/

World War led to product from Eldorado being used in the first atomic bombs, including at Hiroshima and Nagasaki. Such a serious business needed protection and control and as a result, the Canadian government secretly expropriated ("nationalized") the mine sometime between 1942 (according to historian Morris Zaslow) and 1944 (according to the NWT Archives).

This gave the government control of the radium it produced on the east shore of Great Bear Lake, and its uranium mining potential and a processing facility at Port Hope, Ontario. Included was the Eldorado subsidiary, Northern Transportation. Thus, Canada secured two things: access to and control of the uranium, and security of transportation in the North.

NTCL was labelled "The Radium Line." Many of its tugs carried the Radium moniker. The *Radium Charles* and the *Radium Gilbert* (actually a freighter) were named, for example, after two of the Labine brothers who founded the Eldorado Mining Company. Others included the *Radium King, Queen,* and *Prince,* the *Radium Franklin,* the *Radium Dew,* the *Radium Yellowknife,* and three southern-based boats: the *Radium Miner, Radium Trader,* and *Radium Prospector.* It makes for an inspiring photo to see one of the Radium ships pushing a "tow" down river, or a group of them bunched up in a harbour.

And the deliveries were desperately needed, often only once a year, and on which communities, businesses, and individuals relied heavily.

Those barges were loaded with everything from furniture and groceries to oil pipe and drilling equipment, from trucks and food and liquor to, well, anything.

As one-time Inuvik dentist and songwriter Bob Ruzicka wrote in "The First Barge":

You see the smiles upon their faces
As the word spreads over town –
If that rumour's right
You know, tomorrow night
The first barge comes to town.
Everybody thinks their orders on the first barge
But somebody must be wrong,
Or else that barge will be a mile wide,
And forty-five miles long.

They've got fresh eggs, milk, cheese and butter,
Johnny Walker's Special Old,
Baseball spikes and motorbikes
And a brand new still I'm told.

And among other things, it carried:

"long johns and bon-bons and prefabricated stairs,
and 147 identical DPW rocking chairs…

No item was too small, no article too large,
the whole damn world is coming on that barge."[125]

The song reveals the anxious waiting for all the wonders the first barge would bring when it finally arrived after the long, dark winter.

People familiar with the furnished houses supplied to government workers, teachers and the RCMP by the Department of Public Works—all with exactly the same furniture—usually smile at the DPW line.

The river itself is pretty flat for its entire journey, wide and smooth. Although the overall gradient is only about 0.1 metres per kilometre, it is still a powerful, fast river, churning along at 4.8 to 6.4 kilometres an hour. Usually, it is at least 1.6 kilometres wide and often double that; and, in sections with islands, 4.8 to 6.4 kilometres across. Only where a large tributary enters, like the Liard at Fort Simpson, or when traversing the cliffs of the 11-kilometre limestone gorge called the Ramparts or at the San Sault Rapids does change occur, until it flattens into the incredibly spread-out, water-filled delta of the Mackenzie. There, anyone without the right directions could and would get hopelessly lost in its multitude of twisting channels.

The Mackenzie is huge, in all dimensions, replete with superlatives: it is the longest river in Canada with the largest watershed, covering almost one-fifth of the country.[126]

Including the Peace River and that river's tributary, the Finlay River, the

....

125 Bob Ruzicka, writer, "The First Barge," track 8 on *Straight North*, featuring Ted Wesley, vocalist, PET-MAC BMI 1972.

126 Making its drainage basin second only to the Mississippi–Missouri System in North America.

Mackenzie travels "1,738 miles (4,241 kilometres) [from] its head at the source of the Finlay River in northern British Columbia"[127] to its outlet in the Beaufort Sea.

Once past the wide expanse of delta channels, tugs or ships, usually bigger and specifically designed to be ocean going can chug through the Beaufort Sea, and out into the Arctic Ocean, either along the coast or across the sea to one of the Arctic islands. Some are settlements, like Sachs Harbour on Victoria Island. Sometimes, the supply ships just anchored off-shore or, in the case of some converted "Landing Ship, Tank" or LST as the Americans called them from the Second World War, they would run up on the gravel beaches and unload their cargo. Shipping there, in the Arctic, in those days, relied much on weather and chance; sometimes the ice stopped the ships cold, sometimes it was the wind, sometimes a drunk cook or a problem crewman. What might start as a bright and sunny trip may well be closed in by a change in wind or a shifting icepack. Knowing the Inuit communities along the coast relied on that one supply ship a year to get them all their needs for a year, missing a stop was hardly to be contemplated.

Sailing in the north was dangerous work. This is obvious in the Arctic Ocean with its huge waves beating over the shallow waters, added to moving ice, and isolation, but it was also true on the rivers and the lakes farther south. One story survives of a tugboat—lots of names got tossed around—that was heading home on the last run of the season.

It was the last boat out. Every surge of the lake lifted her up, then splashed her down hard into the trough between the waves. Icy spray covered every spot of her exterior. Every wave left more water frozen on the tug's superstructure. Every wave added more ice and therefore more weight on. She didn't sink so much as just get weighed down and down and down until she just went under, kind of in forward slow motion. Luckily, a rescue boat reached the tug in time to take the crew off. The ship itself continued to the bottom.

It was salvaged by those really hardy souls who would do that sort of thing, but the story kept circulating for years after the actual event.

....

127 CanadianGeographic.com. https://www.thecanadianencyclopedia.ca/en/article/mackenzie-river

CHAPTER 25:
Gordon, NTCL, and the Marine Industry

NT Husky entering Hay River harbour;
NWT Archives/Ben Hall Collection/2013-015-0160.

When I finished all my schooling, I worked for Yellowknife Transportation in Hay River for three years and then Northern Transportation bought them out.

HAY RIVER WAS home to Gordon and to the operations centre for NTCL. It was a thriving port and harbour and a logical place for Gordon's working career to start. NTCL was the big fish. It was known all over the north as NTCL, or NT, or for some reason, especially among Indigenous Peoples, as "the NT." This was in contrast to the other large tug-and-barge company, Yellowknife Transportation (YT).

Gordon started with YT in 1961 and stayed on when that company was purchased by NT.

> *With the NT, I did heavy-duty mechanics, also welding, and was shop foreman for the welding department. I also did a lot of mechanical missions up and down the Mackenzie, all the way from Hay River to Tuktoyaktuk* [on the Arctic Ocean]. *Because of my mechanical and welding experience, I went as replacement engineer* [on various tugboats] *on a lot of occasions. This was in the summertime. There was so much I did for Northern Transportation, lots of different jobs. In the winter, I was mostly repairing barges or ships, or supervising crews that did that. I was not a seasonal employee like most people who came from the south for the summer. I liked it. I made good friends at NT.*

One of those friends was Henry Christofferson, the Superintendent of Marine Engineering for NT.

> *Henry used to come and talk to me. Even though most people thought of him as a pompous person with kind of a know-it-all attitude, I liked him, and we got along good. He'd ask me questions, and we'd just talk like two guys. Once, Henry said I was causing him a problem. I asked him why. He said he had to select the next superintendent of marine engineering to be in charge of all the mechanical work, engineering, and maintenance for the tugs and boats and barges. It came down to between me and Bert Stromberg. I told him he had to choose Bert because Bert had his marine ticket, and I didn't. So, he did. But he still came to me for advice. Bert was a great guy, and we were good friends too. I really enjoyed working for Bert. We were friends before, when we were both engineers on tugboats, and we continued to be, even when we used to work in the shop together and even later, after I left NT to set up Northern Arc Shipbuilders.*
>
> *That got Bert into a bit of trouble because I was getting to be a pretty big contractor for NT, doing boat and barge repairs and stuff. He was in charge of that department, and people used to think he was getting kickbacks or some special favours from me. Even though he wasn't, he*

> *was treated badly at the end of his career. But he was a great asset to the*
> *town and to NT.*

Gordon laughs, changing the subject.

> *NT used to have the most underpowered tugs. YT had the* Husky.[128]
> *It was kind of the king of the fleet, the flagship, I guess you would call*
> *it. We'd hear on the marine VHF radio*[129]*—we hung out with the*
> *radio operator at night—that an NT boat was fighting the winds and*
> *waves and would have made only a mile or so since they reported in*
> *that morning or the night before. Then we'd hear the* Husky *talking, or*
> *we'd see it just power through, leaving the NT tugs behind. When NT*
> *bought YT, it was considered quite a high honour to be captain of the*
> Husky. *Kenny Simpson was the captain for a long time.*

About the *Husky*. This was the big boat on the river, for ten years or so, from when it was built in 1959 until the new tugs were launched in 1969 from the Bell Rock Camp. It was all steel, 36.9 metres long and 9.1 metres wide. Like the other Mackenzie River tugs, it was a shallow-draft vessel, although a little deeper, drawing 1.5 metres of water. The *Husky*, like the other river boats, was often far away from any facility out on the river or the big lake. If they got in trouble, the crew's ingenuity became an important aspect of success or failure and sometimes life or death. Often the crew would nurse a crippled ship home to port, much as a friend might prop up a too-inebriated pal.

Once, when Gordon was still working in the NT shipyards, the *Husky* was brought into port, and its bow was pulled up on the slipways for repair. The culprit was a big gash in the bow, below the waterline. Gordon's first question was *What happened?* and his second was *What kept the damned thing afloat?*

> *Ernie Camsell told me that he was sleeping below decks when water*
> *started rushing into the crew quarters. He ran up to the bridge and*
> *yelled at Ken Simpson that there was a hole in the bow and water was*
> *flooding in. "I know," was all he said. Ken Simpson and Ernie Camsell*

....

128 Wikipedia, s.v. "Boats of the Mackenzie River Watershed," last modified April 6, 2022, at 18:59 (UTC), https://en.wikipedia.org/wiki/Boats_of_the_Mackenzie_River_watershed

129 A marine radio generally thought to use FM channels in the VHF (Very High Frequency) range between 156 and 174 Megahertz.

> *gave me the blow-by-blow story. I was involved with the repair once they got to Hay River.*

They had hit a rock and, yup, the captain would likely know. At least it didn't open the hull like a zipper.

> *Ernie told me they took this big tarp and draped it over the outside of the hole in the bow. The ties were stretched tight, as much as they could do, and then they pumped out the water from the bunk area. They stuffed some boxes and stakes and other stuff against the hole, and then Captain Simpson pushed the boat forward. The tarp flattened against the hole, and it worked pretty good. As long as the ship kept going forward, the water pressed the tarp in place, and no water came in. But boy, it couldn't stop! So, they got her back to the shipyard, and we fixed that hole.*

Distances in the North are almost beyond comprehension. They are lonely distances, filled with trees and muskeg and thousands of lakes, and mostly unseen animals and birds. It is a ruggedly pretty land in many places, and a long way from anywhere, except where you are.

The summer nights are at most a twilight. They might be smoky or dusky, but the dark does not fill the sky completely; the horizon is a long way away, if you are high enough in the boat to see over the riverbank. The landscape stretches forever. Photos from airplanes never seem to show the end of the trees or water. The view across Great Slave Lake is never-ending.

And you are often alone with your thoughts, cruising, busy—really busy—for ten minutes every hour. Like baseball, a few minutes of action, or in some cases terror, are crammed into four hours.

There is a rhythm to the throb of the engine, and the shimmy of the deck. The slap of the gentle waves, and the turned swish of the bow wake can be mesmerizing. There are no towns or high-rises[130] or industrial sites or farms like you might see when canoeing a prairie river. On the Slave or the Mackenzie, you might spot a fish camp, or a lone bear. The sight of a village would be a remarkable event, with the anticipation of work if you were scheduled to stop.

Gordon remembers his time on the ships.

....
130 Hay River does have a high-rise, all 17 stories of residential apartments.

A number of times while on the night shift in the summer, when it was daylight forever in the North, I would try to think how the voyageurs must have felt. After leaving the portage at Fort Smith [on the Slave River] there were no more portages and, except for crossing Great Slave Lake, it was all downhill to the Arctic Ocean. With all the daylight, they must have chalked up the miles.

Coming back would be a different story. It would be hard work, paddling all the way back upriver. Their loads were probably a bit lighter then, being mostly furs, but still heavy, and at least there were no portages until they got back to Smith. But it was upriver all the way, except on the dangerous big lake. What a hard life! Imagine all the black flies and mosquitoes, and the other bugs, and the bull dogs [horseflies]. And NO repellent! It would have been a hard job.

The bugs were still a problem in later years, too, but the breeze on board usually kept them at bay. Not on land, however, where they cannot be outrun.

The northern trade was filled with adventure and amazing sights. Some, like an inland sea glistening calm to the horizon, were sublime. The sun would settle on the edge of nowhere late at night, brightening the clear sky with its startling yellow and orange slash. Or the aurora borealis, the northern lights, would dance in shimmering drapes of greens and yellows and hazy purples across the darker skies of August and September.

Other sights rewarded the crews, too. Tributaries would join the big river, a different colour pushing in, and the two currents flowing side by side, distinct, for long distances until the line between them became blurred, and they merged together. It sometimes took several kilometres.

Gordon recalls that before reaching Fort Simpson, *the Mackenzie River is blue and clear from its start at Great Slave Lake, for more than 300 miles.* At Fort Simpson, the big Liard River joins, but it is muddy and brown. The Fort Simpson History and Heritage Organization says that "14 million tons of silt flows down the Liard River to the Mackenzie … and that it takes 100 miles of river travel before it mixes together." (Others say the distance the rivers take to lose their separate colours is more like 300 miles.) The Fort Simpson website claims that 100 million tons of sediment—100 million!—is dumped in Mackenzie Bay at the Beaufort Sea annually. Gordon remembers being told that the Liard moved 26,000 bathtubs of mud per second—per second!—at average flow, and that the hundreds of miles of Mackenzie Delta islands were reputed to be almost all built from the Liard River sand.

> *Mostly the push of silt takes place during spring break up when there is so much fast and powerful water, and also in the summer if there is a big rain or melt up the Liard River, like in the mountains or from the Nahanni River. John Pope had a contract to run the ferry across the Liard River at Simpson for a number of years. He told me that he'd seen the river rise 20 feet overnight, that you had to be really careful there.*

Downstream from the junction of the Liard and Mackenzie, the picturesque Mackenzie Mountains follow the river down its western shore. The mountains and the fish camps, and the communities of Fort Simpson, Deline (Fort Norman), Norman Wells, Fort Good Hope, Inuvik, and others meant there was something else to look at, often a stop, and some news.

Sometimes the news was man-made. Gordon tells his wood buffalo story:

> *We were pushing a house barge north from Bell Rock on the Slave River. The housing* [a building on top of the barge] *was filled with buffalo* [officially, wood bison].[131] *Usually, those house barges had the freight that had to be protected, kept out of the rain, like boxes and food. Anyway, the bison were being transferred from Wood Buffalo National Park to Fort Providence for the big buffalo preserve the government set up there. We pushed the barge up onto the bank of the north shore of Beaver Lake. That's the big wide spot at the start of the Mackenzie. The Parks people had opened up a cutline north to these big hay meadows at Falaise Lake. The idea was that the buffalo would come off the barge and follow the cleared path to the new Mackenzie Bison Sanctuary. Just as soon as we unloaded them, the buffalo took off in all directions, running like mad. It was crazy. But not along the cutline; they went straight into the bush.*

Wood buffalo crammed together, in a building, on a barge, floating, being jostled around, down river and crossing a lake for days. Opening the

---

131 Distinct from the bison (plains buffalo) of the open prairie, the smaller and lighter wood buffalo lives in the boreal forest. Wood Buffalo National Park is the largest park in Canada (bigger than Switzerland), and is a UNESCO World Heritage Site. ("Wood Buffalo National Park," *Natural World Heritage Sites*, https://www.naturalworld heritagesites.org/sites/wood-buffalo-national-park/.)

doors. Hoping for an orderly transference of animals down a nice cut line in the forest. What could possibly go wrong?

* * *

One June, Gordon was sent to the coast of Alaska as the engineer on a smaller tug; his job was to get the MV *Watson Lake* up and running and ready to work after a winter ice-bound at the mouth of the Colville River. The vessel had been sent in the prior summer to do surveying for the proposed harbour at Prudhoe Bay and then had over-wintered in the ice. This was done sometimes when the distance was too great to get back to a port, and especially if you wanted to get an early start in the spring. A ski plane flew Gordon from the nearest DEW Line site to the mouth of the Colville. That is June in the Arctic. Ice in the river and sunshine at midnight.

The DEW Line was a series of radar type installations spread across the far north, from Alaska to the Eastern Arctic. They were remote and strategic, being the first line of defence against an incursion of Russian (then the Soviet Union) airplanes or missiles. This joint Canadian American project was part of NORAD, the North American Air Defense [now Aerospace] Command based in Colorado Springs, Colorado.[132] The sites were difficult to get to because they were the farthest radar line from southern Canada, set up to watch for any approach over the North Pole and the polar region.

> *NT sent me up to Colville River; our job was to get the ship going, and when the river ice broke, the tug would be busy making trips upriver to deliver the drilling rig—the first one in Prudhoe Bay—to the drilling site. There was a big buildup for oil-and-gas exploration then.*
>
> *They sent us in on the Eldorado Aviation DC-3.*

Douglas DC-3s were common in the North then. Eldorado Aviation,

132 Wikipedia describes the Distant Early Warning Line as "a system of radar stations in the northern Arctic region of Canada, with additional stations along the north coast and Aleutian Islands of Alaska, in addition to the Faroe Islands, Greenland, and Iceland. It was set up to detect incoming bombers of the Soviet Union during the Cold War, and provide early warning of any sea-and-land invasion." The DEW Line was started in the mid-1950s, and most of its stations were decommissioned in 1988. (Wikipedia, s.v. "Distant Early Warning Line," last updated May 7 2022, 22:03 [UTC], https://en.wikipedia.org/wiki/Distant_Early_Warning_Line.)

NWT Air, and Buffalo Airways, for example, used the hardy, easily landed workhorses, capable of carrying passengers and freight, up to 2,725 kilograms (6,000 pounds) worth.

Some DC-3s are still active after at least seventy-five years of service. These sturdy, two-engine, all-metal airplanes were first produced in 1935.

Bush planes, like the Norsemen, Beavers, Otters (and the Twin Otters of latter days), opened the North, but they were smaller and more restricted in distance and capacity. DC-3s carried more people and more freight, and they did it reliably just as they once did in World War II, sometimes under the US Army name, Dakota.

In the 1960s and 70s, at least, the Supreme Court of the NWT was famous for its flights into remote Inuit and Dene settlements in the Northwest Territorial Airlines (NWT Air) "Court Plane"—a DC-3 outfitted to carry the judge (Sissons J. and later Morrow J. and likely judges of the Territorial Court as well), the court staff (including a clerk of the court and a court reporter), the crown prosecutor, a defence lawyer or two, and some well-used copies of *Martin's Criminal Code*. Occasionally, there might even be an accused or two being flown back to the community from jail in Yellowknife. The plane would be met by some of the local Royal Canadian Mounted Police detachment, its occupants escorted to town by truck or Chevrolet Suburbans, while the judge would sometimes manoeuvre—or be manoeuvred—into a waiting dog sled and be pulled into the community by the enthusiastic dog team.

Gordon's friend Joe McBryan's Buffalo Airways still flies, at the time of writing, four DC-3s as part of its fleet, which includes the only remaining commercially operated DC-3 that was active on D-Day, June 6, 1944.[133]

But back to the trip to Alaska. That was another first for Gordon, and the first delivery of a drilling rig into the high Alaska oil-and-gas fields.

It was also Gordon's first encounter with international politics.

Before we even got to the boat, the Americans brought in the Jones Act[134]

133 Buffalo Airways, accessed July 20, 2021, https://buffaloairways.com/.

134 The Jones Act was United States legislation designed to protect American jobs. It is described by *Investopedia* as marine commerce law that requires goods shipped between US ports to be transported on ships that are built, owned, and operated by United States citizens or permanent residents. (Will Kenton, "The Jones Act," *Investopedia* (April 30, 2021), https://www.investopedia.com/terms/j/jonesact.asp.

and exercised it. They wanted the tug and barge work for Americans, not us Canadians.

The Americans kicked the Canadians out. There was no fooling around. They didn't want us there anymore; they wanted their people to have all the work delivering the drill rigs and pipe. So they kicked Northern Transportation out, even though it was owned by the federal government.

In fairness to the Americans there in Alaska, maybe things could have been planned a bit better. I remember that NT flew the whole crew into the DEW Line station from Tuk[135] in the DC-3.

The captain flying the Eldorado Aviation DC-3 was told that he could land and offload the Watson Lake crew and the supplies, but then the plane had to turn around immediately and leave, go back to Tuk. The boat crew had to stand outside the airport and wait for the ski plane to take us in to the ship. We had to stay out there on the end of the runway.

Gordon was waiting to get off the DC-3 in the United States. That would be another first for him. But alas, *I heard that NT didn't give much notice, and just assumed they could land. The air traffic controller on the Alaska side said NT didn't have the proper authority to bring us in. Maybe NT or Eldorado just assumed too much.*

Henry Christofferson was with us. He was head of marine engineering for NT. He was furious. He was so mad he stomped down the slanting floor of the DC-3, stopped impatiently as the cargo door was opened, pushed forward, and stepped right into thin air. I guess he forgot to wait for the unloading steps to be put in place. Henry fell right to the ground. Probably 6 or 8 feet. He hurt himself pretty bad.

It was so cold and so windy out there. The Americans had security people to keep us in place. We couldn't even go in the mess hall or the bathrooms. We stood around outside in the wind until the ski plane came.

I was taken in first by the ski plane, with groceries and my tools. It was a Cessna 180, I think.

---

135 Tuk is the universal shortening of the name Tuktoyaktuk, the northernmost NT base and an important Arctic shore community, near where the Mackenzie Delta ends.

After he dropped me off at the tug, alone, the pilot flew a lot of trips back and forth between the MV Watson Lake *and the airport, ferrying the rest of the crew and supplies into the site where the* Watson Lake *was moored. I was happy to see them.*

The snow was drifted all over the place. I had to shovel my way in. First, I fired up the galley stove to get some heat going. The pilot waited to make sure I got into the boat then he flew back to get the crew. I got the furnace going, and melted snow for drinking and washing.

The ski plane made a number of trips to bring the crew in. We were on board there in the ice for about two weeks—until breakup. There is a lot to do to get a tug and the barges ready to work.

One thing was that we had never been in that place [Colville River on the Alaskan north coast] *for breakup before. We didn't know what might happen when the ice started to move and come apart. Sometimes it bunches up something terrible and pushes in every which way. Strange things could happen. Like a fifty-year flood, or it could push us up on the ice or on land or out to sea. As it turned out, the ice around the* Watson Lake *and the barges started to rot. In the twenty-four-hour sunlight, the ice melted fast, and we got out of freeze-up without any trouble.*

That's when we hooked up with the Radium Dew [one of the bigger NT tugs, which had come over from Canada with a drill rig]*, when it anchored in Prudhoe Bay.*

There, the smaller vessel positioned small river barges so the crews could unload the rig pieces from bigger barges brought in by the *Dew*. The *Watson Lake* had a shallow draft. It could push the smaller barges upriver to the drilling site. The sections of the rig were unloaded and put together on site. It took lots of runs back and forth to get the whole thing delivered.

Gordon advises, *You needed the river tug for the river work and the big tug for the Arctic Ocean.*

Both crews got to work and unloaded the drill rig onto our little 200-series barges, and we pushed them upriver.

The 200-series and the 500-, 1000-, 1200-, and 1500-series (they got bigger and bigger as tugs were built that could push and pull the extra weight) were so called because they carried up to 200 Imperial tons of weight, in a combination of fuel and surface freight (or 500 tons, 1,000, 1,200, or 1,500 tons, as the case may be).

The *Watson Lake* stayed around for a while after the *Dew* headed back to Canadian waters, taking soundings for the American company so they could build a proper harbour there. Likely because the smaller tug was already there and wasn't hauling goods from one American port to another, even if going through Canada didn't—apparently—change the rules of the *Jones Act*, they were allowed to do this job for the American exploration company.

> *Once we finished the Alaska job, we ended up bringing the tugboat back to Canada. Oh my God! It was terrible.*
>
> *We had to travel about 350 miles in the Arctic Ocean, and we were pulling barges. The* Watson Lake *was a small tug; it wasn't made for that kind of work, and sure not for the ocean waves. We thought we were going to get swallowed up by all that water.*
>
> *On our trip from Colville River back to the Mackenzie Delta, we got caught in a huge storm. It was real bad weather. After many hours of bouncing around with two barges in tow, the captain was able to get us into some shelter at King Point, north of Yukon Territory. What a relief! That storm, it lasted four days. We would have died if we didn't get protected at King's Point.*
>
> *We had to stay there until the weather calmed and we could get back into the Mackenzie Delta. The captain was George Moulton, and the mate, John Matson. They were good people.*

King Point lies near the outflow of the Babbage River on the Arctic coast of Yukon Territory, approximately two-thirds of the way from the Alaska border to the edge of the NWT. Getting to the point took the MV *Watson Lake* past Herschel Island, where drilling was also prevalent in the exploration days. Sitting just off the northern coast of Yukon at the Firth River delta, Herschel, windblown and devoid of much vegetation, receives a mere 20 centimetres of snow on average per year.[136] To give some context to the wind and exposure the men on the MV *Watson Lake* would experience, here is what photographer and essayist Jim Guthrie said about spring work in the Arctic Ocean there, despite the minimal snowfall:

> Digging out of the snow drifts in the spring could be quite a task at Herschel Basin. It seems like our vessels were the only objects in the way of snow drifting down from the North Pole, as we had snowdrift mountains to contend with… all the steel was completely buried on the Seaspan 250 barge. This wind blasted snowpacks as hard as ice; we used chain saws with very long blades to cut the snow in blocks and roll them down the hill. It was like dismantling the Great Pyramid from the top down![137]

Guthrie added, that after a hard blow, the snow would be drifted in such packs that one could drive a D6 cat over them without hardly making a track.[138] Herschel Island, the westernmost Arctic island in Canada, became Yukon's first Territorial Park in 1987. Surprisingly, it is connected to the Liard River, which seems inconceivable until one recalls that river's flow into the Mackenzie.

> Between land and sea, [Herschel] island's dry polar climate supports a surprising web of life. The answer lies in ocean currents. The huge driftwood trunks that litter the beaches in this treeless land originate from as far away as the Liard Basin. They were delivered by the nutrient rich outflow of the Mackenzie River.[139]

That is one of the things Gordon, like most Northerners, instinctively feels with some awe. How can such a vast and unpopulated area be so interconnected?

The small tug headed for home, but first:

....

136 Measured as accumulation between 16 and 24 centimetres (C. R. Burn and Y. Zhang Permafrost and climate change at Herschel Island (Qikiqtaruq),Yukon Territory, Canada, *Journal of Geophysical Research* 114, F02001 (2009), https://doi.org/10.1029/2008JF001087.

137 Photo essay, June 23, 2021, by Jim Guthrie; self-published.

138 Email to the author. February 2022.

139 Government of Yukon, *A Guide to Herschel Island Qikiqtaruk Territorial Park* (2013)https://yukon.ca/sites/yukon.ca/files/env/env-guide-herschel-island-qikiqtaruk-territorial-park.pdf

We still had a few weeks on the Mackenzie River with the Watson Lake. *We went upriver in the channel past Aklavik, then worked on the Bear River for a while. The barge run there is split in two, at the Charles Rapids. NT had a camp there to do the portage. It brought barges loaded with bags of silver concentrate across Great Bear Lake from the mine at Port Radium and down the top end of the Bear River. The* Watson Lake *would take the barges down the lower section of the Bear to Fort Norman on the Mackenzie. From there, bigger tugs pushed the loads south to Hay River.*

Silver came out of the same mine as the radium and later the uranium there on the east coast of Great Bear. Uranium was hauled from there to Fort Norman to Fort Smith to Fort McMurray and then railroaded out to Edmonton. And that's where the uranium came from for the atomic bomb. We weren't hauling uranium; we were hauling silver. Silver was being hauled to Edmonton at that time by barge down to Hay River and by truck from there to Edmonton. There was no railroad that way then.

Gordon seems more interested in the work and so doesn't expand much about the look of things, the natural elements. Or maybe he knows it, having grown up in the bush, and takes it a bit for granted.

However, the Bear River is a lovely, tumbling, rock-strewn little river, draining Great Bear Lake. Alexander Mackenzie, writing about his epic journey down (and back up) the Deh-Cho (later, Mackenzie) River, described the Bear River as being green when it joined the big river. In NT jargon, it was always Bear River, although shown on maps and referred to in scholarly works as the Great Bear River. The waterway starts at Deline, formerly Fort Franklin, on Great Bear Lake, and descends fast through the Franklin Mountains.

Old NT hands used to say a small tug could make the run from Bear River camp down to the Mackenzie River in six hours or so, but the trip back up was more like two days.

Morris Zaslow described that journey upstream, which Gordon and the crew of the *Watson Lake* were doing, as follows:

The oil, as well as other supplies that could not be delivered by plane [to Port Radium] had to be moved to Fort Norman [now

Tulita] on the Mackenzie during the short open-water period, then hauled up the shallow, rock-strewn Great Bear River with its miles of more or less continuous rapids and finally shipped across the 200 miles of sometimes stormy Great Bear Lake. The process required four different boats to deal with the varied navigational conditions along the route, plus a portage road...[140]

One of those was the *Radium Franklin*, which did the upstream part of the run. Another was the *Radium Gilbert*, which was part tug and part freighter, designed for its work crossing the massive Great Bear Lake.

The NWT Archives report that "(m)any Dene from Deline were hired to carry and transport uranium from the Port Radium mine without any protective gear. The community became known as the 'Village of Widows' after fourteen Dene men associated with Port Radium died of cancer in the late 1980s. [Report does not show causation]."

Gordon loved the experience of going on these trips farther north, to Alaska and up on the Arctic coast or into Bear River. He liked to see more of the North and the differences in scenery, but, he said, *It was the people I liked, they got along so good. The scenery always changed, but what was always there was the people.*

And about his friend Henry Christofferson and the evolution of the North, well, Gordon has this to say:

> *You know, NT named one of its new tower tugs the MV* Henry Christofferson. *That was one of four large tugs NT built in 1973–74.*[141] *They're probably the last river tugs ever to be built for the Mackenzie River trade.*

The word "tower" was used because, for the first time in the NT system, a tall, hollow viewing tower was built behind the wheelhouse, which

....

140 Zaslow, *Northward Expansion*, 182.

141 The other three were the *Jock McNiven*, the *Johnny Hope*, and the *Matt Berry*, all named for prominent white Northerners. Two of these, the *Johnny Hope* and the *Matt Berry*, have been renamed to honour Inuit names.

allowed crew to climb up to see over the cargo stacked on the barges.[142] The ships have been modified and are still the pride of the fleet, now owned by the NWT government's Marine Services Division. Gordon constructed steps on the outside of the towers for reasons mentioned later.

142 "Originally designed by Robert Allan Ltd. (RAL) and built in 1973, the 153-foot [46.6-metre] *Edgar Kotokak* had, as her sister ship *Henry Christoffersen* still does, four open propellers in tunnels for propulsion with twin, transom hung rudders behind each prop for steering. The other tugs, the *Kelly Ovayuak* and *Jock McNiven*, use four *Kort Nozzles* in tunnels, each with twin rudders aft inside the tunnel. All the tugs originally had the same engines." (MarineLink, "Technology: New Nozzles Improve Northern Tug" (October 1, 2003), https://www.marinelink.com/news/technology-northern324581.)

CHAPTER 26:
John Pope and the New Direction

Gordon Gill, Glen Dersch and Ernie Camsell.

When I worked for NT, there were times I would go and work for John Pope at Pope's Construction. It meant a lot of time I would work sometimes fourteen hours a day, all winter long. 1969 was the year I left NT. There was a government job at Enterprise, south of town,[143] that came open, so I applied for the job.

....

143 Enterprise, NWT, is a small service centre located where the main highway splits off to Yellowknife and Fort Simpson.

GORDON LIKED NT and the work, but after eight years, he wanted a change. Maybe it was time to spend more time at home.

> I went to Yellowknife for the interview, and when I got back to Hay River, I told John Pope what I was up to, and this is what he said. "You phone and withdraw your name for the shop foreman at Enterprise now. I will make you an offer you can't refuse," he said. "If you don't take me up on it, I will kick your ass." The offer was, John had this shop 30 by 40 feet in Old Town, a welding machine, and a truck. John said rent-free for one year, more if needed. An offer like that I couldn't turn down. John was setting himself up in the Hay River, New Town. Anyway, I phoned Yellowknife and withdrew my name.
>
> John Pope was a good friend.

He operated a company called Pope's Construction, doing anything and everything—moving houses, salvage work, road construction, Cat work, everything. In fact, Pope invented the Pope International Tree Harvesting Machine for felling trees. He obtained a number of other patents from his inventions. He even did underwater diving and salvage.

One old story is that he made $30 (when that meant groceries) by salvaging a man's dentures, which fell out of his mouth while he was looking down into the murky Hay River.[144]

When a storm caused the loss of a barge full of lumber, Pope scoured the lake and shoreline for it, and gathered the lumber on an island. He also used his diving for salvage, like with *Dredge 251* when it sank. He, as the diver, went underwater, located the vessel, sealed off the portholes, manholes, and doors, or the hole, if necessary, whatever was open, and pumped out the water. On good days, the vessel then rises to the surface. *Dredge 251* got raised that way.

Small towns breed some ingenious people. And generous ones. Like John Pope, who recognized in Gordon something worth pushing and trusting, and was willing to take a risk to help Gordon along to the next step in his career. There are two heroic actions here. Pope for seeing Gordon for the honest, capable, and trustworthy guy he is, and for acting on that, putting his money where his mouth was. That is not so common.

144 Mary Pope, in Collins, *Ever Since*, 131.

There is the other heroic act here, that of Gordon Gill (and Treena) taking the plunge, acting on the offer, and making a big career move. It was also a move into the unknown. Gordon had never owned a company or a business before. So not only was he prepared to listen and act, but he was also prepared to learn what he needed to, and to exercise the courage to do it on his own.

> *After I talked to John, and withdrew my name for that job, I went home and told Treena what I had done. Not knowing what to expect, I was on pins and needles, but to my surprise, Treena said, "I wanted you to take the Enterprise job so you would be home more, but that's not going to happen, so I will be your bookkeeper, starting today." She put in her notice at CN Telecommunications, where she was a telephone operator.*

So Gordon started to work on his own, and within six months he had enough business to hire both Ernie Camsell and Glen Dersch away from NT. They came over to Northern Arc, the first two non-Gill employees. They were his "guys", number one, and a close second, for the rest of their lives. Glen also followed Gordon to Northern Crane Services and the move south, and even after they both "retired", Glen and Gordon still worked together until mid-2022.

That welding truck and shop, and Gordon and Treena's partnership, and the work of people like Ernie and Glen, translated over time into barge and ship repair, then fabrication and then into one of Western Canada's large crane and haulage companies.

> *We worked as a team for thirty-seven years, 1969 to 2006. Treena worked hard at home and work. As for John Pope and his offer, in less than a year, I had bought the land, shop, welding machine, and truck; it all worked out so good. John was happy, Treena and I were happy, and life was good, work, work, work. Little did I know, but the real work was just beginning and ran for thirty-seven years nonstop.*

CHAPTER 27:
Northern Arc Shipbuilders Ltd.

NAS barge construction at the mouth of the Hay River,
Roman Catholic mission and church across the river.

Nothing but good came out of my time at NT, even leaving.

IN 1969, Gordon and Treena set up Northern Arc Shipbuilders Limited
to repair barges and tugs. Later they built ships, oil platforms, and barges,
anything that floated, and some things that didn't.

For example, Northern Arc worked for Imperial Oil at Norman Wells
for two years in the early 1970s. They built the gathering system and com-
pressor station and did the pipeline work to connect the oil being pumped
from the islands—natural and man-made—in the Mackenzie. Goose
Island and Bear Island were two of them. Gordon remembers that the

welders were afraid they'd get snuck up on by a bear, that face down and buried in their welding helmets, they might miss seeing the bears. Gordon arranged for spotters to watch out for the animals, just in case.

He explains about Northern Arc (the "arc" being the bright spark given off by a welding rod). *The biggest part of our business was repairs. You know, barges or tugs. They'd hit a rock somewhere, and maybe have a 200-foot-long [61-metre-long] crease along the bottom. Or the captain would run a tug into the wharf too fast. We'd fix that. Or the propellers. Sometimes those engines were so powerful that they would spit rocks through the props; they'd be severely damaged. Or there would be a big crease down the hull from scraping along a rock.*

We worked for Northern Transportation, and Coast Guard, and other marine companies. They were good customers.

It was a busy time, what with all the oil-and-gas exploration in the North, especially with the boats and barges and especially in Hay River. So, we got lots of work.

Gordon is the first to credit others; he repeats a mantra. *Help people look good, help them do what they need to do, and do it willingly and well. If you do, they will help you.* He is a man appreciative, perhaps more often more than necessary, of those who helped him. He remembers those who gave Northern Arc a chance, a job, awarded them a contract, or gave advice. He appreciates those who told him things or answered his questions.

He constantly reminds others of how "nice" people were to him, how friendly and helpful, and of what "good people" there are in the world and how he just wanted to help them look good in what they were doing.

> *I always wanted to help to do more than I was asked to do. I spent a lot of time helping others look good, and it really paid off. In a lot of cases, any favour I did was returned many times over.*

Is this a function of his culture and upbringing? Gordon says he always had that attitude and attributes it to his upbringing.

Gordon has a quiet manner, but he was always a hard worker and (quietly) ambitious. As he said: *My ambitions were always to do with work, cutting wood, shoveling snow, and later building things, setting things up.*

We didn't really plan what we were doing. Like we didn't have any of it mapped out.

There were no business degrees present, no strategic plans, or human resource departments. Gordon and Treena just watched for things that looked like they needed doing.

One of those involved another first in the north, although not directly by Gordon. NT had tried using a hovercraft in the Arctic, thinking that it could move atop the ice or water, or both, easier than through it. When asked if he had anything to do with this short-lived experiment, he said no.

> But, after NT decided the hovercraft was not working out, it was sold to someone on one of the big Ontario lakes. Apparently, it was used as an ice breaker, with a notch cut out of its bow. That craft was so heavy. It was set up so that it forced air underneath itself with great pressure. So, it didn't work on the ice but it made a good icebreaker. It would get up on the ice and force it into like a dish or a trough, and the ice would break.

With his track record, it would not have been surprising if Gordon had worked on that vessel as well. But surprisingly, his next words were *I never worked on it*.

Then, after a pause, Gordon added:

> I did get the job of cutting it into three pieces for shipping south from Hay River though. And we got a very nice letter from the new owner in Ontario thanking us for the beautiful job of cutting the hovercraft. The new owner said it was cut so smooth and clean that putting it back together, welding the three pieces together was easy!

CHAPTER 28:
Bell Rock Camp – A New Era Begins

Northern Trader at Bell Rock, winter;
NWT Archives/Bobby Porritt fonds/N-1987-016-0513.

I was down to Bell Rock many times. I was the last
engineer on the Radium King. We took the King
to Bell Rock for its final trip; it was pulled up out
of the river and stored. Retired, I guess. It later
was taken into Fort Smith for its museum.

THE TIMES, they were a-changing. Bob Dylan wasn't singing about Bell Rock Camp in 1969, but he could have been.

That summer, a large Vancouver company, Allied Shipbuilders, built three large, modern tugs and some of the largest barges ever contracted for by NT.[145] The construction site was at the NT camp at Bell Rock, on the Slave River, 13 kilometres northwest of Fort Smith at the end of the Fitzgerald Portage.

The tugs—the MV *Angus Sherwood*, MV *Kelly Hall*, and MV *Knut Lang*—were named for two prominent early Northerners and an NT man, notably all non-Indigenous. No one seemed to notice. Sherwood was a trader and merchant in the Sahtu (Norman Wells) area, Kelly Hall an NT captain and executive.

Lang, a Danish trapper and trader in the Aklavik area, was a member of the NWT Council. When the government directed the people of Aklavik to vacate the place in favour of the new community a bit north on the Mackenzie Delta (since Aklavik was supposedly sinking into the river), it was Knut Lang who suggested the name Inuvik.

The largest and most advanced tugboats yet were downright spiffy and capable of sailing in the Arctic. The new barges were designed for the new world of the 1970s. Fuel would be a major cargo inside the barges; drill pipe, trucks, and other equipment would be topside.

The next years, the 1970s and most of the 1980s, were boom times. The Hay River and other NT camps up the Mackenzie, at Inuvik, and Norman Wells, as well as at Bear River and at Tuktoyaktuk were busy with workers; the docks and warehouses were packed with cargo and new tug and barge companies entered the market. The Vale Island shipping areas, overhaul facilities (including a significant marine synchro lift), and rail access were built or greatly expanded, in part by building an artificial island in the river. In 1973/74, a new mess hall and kitchen were erected for the Hay River camp. The highway was busy, filled with heavy truck traffic and thick, killing dust. The rail line was full of tanker cars and freight.

Just as it was a transition time for Gordon and Treena, it was also—in the late 1960s and early 1970s—a time of transition for the world. The Americans had suffered violent race riots, Vietnam War protests continued, and two political assassinations in 1968 (of Bobby Kennedy and Martin Luther King) had the Western world on edge.

The summer of '69, was also a new time for the North. In addition to

145 The barges were large. There were twenty-four 1000-series and seven 1500-series barges. The descriptor number refers to the number of tons the barge could carry, in a combination of liquid, usually fuel, inside, and freight on the cargo deck.

the three new, brilliant-white masterpieces of tugboat construction and the fabrication of the largest barges ever for NT, other portents of the future took place that summer. One, international in scope, was Neil Armstrong taking a "small step for man" on the moon, which wasn't even seen by those in the Bell Rock Camp that summer. Without the wonder of radio, television, or internet, the moon landing was like it never happened. That alone marks the distance in time and technology between the northland and the populated southern part of Canada.

The second was more local but also a harbinger of what was to come, in a couple of ways. It was not really an event, but rather a sign. In the same shipyard now producing the new barges and three gleaming vessels, at least three older NT vessels sat drooping on slipways, never to float again, their life and purpose ended.

As Gordon said, the *Radium King,* NT's former flagship, had been delivered to Bell Rock. There, it was pulled up onto huge, squared timbers and left to sit with long grass and weeds and northern wildflowers rubbing its hull. It seemed to float across the greenery, perhaps remembering its important prior life on the river. It was the *King* that carried famous Canadian writer Hugh MacLennan "down north" years earlier, from which he wrote the aptly and perceptively named *The Mackenzie, Into the Future Kingdom.* The story of the river, and the portage and the trip to Aklavik and the transport business in earlier days, forms part of *Rivers of Canada,* published by MacMillan in 1974.

The *King* was dwarfed by a former US Navy landing craft settled there by its side. Built in 1943 for the United States military effort, it became redundant as war surplus; YT bought and converted it in 1949 into a freight-carrying vessel, naming it the YT *Expeditor.* While it initially provided a scheduled cross-lake direct service for passengers and freight between Hay River and Yellowknife, this only lasted for three seasons: 1949, 1950, and 1951. In 1951, the large ship was damaged when it hit a reef. In 1955, it was rebuilt as a tug. The big difference was that fully half of the vessel, the front 18 metres (60 feet) were cut off. This allowed more effective use and a shorter turning capacity, since by attaching pushers to the flattened bow, the *Expediter* could move barges. It didn't need the room where previously passengers and freight were carried.

In the late 1950s, the YT *Expeditor* moved freight between Hay River and Aklavik on the Mackenzie River. Later, the *Expeditor* remained in the Western Arctic, frozen in the ice over winter and servicing communities along the coast in summer. After YT's sale to NT in 1965, the vessel was taken out of service and pulled up on the slip to rest beside the King.

These two soon-to-be-forgotten relics were joined by the NT *Saline*. It was smaller, about 21 metres long, 4.5 metres wide, with a 1.8-metre draft and relegated to a lesser position, farther away from the Slave River and closer to the encroaching stand of poplar and birch trees. The US Army initially owned it, using it at the Norman Wells oilfields during the war, when the Canol Pipeline was being built from the Wells through to the Yukon for wartime use. Imperial Oil bought it in 1945, and then Yellowknife Transportation took it over in 1946. It sailed the Mackenzie River and Great Slave routes until 1956, when it was rebuilt in Hay River with a new superstructure. It was renamed the YT *Saline* and worked the Slave River and Great Slave Lake trips[146] before being relegated to the long grass beside the road. It looked even sadder than the *King* and *Expeditor*.

And they got very few visitors. The old tugs, I mean. The big new ships, well, they got a lot of lookers and visitors, all of whom were impressed and vocal in their admiration for such clean, and princely vessels.

Then one day, in the heat of a mid-summer day of 1969, those lookers got another surprise.

There arrived, unannounced, a clanking and rumbling of steel on rock, great clouds of dust and the roaring of tractor engines. Was it war? Running out the various doors of the camp, those present could see at the top of the rise above the camp an apparition of some sort. What at first appeared to be a ghost ship, floating on dust down the hill toward the Slave River, turned out to be, in fact, an actual ship.

"My God, there's a tug coming down the hill!" exclaimed at least one excited teenager.

After the initial shock, it was clear that one of the (until then) bigger Radium Line tugboats was propped up on extended low-boy trailers. These were pulled and pushed by Caterpillar tractors along the 26-kilometre portage, which gave birth to this camp and shipyards in the first place. It was one of the last portages from the now pretty much obsolete southern

....

146   Wikipedia, s.v. "Boats of the Mackenzie River Watershed."

route of the Athabasca/Mackenzie River system; what killed the southern section off completely was the closing of the uranium and other mines on the north shore of Lake Athabasca, on the Saskatchewan side. Perhaps that was, in its own way, another sign—the passing of another era.

*   *   *

The new era of oil-and-gas exploration in the Arctic came over the north with a rush. The three Bell Rock tugs were the first sign, of course, but then, in 1970, southern contractors built the NT *Lister* and the large MV *Vic Ingraham*.

The latter was named for a well-known Northern businessman and pioneer. Ingraham had partnered in one of the first businesses, Murphy Services (sawmills, store, post office, mining office), where the new mines were getting going in the early 1930s at Cameron Bay on Great Bear Lake. He also operated the *Speed II*, hauling freight and ore across Great Bear. One trip resulted in an explosion and fire, the loss of two men, and the *Speed II*. Ingraham was badly burned and stuck with other survivors who cared for him for two weeks on a snow-covered beach in the cold, eventually having his legs and fingers amputated. Later, he built and managed Yellowknife's first hotel.

Cameron Clement, the former NT president, said about the *Vic Ingraham*, that it was the only new vessel that was such a shallow-draft vessel that she was never used for Arctic service.[147] The Coast Guard vessel *Nahidik* was built using the *Vic Ingraham* design, with the express function that in an emergency, she could be used as a pusher tug.

The new tower tugs were, like the Ingraham, also named for Caucasian Northerners Jock McNiven, and Matt Berry, and another NT man from the south, Henry Christofferson.

Clement said something that reflects those Northerners as well as Gordon Gill and people like him. "At NTCL, we have always gone about our business quietly, without fanfare, which is the northern way."[148] The Northern way. Many people use that phrase.

And the Expeditor mentioned earlier? Well, Gordon had forgotten to

147 Clement, email to the author.
148 Clement, *Tides*.

talk about it. It was the first commercial tug he worked on, owned then by Yellowknife Transportation, and later taken over by NT. Gordon did a trip down the Mackenzie from Hay River to the Arctic as the second engineer on that vessel, when it was still under the captaincy of the well-respected Cec Kirkland, one of the senior captains, and later one of the executives in the marine department at NT. Gordon's future partner, Don Tetrault, served as captain of the Expeditor in his first northern tour of duty; Gordon worked with most of the captains and other leaders in the northern marine transport business.

They all grew into their manhood and their careers together.

CHAPTER 29:
Gold!

Au.Nugget Gold Dredge, Liard River, NWT.

We built a gold dredge and called it Au.Nugget
and a housing barge named the Ag.Bar. Au is the
chemical symbol for gold, Ag for Silver. So, we
worked the Gold Nugget and the Silver Bar.

EVEN GORDON'S HOBBIES sound more like work. One photo shows
Gordon "on holiday," looking after the equipment at a gold mine in the

Lillooet, BC, area. It wasn't a job or a contract. He kind of just fell into a little partnership with the chief of the Lillooet [BC] band, through some people he knew from work. It didn't pay, but it actually got him a more focused start on dredging for gold, which we talk about later.

Gordon always has had an interest in mining, and especially the combination between dredging and mining. He had experience in both by the time he was twenty-three.

Gordon also grubstaked prospectors and feels good that he helped Fred Nelson, who discovered what became Cadillac Mines near the Nahanni River in the western NWT. Gordon is actively watching what happens there. Now called Norzinc, the NWT government has recently given the company the "go-ahead" to mine, and to build a road from the Liard Highway west of Fort Simpson to the mine site on Prairie Creek near Nahanni National Park. Interestingly, one of the minerals that the mine will target is cobalt for use in new technology, like batteries. So Gordon, here too, has been involved in the old North, initially grubstaking a prospector—many years ago—who was pursuing lead-zinc leads, and the New North, investing in the same mine but with an eye to the future, for new minerals and new times.

Gordon's interest in gold led to Northern Arc's construction of the *Au.Nugget* gold dredge and the *Ag.Bar* house barge. The object of these vessels was summer exploration for gold on the Liard River. The effect was to keep people working. Much of the fabrication of this equipment was done on the shore in West Channel, the old fishing sector of town.

Gordon and his friend Ernie Camsell took both vessels down the Mackenzie and, at Fort Simpson, turned up the Liard River. They based at the old Lindberg place, now the site of Blackstone Territorial Park.

Upriver from Lindberg's Landing is the small village of Nahanni Butte, home to a few hundred Dene people. Overlooking it is a large, squarish, dominating mountain, the Butte, which channels the Nahanni River to its meet-up with the Liard. Now the home of a national park and brought to some prominence by the canoeing Prime Minister Pierre Elliot Trudeau, it is emblematic of the Canadian mountain wilderness. Rugged, stunning, and isolated, the number of park visitors is probably under a thousand a year. (In 2019/20, Banff National Park, by contrast, welcomed 4.12 million visitors.)

The Nahanni is home to the spectacular Virginia Falls, twice the height of Niagara. The crashing water carves its way through four canyons, rising in height to 1,210 metres above the rushing, powerful river. Many rapids toss tourist rafts and flip canoes. Three of them at least—Hell's Gate/Figure Eight Rapid, Lafferty's Riffle (which is anything but), and George's Riffle (more of a roller coaster)—are famous amongst canoeists and rafters. And there are spectacular natural features, like Kraus Hot Springs, which seem to seep right up from the river before they are captured in a riverside pool by a circle of rocks, while maybe a mile upstream, one of the shortest "rivers" in the world rushes out of a spring, cold as ice, just above freezing.

This quite spectacular national park is a land of contrasts—high mountains, glaciers, narrow, incredibly deep canyons, creeks, and tufa ponds. The names say it all: Pulpit Rock, rising hundreds of metres above a narrow defile in the canyon; Figure Eight Rapids; Prairie Creek with its wide-open spaces; Third and Fourth Canyons; and Virginia Falls, which deserves a second mention.

The top and lower ends of the river wind through sprawling distances of wide, braided channels, filled with gravel islands. There are the Rabbit Kettle Hot Springs, Dall mountain sheep, exotic rock formations, and, unbelievably, writing on rock that matches the unique style of one of the Native American Peoples of Arizona.

The Nahanni Valley may also be the source of gold for which Gordon and his good friend, Ernie Camsell searched. At least, it is the site of the Headless Range, Deadman's Valley, and other spookily named reminders of the days when men came in search of the golden treasure, never to be seen again or, in the case of a couple of poor brothers (McLeod by name) found without their heads.

The Camsell name is synonymous with the North. Ernie's great-grandfather left the British army to join the Hudson's Bay Company and worked out of Fort Simpson as the director of the Hudson's Bay Company Mackenzie Region. He and his Métis wife had many children, including Ernie's grandfather Fred, a "Hudson's Bay Man" too, who had been educated in business administration at university in Winnipeg, and Dr. Charles Camsell,[149] a well-known doctor educated in the south. Both came back North. The federal

....

149 Terry Camsell, in Collins; *Ever Since*, 16.

government hospital in Edmonton, initially set up for Inuit and Indigenous Peoples from outlying regions, was named for Dr. Camsell. Camsell Bend on the Mackenzie and the Camsell River system between Great Bear and Great Slave are also named for the family. Ernie himself was the son of a part-Inuit mother and a Dene/Métis father. His maternal grandfather was part of the tragic "Lost Patrol" of RCMP members who perished when they took a wrong turn on a patrol to Dawson City from Fort MacPherson.

Ernie worked for Gordon as a welder at both NT and Northern Arc. *He was a great friend and employee. We went to the Hay River Federal (Indian) School together. His family lived in the Indian Village across the river from the main town. We'd have kept on with the gold dredge on the Liard if he hadn't died when he did.*

That dredge was kind of Ernie and Gordon's pet project.

The *Hub* newspaper in Hay River did a big spread, in its July 27, 1988, edition about the gold dredge. Reporter Vicky Latour wrote:

> If you have a dream and a specific purpose in mind, it is sometimes easiest to pursue it by designing and producing your own vehicle (in this case, "vessel").
>
> When the *Au.Nugget* sails out of Hay River, Gordie Gill… will be demonstrating just such a precept.
>
> "This kind of operation placer mining is something I spent nine years on the Fraser River doing," Gill says. "There is more here, with the *Nugget* though; I guess it's diversification."
>
> [T]he shipbuilding business hasn't been great recently; as on the Atlantic and Pacific coasts, Canadian shipyards have closed or laid off workers. The economic recession of the early '80s took its toll here, too, but Gill is a survivor: "Even if there's a drop in marine activities, you have to continue to live." he says. The *Au.Nugget* is an example of Gill's ability to diversify—and survive. "Just building the vessel has probably created approximately nine man-years of work since the end of February," Gill says.
>
> She is an "exploration vehicle" designed to dredge the treasures of precious metals found in NWT rivers, "designed to our own

specifications to determine the viability of such an operation." The main "body" of the vessel was a barge Northern Arc had built for an owner who never used it; once they bought it back, Gill and his crew began the modifications needed to accommodate the special equipment mounted on the deck… "It is built in such a manner," Gill explains, "that if we want, we can take off the wheel-house and engines and just push it around (at the site) with the smaller workboat." Doing this would decrease the draught (draft) of the *Nugget*.[150]

When Gordon was interviewed by the Hay River newspaper for that article on the gold dredge,[151] it was his hope that the exploration would expand into something good for the town, like a small refining plant. Unfortunately, at least in terms of Gordon bringing that forward, it wasn't in the cards. Ernie Camsell's death, and that of Herman "Moose" Earnshaw, who died just before Ernie, took the wind out of the exploring sails for Gordon. Herman had been an encouraging voice in the search for Liard River gold, and a friend out on the river. He and his sister, both veterans of the war, along with Edwin Lindberg, who lived near Herman's cabin on the Liard, played, in Gordon's words, *a big role in getting us* [GNWT] *water use permits that we needed to work the river. He was also a friend, like I was, of Albert Eyrie, from Arc Nav* [Arctic Navigation, a competitor of NT during the Arctic exploration boom].

The exploration ceased when Ernie died. Gordon never went back. He was too busy anyway, but (as he says), *There was no Ernie. We were great friends. And when you lose your key guy, well…*

Gordon sold the dredge and other equipment to a fellow who took it to Inuvik for work in the far north.

150 C. Brodeur, "Exploration vessel designed, built here, sailing soon," *Hay River Hub* (July 27, 1988).
151 Brodeur, "Exploration Vessel," *Hay River Hub*.

CHAPTER 30:
Northern Shipbuilder

Abraham Francis ferry, Peel River, Ft. MacPherson, NWT.

NT seemed to like us. We worked hard,
and got the work done fast.

WE REALLY GOT GOING *in the spring of 1970 into the welding,*
building-boats business and barges. Our company name was Northern
Arc Shipbuilders. We operated out of the shop and that block of land
on the river I bought from John Pope. As many as possible, we hired
local men. We never were unionized, but we also didn't have any labour
troubles. We hired lots of men through the union; they were happy to
have the work, and they sent us good men.

> *Treena and I, and* [sons] *Bryan and Trent were shareholders; there were four of us. When they were old enough, both Bryan and Trent got their trade papers and they both worked for the company. We were a good team. Their ambitions were different from mine and eventually they went on to other things.*

Gordon is calm; he has what are now called people skills. He has a ready laugh which he thinks is like his mom's and part of his Métis culture. He isn't a worrier, and that seems to rub off on people.

Gordon's timing couldn't have been better to start his own company.

In the 1969 construction of the new larger barges, the amount of steel used was awesome. Gordon says he was averaging 600 tons of steel to make one 1,500-ton-carry-capacity barge. And that was for a single-hull vessel. Later, when for environmental reasons, the barges had both an inner and outer hull, the cost was incredible. Added to that was the establishment of a camp at Bell Rock and the feeding and caring for about 250 unionized workers from Allied Shipbuilders in Vancouver. There must be a cheaper way.

In 1973, four tower tugs were built in Vancouver, and sailed up the west coast of Canada, through the Bering Straits separating Alaska from Russia, and into the Arctic Ocean. From there, the tugs' path traced the northern coast of Alaska, Yukon Territory, and the western Northwest Territories to join the Mackenzie system at Tuktoyaktuk.[152]

Again, the costs must have been huge. There was obviously business to be had, and the North was booming.

A smaller but powerful and maneuverable "yard boat" called the *Kakisa* was also built then, for moving barges around the Hay River harbour and helping the big boys get set up for their long journey to the northern oil fields.

The clear northern air was filled with excitement and anticipation in those days. Big things were happening, and new people and projects filled the boats and airplanes and work camps of the North.

Bob Ruzicka, "the singing dentist" and a great songwriter who told so many wonderful stories of the North, lived in Inuvik in those days and evoked the tone (of at least some people anyway) in his song "Northland Destiny," which Ted Wesley performs on his 1972 recording, *Straight North*:

152 Tuk is known for its place at the top of mainland Canada, for its transshipment of freight and fuel along the Arctic coast, its marine repair facilities, the ice centred hills called Pingos, and the always popular "University of Tuktoyaktuk – Tuk U" sweatshirts.

A hundred years have passed,
The changes now are coming fast,
Progress calling for the new breed to come forth,
The visions and dreams
Fulfilled by man and his machines
As a breath of promise blows across the north;
Men of vision firmly stand
To face the challenge of our land,
We learned to walk where once we had to crawl.
And a promise of tomorrow is the end of all our sorrow,
For this land is surely rich enough for all.

Oh, Canada, look north to see
This sleeping giant's breaking free
Come help us make our dreams a reality,
We need your hands, your heart,
Your willingness to play your part
In the shaping of your Northland Destiny.[153]

Ruzicka also wrote of the "winds of change blowing over the big land" and the risks facing a people who told "time by the sea and sun and seasons." He has an Indigenous-man lament that "my kids' books don't say nothing about traplines."[154]

It was the same lesson Gordon and his family had to learn a generation earlier, the one his mother taught from his birth, the one she chose to make his life easier. She clearly saw the winds of change and faced them squarely, teaching Gordon hard work, adaptation, and how to succeed in a changing world.

And if that change was coming, and if the distances were great and the costs high, well, perhaps a local outfit, especially one with Indigenous ownership and workers, would be a positive step?

We did lots of work for NT and other companies; DPW too. Like on

----

153 Bob Ruzicka, writer, "Northland Destiny," track 6 on *Straight North*, featuring Ted Wesley, vocalist, PET-MAC BMI 1972.
154 Bob Ruzicka, writer, "Winds of Change," track 7 on *Straight North*, featuring Ted Wesley, vocalist, PET-MAC BMI 1972.

those four new tugs built in 1973 to 1974. They called them tower vessels because they were the first tugs to have conning towers to see over the barges better, because they were piled so high with freight and drilling equipment. The towers had small stairs inside, which led to the upper cabin. You could see over the freight and steer the boat from there. NT asked us to build circular stairs around the outside of the tower to the top. Some of the captains and mates were claustrophobic and hated the thought of being in those narrow towers, where the stairs went straight up. And some of those guys weren't in the best of shape weight-wise, so they were happy to have the outside stairs we built.

CHAPTER 31:
Justice Berger, the Mackenzie Valley Pipeline Inquiry, and Its Impact on Northern Arc

Gordon and crew

The oil-and-gas boom had another effect.
Many were worried about the potential
impact on the Northern peoples.

WITHIN A FEW YEARS after setting up Northern Arc in 1974, Gordon met a man who was to be integral to decisions affecting northern businesses, and specifically the rate and perhaps the fate of development in the North, Justice Thomas Berger of the BC Supreme Court.[155]

....

155 Coincidentally, Berger served as a board member of Frontier College, founded by Alfred Fitzpatrick, and referred to in Chapter 10, in the late 1970s, a position the author presently holds.

Imperial Oil Limited—an integrated company (and a subsidiary of huge American oil giant ExxonMobil) long operating in Canada in general and the North in particular—and others had promoted the idea of a 1,600-kilometre (1,000-mile) gas pipeline from the Arctic gas fields of the Beaufort Sea to the south through the Mackenzie valley. It was to be the "Canadian Route," designed to ship the huge amounts of natural gas then being discovered off Canada's northern coast. Proponents of construction, including many in the NWT government and the small NWT business community, spoke of the benefits of building the pipeline, the jobs, supplies, payments, and training that would flow, along with the gas. The opponents were concerned with the potential harm to the environment, the disturbance of the way of life of the local residents, and the negative impacts on Indigenous Peoples of the North.

Some, including federal civil servants[156] and some in the Roman Catholic and other churches, were of the view that many Indigenous people didn't understand the demands of employers, or if they did, they did not want to be part of, or could not readily adjust to, that system.

Many First Nations, Inuit, and Métis people in the North still relied on hunting, fishing, and trapping for subsistence. The seasons of the year and the weather were just as important as the clock—maybe more so. It was a difficult time to be an employer but also to be an employee. As well, serious concern was raised in the media about the effect of an economic boom on Indigenous women. The North had seen already what alcohol, southern workers with money and drugs, and prostitution could do to women—and men, for that matter. It was devastating, psychologically and physically.

The court system wasn't helpful; many Indigenous people struggled with the loss of their language and culture, their way of living. Poverty, poor nutrition, and other effects of the collision of north and south abounded, especially problems with alcohol. Fines imposed often weren't paid; jail time resulted. Family life and work life suffered. It was a vicious circle, a merry-go-round of crime, often petty or as a result of drinking or drugs, arrests, shame, court, no money for a lawyer (if one was available), little understanding of the system, jail time, followed by release, then a party, a fight or a domestic assault, another arrest, and around it went, again and again.

....

156 See Robertson, *A Very Civil Servant*.

Legal Aid lawyers did exist in some communities in the North, and also by way of a circuit court, but while good intentions abounded, most of those lawyers were young, non-Indigenous, and from the south. There was no sensitivity training and, in some cases, little understanding of the history and background of the local people. Time and resources were often in short supply. There were not many cases on Indigenous Rights or legal requirements to protect Indigenous defendants, especially before 1980, and much of criminal law practice on circuit was based on what could be gleaned from a copy of *Martin's Criminal Code*.

Often, Indigenous Peoples just pled guilty, got a fine or maybe jail time, and went on their way without counsel and without, initially at least, any real alternatives to the "crime and punishment" circle. Later, more understanding led northern judges and communities to investigate "sentencing circles" and other community and social remedies.

Meanwhile, the police, the establishment non-indigenous people, and the employers got more and more fed up, and goodwill became harder to find, especially sympathetic goodwill—helpful goodwill. The level of frustration with crime and the revolving-door nature of offenders was high.

Often, in the late 1960s and 1970s, at least, the clash of cultures was like two ships colliding in the dark of night, as if they were coming at each other with neither vision nor understanding. There was little means of explaining and understanding what the other wanted and needed. They weren't talking the same language. The divide between the "law and order" of the English judicial system and the traditions and methods of the local, especially isolated, communities now in the path of development was great. Jail was commonplace, but it sure didn't improve the lives of many offenders, and it was terribly disruptive to families and prospects. It was a mess.[157]

The opponents of the pipeline wanted it stopped or at least delayed to provide time to work on solutions to these problems and transitions for the people. There was much talk, then, about the serious impacts of development on local people, and the beginning of a look at the effect of residential schools. Given the factors already facing Indigenous Peoples—including losing culture, language, customs, ways of decision-making, and dignity—it

....

157 See J. H. Sissons, *Judge of the Far North* (Toronto, ON: McClelland & Stewart, 1968); and William J. Morrow, *Northern Justice; The Memoirs of Mr. Justice William J. Morrow* (Toronto, ON: University of Toronto Press, 1995).

was proposed by Indigenous Peoples and social-justice advocates alike that consultation and education were necessary before another onslaught of southern workers arrived in the North. It was also an opportune time to look at outstanding Indigenous land and other claims.

Accordingly, in March 1974, the government of Prime Minister Pierre Trudeau appointed BC Supreme Court Justice Thomas Berger, and former leader of the New Democratic Party in that province, to act as a commissioner to investigate and report to the federal government on the construction of what was going to be called the "Mackenzie Valley Pipeline."[158] As commissioner, Berger would travel the North and conduct hearings into the advisability of the construction and how to mitigate any issues that would, no doubt, arise from such work.

The investigation, known as the Berger Inquiry, was notable, it has been reported, for the voice that it gave to Indigenous People about what was to happen in and to their traditional territory if the pipeline were to proceed.[159]

Justice Berger dropped in to visit Gordon one day. He was in Hay River, likely before he started to conduct hearings about the pros and cons of the pipeline. This sophisticated ex-politician and now judge from BC climbed up a ladder to visit Gordon while he was working on a barge in the shipyard. He wanted to have a chat.

Justice Berger wanted to know what benefit the pipeline would bring to the local economy and the local people. It would seem that Gordon—unlike many Indigenous northerners—would have supported the pipeline, or at least the work that would come out of it. This was at a time when the petroleum industry was driving much of the country's economy. Exploration was booming all over Canada, especially in the far north; government subsidies for drilling and other work spurred the largely Alberta-based oil industry to new heights, and dollars were flowing. Gordon wasn't that concerned about the pipeline.

Most of us thought they would be exploring and stuff like that for fifty years without ever thinking about the pipeline. I was just happy for there to be exploration, he said, looking back on the early 1970s, a time quite a bit before the

158 Thomas R. Berger, *Northern Frontier, Northern Homeland: The Report of the Mackenzie Valley Pipeline Inquiry* (Ottawa, ON: Mackenzie Valley Pipeline Inquiry, 1977).
159 Wikipedia, s.v. "Mackenzie Valley Pipeline Inquiry," last updated February 4, 2022, at 06:38 *(UTC), https://en.wikipedia.org/wiki/Mackenzie_Valley_Pipeline_Inquiry.*

boom later that decade and into the '80s.

The decision was made.

> As Commissioner, Berger recommended that, "on environmental grounds, no pipeline be built, and no energy corridor be established across the Northern Yukon" and that any pipeline construction be postponed until native claims could be settled.[160]

In due course, the federal government placed a moratorium on building the pipeline. That changed the complexion of northern business and the force of the pro-pipeline groups. However, in the not-too-distant future, aided by the world oil crises of the late 1970s and various federal government policies, the exploration continued and increased and eventually took over the North like a runaway train, notwithstanding what Berger thought about the pipeline. There was, in the end, a lot of exploration, southerners coming north, social pressure, and displacement—even without a major gas pipeline, as had been proposed.

In reporting on Berger's death at eighty-eight on April 28, 2021, *The Vancouver Sun* quoted BC Premier John Horgan as saying:

> Thomas R. Berger believed in justice. That meant he needed to address injustice. Mr. Berger was counsel for the Nisga'a elders who were plaintiffs in Calder v. Attorney-General for British Columbia (1973), a historic case in which the Supreme Court of Canada first acknowledged the existence of Aboriginal title to land.
>
> His work as commissioner of the Mackenzie Valley Pipeline Inquiry resulted in a report highlighting unresolved land claims, as well as the threat to wildlife upon which the local Indigenous Peoples relied on for survival. An unprecedented public consultation process helped highlight what was at stake for the Indigenous Peoples of the north.
>
> As a lawyer, judge and commissioner, he helped countless ordinary people in their struggles against powerful interests. He changed life in this province and in this country for the better.

----

160 Wikipedia, s.v. "Thomas R. Berger," last updated December 1, 2021, at 00:15 (UTC), https://en.wikipedia.org/wiki/Thomas_R._Berger.

Horgan, in the same article, describes Berger's view of his inquiry.

> "It's part of the Canadian experience, coming to terms with the people who were here first," Berger said in 1997. "Any civilized society has to do that—and it ain't easy. We went to every village and listened to everyone who had something to say. It was an education for me and, because it had such a high media profile, in a sense an education for the whole country."[161]

From Gordon's perspective, the impact of the Berger Report was to delay the real explosion in work for six or seven years, but in the long run, Northern Arc was still busy enough, and it gave Gordon the time to learn more about business and perfect his fabrication techniques.

While Justice Berger eventually sided with the views of the National Indian Brotherhood of the NWT (later the Dene Nation) and adopted the idea of a ten-year moratorium on the building of the Mackenzie Valley Pipeline, the other side of the spectrum was advanced by another prominent lawyer, David H. Searle, QC.

Searle was notable in many ways, including for his candid and outspoken views on the politics of the time. As the member of the legislative assembly for Yellowknife, the first elected legislative speaker of the NWT, the head of the largest and most prestigious law firm north of the 60th parallel, with offices in Yellowknife, Hay River, and Inuvik, and lawyers flying the entire territory on court circuit, he was the putative leader of the pro-business and pro-development voice. David was a lifelong Liberal and a federal Queen's Counsel. His views were sought out, freely given, and carried a lot of weight.

On Searle's passing, the Law Society of the NWT published this comment:

> David Searle was first elected to the NWT Council, the precursor to the Legislative Assembly, in 1967. He served on the council and assembly for 12 years and became the first elected speaker in May 1975.

---

161 John Mackie, "Obituary: Former B.C. NDP leader and legal legend Tom Berger dies at 88," *Vancouver Sun* (April 28, 2021), https://vancouversun.com/news/local-news/former-b-c-ndp-leader-and-legal-legend-tom-berger-dies-at-88.

In 2000, Searle was appointed a member of the Order of Canada for his role in shaping the government of the NWT, including bringing a representative, fully elected government to the area and helping to devolve federal powers to the territory.[162]

Raised in Yellowknife, he returned to that city to practise law after law school in Alberta, becoming, in due course, the dean of Yellowknife lawyers. Searle acted as the Crown Prosecutor for the NWT during the flying-court days of Judge Jack Sissons and again during the early tenure of Justice Bill Morrow. He also served his profession and the public as the first president of the Law Society of the NWT. Moreover, David Searle was a plain-spoken advocate for many causes, especially northern development, and was specifically against the idea of a moratorium on building the Mackenzie Valley pipeline.

Searle disagreed with Berger, strongly. He reflected the views of large numbers of businesspeople from all over the country, including many of the non-Indigenous people resident in the NWT. His stance was not popular with the federal government nor much of the Indigenous community and their supporters. His views did not prevail at the time, although some road and pipeline work did happen over the ensuing years. But that ship—the Mackenzie Valley Pipeline as saviour and catalyst for northern development and petroleum production—seems to have sailed. What benefit was achieved by the ten-year moratorium and at what cost, and what would have happened otherwise are very difficult to conceive.

Interestingly, Searle and Berger both died, within about a month of each other, on the West Coast in the early part of 2021.

By the way, during the time of the Berger Inquiry public hearings in Hay River, the local newspaper published a photo that was in itself a sign of the North in those years. Prince Charles, the first son of British Queen Elizabeth II and heir to the throne, was on a royal tour of the North. The photo shows him shaking hands with local Dene Chief Daniel Sonfrere. The fact that no security people were gathered around, nor appeared even close, was not even deemed noteworthy in the Hay River newspaper of 1974. It was, after all, the North.

....

162 Law Society of the Northwest Territories, "David H. Searle QC Remembered," https://lawsociety.nt.ca/.

CHAPTER 32:
Expanding the Business – The Panarctic Years

Hay River Hub news clipping: "Northern Arc launches Dome barge".

Northern Arc didn't stick to repairing tugs and barges.

FOR STARTERS, Gordon says, *we also built four 1200-series barges for Northern Loram. They were used to haul rock to build islands in the Mackenzie at Norman Wells for drilling. We built other vessels too, like the ferry we built for the government of the NWT. It was the one that crossed the Peel River* [another major tributary of the Mackenzie] *at Fort MacPherson.*

The North saw the start of the petroleum exploration boom in the 1960s. Many of the exploration companies and the Canadian government formed a partnership in the Arctic called Panarctic Oils Limited.

Panarctic Oils Limited was formed in 1966. This was both the first direct entry of the Canadian Government in the oil and gas business, except for some action in the Second World War, and it was an expression of Canadian sovereignty in the region. That company consolidated the interests of seventy-five companies and individuals with Arctic islands land holdings plus the federal government as the major shareholder. Panarctic became a major player in the development of the petroleum industry in Canada, spending large amounts of money, doing a lot of the drilling in the Arctic and discovering both large gas fields and oil.

As Morris Zaslow explains in a comprehensive report on northern development, Dome Petroleum, based in Calgary and run by the flamboyant Jack Gallagher, played an oversized role in promoting and then managing the arctic exploration.

> Dome Petroleum agreed to manage the company until Panarctic secured its equipment and built up its own staff. The original partnership being 76 percent Canadian-owned was eligible for all the subsidies and other concessions available to Canadian firms. The resources continued to be developed with no returns to the developers, but the governmental participation and spending over the next decade… in the Panarctic syndicate would mushroom to gigantic proportions.[163]

Panarctic was a pioneer in exploring offshore and this impacted Gordon and the businesses in Hay River. Panarctic began drilling wells from "ice islands"—not really islands, but platforms of thickened ice created in winter by pumping sea water on the polar ice pack.

The exploration boom came at the right time for Northern Arc. There were workers available, and more of the local men had been trained as welders and steel workers. Gordon had set up shop and the local competition was virtually non-existent. Hay River was the base for most transportation and Northern Arc was right there.

> *In 1971 we got our first big contract to build a work barge complete with a camp, workshop, and helideck for the Arctic. Oil-and-gas exploration was becoming big business in the North. The barge was called the Canmar (for Canadian Marine Drilling), built for Dome Petroleum. It was the first of its type for Dome, which had a major presence, the leader, you might say, in Arctic drilling.*

....

163 Zaslow, *Northward Expansion*, 349.

> *The barge had a cutout notch in its stern, built that way for dropping caissons, big steel culvert kind of things that would sit on the ocean floor to protect the drill well-head.*

The *Canmar* earned Northern Arc another *Hub* headline: "Northern Arc Launches Dome Barge,"[164] along with appropriate photos. In one, the barge spills over two pages of the newspaper. The photo is too small to properly reflect the extent of the fabrication or the size of the barge.

One thing Gordon still thinks of as pretty remarkable:

> *The* Canmar *was a work barge, must have weighed 700 tons. It had a small machine shop and room for a 150-ton crane, in addition to the camp, helideck, and work areas. Just to build it, we used thousands and thousands of welding rods. I figure we used about fifty tons of welding rods that year just on construction and repairs.*

Welding rods were typically a third of a metre (14–16 inches) long and up to 6.35 millimetres (a quarter of an inch) in diameter. The rod is the part of the welding rig that gets "powered." The rig has two lines, one grounded and one called the "stinger." The rod is attached to the stinger and heated. When the rod gets hot enough and touches the objects to be welded, like two parallel steel plates, it melts both plates and the rod material to form a bead. When that cools down, it bonds the steel. Then, voilà, the steel plates are joined. Pretty soon, you have a whole barge. And you have used an awful lot of welding rods. Thousands, at a rough estimate.

Once the welding and fabrication were complete, NT moved the *Canmar* down river to the Beaufort Sea. This Arctic work was all new. One of the big issues in the Beaufort was its shallowness.

> *The bigwigs said the average wave in the Beaufort should be about two feet or so. I used to wonder if that average took into account that the sea was frozen for nine or ten months of the year, because when those western winds came up, the sea water would crest up at 20 feet. It would drown these man-made sea islands, submerge them right there.*

Gordon was getting the hang of this work and getting his name known. Next up were the *Arctic Star* drilling platforms for use in the Beaufort Sea,

---

164 C. Brodeur, "Northern Arc Launches Dome Barge," *Hay River Hub*.

in the Arctic Ocean, another impressive first for Northern Arc.

> *The* Arctic Star *was the first submersible drilling platform for the Arctic. The platform measured around 225 feet long and 110 feet wide. The owner was Sun Oil, and the main contractor was BC Marine. We went to BC to cut up some railway barges that were used to cross the Okanagan Lake.*

The plan was to disassemble the steel railway barges, cut them into pieces, and ship them by truck to Hay River. There, the barges were reassembled as the outside base of the structure, and a central portion was built as the drilling platform. It had to be shallow enough to float down the Mackenzie River, and sturdy enough to be hauled out into the sometimes-treacherous Beaufort Sea.

The Beaufort is shallow, which is good and bad if you are setting up drilling platforms. As it affects this work, Gordon recalls that:

> *The Delta is so wide open but so shallow It is hardly more than 10 feet deep, in places, and it is so wide and complex, with so many channels. I think the Delta is around 100 miles wide at the top. The river carries so much silt out into the Beaufort Sea that it goes for miles. It creates ledges and shallow waters. That is where the* Arctic Star *worked, just off the end of the islands in the Delta.*

The need for equipment to handle these big jobs also presented other opportunities for Northern Arc. For example, because they had large cranes (to lift the steel into place for the barge and tug work), Northern Arc also did a lot of other things too. Gordon adds:

> *We did a lot of pile driving and dock work; we drove piles for housing in Hay River and Fort Simpson; we did bridge piling work on the Liard Highway. Everything we could do to keep busy.*
>
> *People used to ask how I got all this good work, especially when NT and the BC companies were union. Some people thought all the work would go to companies connected with the Liberals and maybe it did, outside of Hay River. I was never political. All I was involved with there was work, and curling. I was a member of the Métis group too but that's all.*

That's where Bert Stromberg got in a bit of trouble. He came to me one time. Said he was accused of taking kickbacks, bribes to give us work. That wasn't true. I never even thought of that. I never in all my life did that. Bert wouldn't have allowed it, either. But people talked like that. And if ever either of us would have suggested something like that, it would have ended our friendship.

It is interesting discussion, though, in business circles. Where do you get and how do you get customers? Take the *Arctic Star* project, mentioned above, for example.

Gordon explains its genesis:

The Arctic Star contract was because of Albert Iryie. So was the Canmar barge; it was for Dome Petroleum. Both those projects were contracted to BC Marine. Albert had been a captain for NT. I had known him because when he was the captain of the Radium King, he would bring her in to port. I would go see him to ask if he had any problems or any repairs he needed.

Albert was also a welder; he was always amazed at what our welders could do.

Anyway, Sun Oil wanted a submersible drilling platform for the Arctic. They contracted BC Marine to do it. Albert worked for Arctic Navigation, which was partly owned by BC Marine. He recommended us to do the job.

I said I couldn't do that. Albert said I could. I said, "No," but he believed in us, and insisted. It was our first really big job of this type, and the first submersible to go into the Arctic.

About this time, it was starting to be important to help Métis and Native companies and people get work, especially in the North. That must have helped us.

Before BC Marine would give me the contract, though, I was asked to fly to Vancouver to have a meeting with the head of engineering. So, I took the jet from Hay River, and when I got to Vancouver, I stayed at the Waldorf Hotel, which was pretty dicey. The next morning, I went to the office and met the head of engineering. He had a reputation as a very tough guy, but I didn't see that. He and I got along great.

At the meeting, there was the head architect, the head engineer, and about eleven other engineers from BC Marine and me. The main ship architect asked me if I had looked at the plans.

The plans he mentioned were for a unique 800-ton drilling platform, with a lowered section in the middle, constructed between two barges. Gordon had not seen the plans until the meeting.

The head architect, Captain Steele, rolled out the plans. He asked me what I thought of the design. And to be truthful.

The head engineer, Bill Tollefson, and I looked through them, and then I said I didn't like the plan. There was some silence, but Steele asked me why. So I got out a package of cigarettes (I smoked then) and asked him for his pack. I put them side by side on the table. I explained that the drilling platform was like these packs of cigarettes. And I pushed with my fingers on the inside edges of both packs. They kind of squished and separated. Everybody could see that's what the Star *would do under strain.*

Not only was the platform itself about 800 tons, but with the added weight of the drilling rig, pipe, and other equipment, it was going to be *really* heavy; Gordon puts that weight at hundreds of tons, and it needed a lot more strength.

I told them it would be better if there were some cross-bridge beams between the two barges—extending past centre on each. This would take away the stress in the centre, better than the way they had it drawn up.

Then there was a real silence.

After a bit, Bill, who had been sitting on my side of the table, looked at the eleven other BC Marine engineers and spoke. "Well, boys, you got your work cut out for you."

So, they redesigned the platform and added in those cross beams and some extra longitudinal ones too.

There weren't any other questions. Northern Arc got that job.

Later, the head of engineering came to Hay River in winter, when it was "cold as hell." He walked across the frozen river with Gordon through deep snow to check out a barge. On the way back, he had a heart attack, right in the middle of the river.

> *I was shocked. I took my parka off and wrapped it around him* [Bill]. *Then I ran like hell, through all that deep snow back to the Synchrolift. I thought I was going to have a heart attack too. I was able to get help and an ambulance there. As soon as I got help coming, I ran back to him. It was about 1,500 feet each way. Man was it cold. I am so glad that he* [Bill] *survived.*

*   *   *

Gordon takes real pride in his and his team's hard and fast work. He tells of times when they would be done a project before the NT employees or some of the union guys were halfway started.

> *Bert Stromberg would purposefully put his team against ours, just for the competition.*

Gordon fondly recalls the memory of how well his team did; how fast and well they performed as a group. He doesn't make fun of the other guys or say anything negative about union workers; he often called the union for more men, and he was friends with them and other welders and even the "bigwigs" in the marine fabricating concerns in the south.

Gordon is very proud of the work Northern Arc did. He took pride in "finding a way" and in getting the job done. One of those ways was to hire local Indigenous workers whenever possible.

Gordon's view is that companies wanted to hire local Indigenous people and businesses if they could. This worked for him and for his goal of hiring Métis people too.

> *They wanted to work, and they worked hard. But at the same time there was a lot of joking around and they didn't take themselves very seriously.*

Those are Gordon's words, but they make you wonder if he is just describing himself and the example he set. In any event, they got work, and they got it done.

> *There was lots of work in the north then. Everybody needed workers. Some of the southern companies, even northern ones, for that matter, had trouble understanding the local workers. Lots of times, the guys wouldn't show up, or they'd leave and then that was that. They'd get fired, and then the companies had to find other men, and train them, or they'd not hire Dene or Métis guys at all. We were lucky, we weren't as strict about that kind of thing, and we did what we could to keep our workers. If they needed a little break, or if they didn't show up, we just carried on until they got back.*

Gordon emphasized more than once how building vessels or doing a crane job was like any other job; like lawyering, accounting, or anything. You have to get the work, plan it, and get it done because if it is just sitting there staring at you, or if you can't let it go, it isn't making money for anybody. Sometimes, Gordon believes, you have to say, "That's enough; it's done."

In those NT work competitions, he never sensed any animosity. The other workers were always good to him and his men. They didn't seem to feel they were being "shown up." Gordon is clear that shipbuilding, at least at his level, was pretty fraternal. *If I needed help, I would call someone, like Allied that had good history in the North, or BC Marine, or the NT guys. And if they needed help, they would call me. We helped each other.*

Pricing apparently wasn't an issue either.

> *On our first job for Kap's Transport, we were building a section of the wharf at Hay River for them to use. Vic Kapchinsky, he was one of the owners or the brother of the main owner; he called me in to see him when I sent him the invoice. "You can't send me this bill," said Vic. "What's the matter with it?" I was kind of confused and worried. "It's not enough. You gotta make it at least ten times more. If you don't, they're gonna wonder what the hell I am doing up here with all my other contractors."*

Apparently, that isn't the usual response to an invoice from a sub-contractor.

* * *

In 1981–82 particularly, Northern Arc Shipbuilders was tremendously busy. It received a number of contracts for quite a variety of vessels.

One such project involved a new ferry for vehicle and passenger traffic over the Peel River crossing near Fort MacPherson, NWT. It is a nice-looking unit. That project, for the GNWT, also gave Gordon the chance to spend some time on the Peel River (west of the Mackenzie) when he arrived to establish the cables that held the vessel in place and get it operating.

Northern Arc also fabricated the four Northern Loram barges. The importance of these platform barges was their use to create drilling islands in the middle of the wide Mackenzie, at Norman Wells. This work would allow Imperial Oil, the owner of the Norman Wells oil refinery, to access more product by expanding their drilling capacity.

These projects were all in addition to Northern Arc's regular repair work.[165]

Perhaps most impressive, however, and certainly the most newsworthy, was Northern Arc's design, expediting, and fabrication work on the ocean-going tug, which came to be called the MT *Gordon Gill*—and its eventual loss. More on that later.

165 John M. MacFarlane, "Vessels Built by Northern Arc Shipbuilders Ltd.," *Nauticapedia* (2015), http://www.nauticapedia.ca/Articles/Vessel_Builders_Northern_Arc.php.

CHAPTER 33:
The MT *Gordon Gill* – Part 1, Launch

The Hub

Hay R
Pine P
Northw
(

WEDNESDAY, SEPTEMBER 29, 1982   If undeliverable return to Bo

Gordon Gill launched

The Gordon Gill, newest addition to the Arctic Offshore fleet, was launched into the Hay River Wednesday morning after an unsuccessful attempt the previous day. The vessel slipped on the launchway Tuesday and had to be righted. The tugboat will serve in the Beaufort Sea with the company's other three ships - the Norweta, Orion and Pilot II. The purple coloration of the boats will make them easily identifiable as those of Arctic Offshore. See feature article on pages 4 and 5.

Hay River Hub front page: "Gordon Gill launched".

"[N]ortherners from Hay River are showing . . . that big jobs can be conceived, planned and executed in the north by northerners." Hay River Hub.

IN 1982, Northern Arc was contracted by Arctic Offshore to build a serious ocean-going tug to clear ice and do other supply and logistics work for Dome Petroleum, especially involving its dry dock in McKinley Bay, east of Tuk, in the Beaufort Sea.

Some dry docks are just a series of parallel squared timbers laid on the ground up onto which a boat might be pulled for repair. Some dry docks look like a big, empty ship with doors that can be opened to let water in, flooding the centre. Some do this with a submerging exercise. The vessel needing checking or repair can then just power into the centre, the work-place. Then the doors are closed, and the water pumped out. The vessel is now open to the air so workers can see what problems exist and design the repairs needed. In the Tuk harbour, it was the latter, like a wet dry dock, and it was so large it needed a very powerful tug to move vessels, clean debris, and other assorted chores.

This was the contract Arctic Offshore was to fulfill and which it did with Northern Arc as the shipbuilder. Thus, came about the deep-sea work tug that became the MT *Gordon Gill*.

The *Gordon Gill* was short and stubby. It had to be because it did most of its rugged work—90 percent or so—*inside* the dry dock itself. However, the tug was a workhorse out there in the Arctic Ocean, so strong, so ice-strengthened, Gordon says, that it was *built like a tank*. It was an interesting and different kind of tugboat, built for a specific purpose, a steel-hulled, twin-screw 1600-HP work boat. Its gross tonnage was between 148 and 160 tons.

At 21.7 metres long and 9.3 metres wide (65 by 28 feet), the *Gill* had a 2.1-metre (seven-foot) draft. Normal river tugs drew maybe 1.1 to 1.4 metres (3.5 to 4.5 feet).

The deep draft posed a problem. Not in the dry dock in the ocean but sooner—in fact, quite immediately. Gordon explains how they moved the ship down the often-shallow Mackenzie to the Arctic:

> *The hull of the ship went too low into the water and wouldn't be able to float the river, so we took two barges and filled the insides with water. They sank in the river. Then we secured the* Gordon Gill *in the middle of the barges with some bridgework fore and aft and slung cables under it. Then we pumped the water out of the barges, so they came up again.*

> *The ship floated at about 4-foot depth [draft] so it could go down the river.*

When asked if Gordon thought that up, he said yes, a pause, then, *Well, me and Don Tetreault.*

The *Hay River Hub* newspaper announced the launch of Arctic Offshore's MT *Gordon Gill*, "the latest edition to its purple fleet of ships."

> We have been working the Arctic for the last seven years and we've been lost in the crowd up there [the Beaufort Sea], but this year we are getting all kinds of remarks, good, bad or indifferent on our ships' colour, but people are talking about us," said [Don] Tetrault, president of Arctic Offshore and the man who wanted northerner Gordon Gill to build the latest addition to Offshore's fleet right here in Hay River.
>
> The colour of its ships is the least of the reasons why the oil companies with the majority of the action in the Arctic are starting to notice the flamboyant… Tetrault and the more reserved but equally hard-working Gill.
>
> She [the ship] is ice strengthened to an exceptionally high degree and meets Canada Arctic Standards 'A'.
>
> The Gill will also assist [ships] to anchor securely in the [McKinley] Bay and can lift up to 40-ton anchors used to secure drill ships.
>
> The ship was built in sections by Brisdale Marine in Vancouver and shipped by truck to Hay River where the sections were welded together. Northern Arc then fitted the engines, all the other fittings and electronics, [and completed the ship with local subcontractors].
>
> These two northerners from Hay River are showing… that big jobs can be conceived, planned and executed in the north by northerners.
>
> Gill had up to 40 men working at one time on the boat with his own company alone. At the same time, he had about the same

number constructing barges for Northern Loram for the Norman Wells project.

[Gordon was quoted about the effect.] Just about every business in town has had a hand in this ship; the spinoffs on a project like this are astronomical in a small town like Hay River. Before, all the benefits … would have gone south …

Gordon's nature comes through in this quote from the same article:

The Tugboat is the most ambitious project his company has undertaken since he stopped welding for NTCL as an employee and formed his own company eleven years ago. Building tugboats is the more glamourous part of Northern Arc's business but Gill does not forget the earlier days when barge repair was the mainstay of his business. "In fact," says Gill, "our bread-and-butter business is barge repair. That keeps us going through the slower months and we can't ever forget that part of our business."

As completion of construction of the still-nameless vessel neared, Gordon repeatedly pressed Offshore's Captain Tetreault for the name of the tug, so he could get the nameplate crafted and welded on. Tetreault—himself an ex-YT and NT ship's captain—said, "The *Gordon Gill*." Gordon said he was so surprised; "it was the best-kept secret," and he was a director of Arctic Offshore, along with other Northern notables.

The paper went on to say:

Captain Tetreault pointed out that neither the choice of the name of the tug nor its [purple] colour scheme had anything to do with Gordon Gill. "We wanted to recognize his contribution before he died so we named it after Gordon," said Tetreault, who explained the choice of the name originated with Irene Tetreault, Capt. Tetreault's wife.

Chris Brodeur, publisher of the Hay River newspaper, advises that the purple colour was in fact selected to match the colour of the high school in that town, chosen by the student body. Famed Métis Canadian architect Douglas Cardinal designed the unique structure, built with his trademark rounded walls.

And that photo of the new MT *Gordon Gill*, painted purple, which graced the front page of the *Hub* newspaper on September 29, 1982? Well, it was another first for Gordon, in a way. It was the first coloured photo ever used in the newspaper, befitting the occasion of a new ship launched from the Hay River shipyards, built by a local shipbuilder, for a local company. Oh, and painted to match the local school[166]

Gordon Gill was described in the same article as "reserved" and "hard-working" and then quoted as saying, "I didn't particularly like it but I had no choice." He later explained that the *Gill* was probably named as a thank you for what he had done to help Don Tetreault and Arctic Offshore.[167]

Jim Guthrie doesn't know Gordon personally and was only connected to this story because of his photos and descriptions of working in the high Arctic, but when the name Gordon Gill was mentioned, Guthrie said: "One of the small but excellent vessels both BeauDril and Canmar chartered from Arctic Offshore Services owned by Don Tetrault from Hay River, was the *Gordon Gill*."[168]

The MT *Gordon Gill* was equipped for icebreaking. Oversized tow lines and bigger deck space allowed the *Gill* to transport large containers to drill ships, and to clear ice from the submersible dry dock. It also acted as a "tender," a kind of a delivery vessel, working in the Arctic until late in 1986. But when the federal government cut the Petroleum Incentive Program (PIP) grants, all work in the Beaufort stopped. Dome was done, and the work ended. Arctic Offshore had to move all its boats from the area.

> And then, in 1986, there was a big crunch, a big crash. All that Arctic exploration just stopped. It was coming prior to '87. I wasn't in Hay River to see the start of the marine industry, but I sure was there to see the end. It was the end of an era.
>
> Northern Transportation was still the big dog on the river, but after that, there was no more building.

166 Chris Brodeur, telephone interview with the author, July, 2022.
167 *Hay River Hub*. September 29, 1982.
168 Email to the author, February 2022.

CHAPTER 34:
The MT *Gordon Gill* –
Part 2, Survival

The MT Gordon Gill on duty amid the ice flows of the Arctic Ocean.
Photo courtesy of Brent Kobbert.

I was sure it didn't sink.

THAT'S WHAT GORDON said about his namesake tug.

So, what about the MT *Gordon Gill*, until then on-duty in the Beaufort Sea?

The dramatic drop in oil prices left the *Gill* without work in the Beaufort Sea oil fields in the mid-80s. So it was that it came to be transported west, through the Bering Sea and around to the Pacific, through the Panama Canal, and to eastern Canada. A route directly eastward, through Canada's Northwest Passage, was not possible due to ice.

With all the Arctic work gone, the MT *Gordon Gill* was being sent to Canada's east coast. The long way. Think of the journey, being pulled behind a tow tug on the end of heavy steel cables 610 to 915 metres [2,000 to 3,000 feet] long, along the Arctic coast of Alaska, through the Bering Straits, and into the stormy seas surrounding the Aleutian Islands. And that was only the start since the *Gill* was on its way to Vancouver and then Halifax. Near Dutch Harbor in the wild waters of the Alaska panhandle, a major North Pacific October storm shook the boats and took hold. The long tow cables frayed and snapped. Immediately, the boarded-up and unmanned ship, the MT *Gordon Gill,* was gone.

The insurance company hired oceanographers and other experts to chart the ocean currents to determine where the big tug should have gone. Two huge Hercules aircraft with spotters flew grid-style search missions all over the area. Despite all that and other extensive searches by helicopters, and other Arctic Offshore tugs, the *Gordon Gill* was nowhere to be found.

Gordon was convinced it was still afloat. The ship had a beacon system in it, which would have reported it sinking. Nothing like that showed. However, in four long winter months in the North Pacific, not one report of a sighting was recorded. Northern Arc was still owed a substantial sum of money for the construction of the tug, and, in due course, an insurance claim was made.

Then, as the *Vancouver Province* newspaper of February 26, 1987, blared in its headline: "Ghost Boat Comes Home; Tug adrift 4 months."

The paper goes on to quote a US Coast Guard spokesman, who said, "The tug was in perfect shape after spending four months on the North Pacific." He continued, saying, "And there's some bad weather out there." Only a few dishes were broken, and some maps dislodged.[169]

....
169 *The Province.* Steve Berry. February 26, 1987.

The *Los Angeles Times* also got in on the story, saying the "Unsinkable Gordon Gill Tugs at Their Heartstrings."[170]

Perhaps the fact that long-serving northern Anglican minister and character Turk McCollum christened the *Gill* on its launch helped. A fisherman found it 40 kilometres from Dutch Harbor and towed it there. The fisherman claimed the tug had been abandoned, lost at sea, and by maritime law, the salvage rights belonged to him. A legal dispute ensued, which ultimately ordered the insurance company to pay a significant amount of money to cover the fisherman's costs and lost opportunity.

The court record found the salvage of the boat by the fishing rig *Sea Star* and its captain Larry Hendricks took place about 4 kilometres east-northeast of Egg Island, a tiny spot in the Aleutian Islands where the boat was spotted on radar. It was boarded up, with no one on board. The Alaskan court found it to have been a difficult and hazardous process, in the late-February below-freezing temperatures. The *Sea Star* and the *Gill* faced 20–30 knot winds and 2.4- to 3.7-metre [8- to 12-foot] seas. Running up through the pass between Unalaska Island and Alutan Island (to the secure anchorage at Dutch Harbor) meant traversing a passage with conflicting winds and current, north from the Pacific Ocean into the Bering Sea. Tow lines snapped more than once. Hendricks was awarded damages for his role in the rescue.[171]

Gordon is proud that the ship was intact and afloat after four long, cold, icy months in that inhospitable ocean. Yet, he doesn't seem to have any regrets or sad feelings about his namesake boat or its ultimate sale and renaming.[172] When asked how he felt about the tug's loss, he said, *I learned early in business never to get too emotionally involved in what we built. I never got married to a piece of iron in my life. To be quite honest, I was happy the insurance money came through... we were still owed quite a bit by Arctic Offshore.*

Who knows what plays a part in the stories of man, his successes, and his near failures?

> *We cashed the cheque.*

....

170 https://www.latimes.com/archives/la-xpm-1987-02-27-mn-3724-story.html

171 *Hendricks v. The Tug Gordon Gill* No. A87-313 CIV (January 12, 1989), https://casetext.com/case/hendricks-v-tug-gordon-gill

172 The tug is now called *MANTAYWI-SEPE.* It is owned by Hudson's Bay Port Co. of Churchill, Manitoba.

CHAPTER 35:
Northern Crane Services and the Move South

Northern Crane Services Mobile Crane. Photo by Bob Van England.

*I always thought: if nothing's happening,
you make it happen.*

AFTER 1987 [with the decline in the marine business in the North], *there was no more building of any kind for us, no barges or tugs or other vessels. We still had repair work, but that was falling off too. Then after 1993, there wasn't even much in the way of repairs. NT could handle what they needed in-house. There wasn't much for us to do.*

Northern Arc had a little division called Northern Crane; that was before 1987. After 1987, we applied all our effort to Northern Crane.

You might ask how a mechanic on a small tugboat (called the "engineer" because they keep the engines running) becomes the owner of a well-respected crane and heavy lift company working in the oil field service business in the Alberta oil sands and elsewhere in the south. How does a young man without much education start welding in the company shop, repairing ships and barges, then become a shipbuilder, and when the boom era of barge transport and shipment comes to an end as times change, take his knowledge of cranes (as a crane operator, lifting heavy steel plates to be welded in place to form part of such vessels) and become a southern businessman, eventually selling his company to an international consortium?

In the early 1980s, two fellows came to our office and asked to see me. One was from Imperial Oil [Esso], and the other was a Native fellow. They asked if I would agree to be appointed to the board of directors with Shehtah Drilling. I didn't know them, but they had got my name and seemed to want me. So, I did become a director of that company. Shehtah Drilling was 50 percent owned by Esso, and 50 percent owned by Natives (25 percent was the Métis and the other 25 percent was the Natives). Esso had two directors, the Natives had one director, the Métis had one director. I was the fifth director, the independent one, in case they needed outside advice or a tiebreaker. I had no monetary involvement; they would call and say they were having a meeting and then send a Learjet to get me.

I was on that board for five years, and that was an enjoyable part of my life. It was then that I learned that the Beaufort Sea was shutting down because the government had cut off all the PIP[173] grants, so the government was cutting off all the work in the Beaufort Sea. Had I not been on

173 The Petroleum Incentive Program was established by the federal government to encourage exploration and production of petroleum products, especially in difficult-to-access areas where intensive and extensive capital was required. Per *The Canadian Encyclopedia*, "As petroleum became the critical energy resource of the 20th century, governments became more intimately involved in the operations of the petroleum industries—especially during the 'crisis' years of the 1970s and early 1980s." (Robert D. Brott, "Petroleum Industries," *The Canadian Encyclopedia* [January 7, 2016], https://www.thecanadianencyclopedia.ca/en/article/petroleum-industries.)

the board, I would not have known that this was happening. But what Esso told Shehtah to do, I applied those ideas myself with Northern Arc Shipbuilders. So, then I was downsizing and getting ready. I knew this wasn't going to be a pause. This is for real. The Beaufort Sea is shutting down, companies are moving out, and there's not going to be no tomorrow here, and that was the word from Esso, basically.

After the closing of the Beaufort Sea activity, Gordon had to tell Treena that things were bad, and going to get worse. The country's serious economic decline meant they would have to sell their house at Delancey Estates south of town. When she asked why he didn't sell a crane instead, he said: *Because that's what makes the money.* And Gordon wasn't giving up.

I was doing crane work in Hay River and Fort Simpson and Fort Smith, Yellowknife and even in Rainbow Lake [northwest Alberta]. I had been doing a lot of crane work all around the country. Treena would keep everything separate for Northern Crane and Northern Arc Shipbuilders. I operated crane lots; in those days in the Territories, you weren't compelled to have a crane operating licence. That came later. But I had my heavy-duty diesel mechanics so I could repair any part of a crane. If I was licensed to repair it, I should be able to drive it. Being an owner, you study the books, the manuals on all the equipment and cranes, but I operated the crane lots.

For example, we got involved in lifting and moving the houses from Pine Point when Cominco closed the mine because it was a company town, and it closed too.

Gordon's way was to seek all kinds of work and to diversify. He was adaptable and determined to find work where and how he could.

NT had cranes, and they weren't busy, so I rented some from them. We did all kinds of work to keep alive, like pile driving. Whatever we could do.

(Gordon had initially thought to chase work from the diamond mines planned for north of Yellowknife).

Long-time accountant Jonathan Smethurst recalls driving south to Grande Prairie, Alberta, to meet Gordon about the financial statements and year-end. Gordon was the president of Northern Crane, but he spent the winter in that northwest Alberta city operating a crane and doing pile driving; he was always working, going to where the work was, as necessary.

> *So, I applied what Esso said to the business, and that's when I decided. I had hired these guys from Edmonton, and one of these guys was Leo Davis, and he had had experience in Alberta with a crane company of his own, which got caught up in the economic problems in Alberta. So, he knew a lot of the people and a lot about cranes, and I hired him to work for me, and at that point, I decided we should take cranes to Edmonton… in 1987. Leo worked tirelessly, and we did well together. It paid off when we sold the company.*
>
> *And then we officially moved out of Hay River in 1993; up until then, Treena and I were back and forth between Edmonton and Hay River, which made it very difficult. I mean, it was a 10- to 12-hour drive, and that was a waste of time. If the weather got bad, it was worse.*
>
> *Hay River was continuing to go downhill and in 1993 is when we decided to permanently live in Edmonton.*
>
> *The marine industry, the downturn in the economy, and the new highway to Inuvik, well that was basically the end of it; it was just sort of a thing that happened all across Canada very similar to the voyageurs with their freighter canoes, and development coming West. The marine end of it dropped off, and the same thing happened to the North; as soon as development came, in came the road up to Inuvik, and that ended a lot of the marine traffic that we used to have, and that gave us our work. It was never going to come back.*
>
> *Now the government in the Northwest Territories has taken over NT, and they're doing it mainly just to resupply some of the communities in the Arctic. It's a commitment they can make—either take freight in by boat, or they can fly in the freight. It's costly either way. So, they can use both air and boat. It is the end of another era.*

In 2020, the NWT government announced the opening of a road to Tuktoyaktuk, the first Canadian all-weather road from Inuvik to the Arctic coast. Now, Canada is drivable from sea to sea to sea. In 2021, the MV *Vic Ingraham* was featured in a news story. There it was, in the Yellowknife Harbour for the first time in thirty years, its two barges loaded with equipment. Cheetah Resources, the operator of Canada's first rare-earth minerals mine, Nechalacho (the old Con Gold Mine), said it plans to move ore by barge, too.[174]

> We were lucky to do well in the crane business, especially with all the work coming out of the oil sands at Fort McMurray. Our competitors were mostly large international companies. We had good people and good friends, and they helped us. The contractors liked to have us work with them; I think it was because we were smaller and local, and we could bid jobs cheaper than the big boys. That we were Aboriginal was a help too.

However, here too, Gordon is likely too modest. In addition to being the first crane company in the oil sands to bring in truck-mounted cranes, Northern Crane brought the first Spiering crane into the country from Europe. The key aspect of this equipment was the main boom, which could rise out of itself straight into the air. At the appropriate spot, a "jib" boom extends flat, straight out, at a 90-degree angle. As Gordon explains,

> The benefit was that the crane could get right up beside a building or structure. You'd raise the boom as high as you needed and then have the jib extend over the building. It was just like a tower crane but not fixed to the building. It was still mobile. We could just drive up to site and drive away when we were finished. That was great because we didn't have to dismantle it like a tower crane, and we could move in and out a lot quicker and maneouver wherever we had to.

The move south, however, took Gordon and Treena into the world of "big business." Gordon personally didn't see much difference in the business world, in either place. He was not intimidated. For one thing, he had been told numerous times by people he met, from the oil companies and construction people, "You could make it in the south anytime." So, he wasn't worried and didn't hesitate to make the move.

---

174 Ollie Williams, "Freight Barges, a Rare Sign in Modern Yellowknife, Dock Near Con," *Cabin Radio* (October 15, 2021), https://cabinradio.ca/76296/news/yellowknife/freight-barges-a-rare-sight-in-modern-yellowknife-dock-near-con/.

I really enjoyed the shipbuilding and the early crane years. I didn't claim to know it all. We hired the people who knew what to do, like we'd hire naval architects to work with or other experts. But that was work I would do with the employees. The crane business, especially in the south, was different. It was still problem solving, but it was bigger, more at a distance. Our biggest competitor was Sterling, which Warren Buffet eventually took a big interest in. It was American and huge. We got along great with them, rented cranes from them, and worked with them too, but we were able to get a foothold because we were smaller, and there was a hunger for competition and for Indigenous-owned companies, especially in Fort McMurray.

However, it wasn't a piece of cake or easy. For the first five years, the crane company lost money. It was the lines of credit and the reserves from the previously successful Northern Arc that kept it going.

One thing I think about is how close it came to failure. We were buying lots of cranes; at one point, we had about ninety of them, including huge German ones from Leibherr. They were big too—some of them, like one of those Leibherrs, was $3.7 million dollars and could lift 1,000 tons. Our first one was an LTM 1300, 360-ton and then later we got the LTM 1550, 1,000-ton.

We financed some of them with equipment financiers, like John Deere Credit. But most of our borrowing was through the Royal Bank. One problem was that the bank only lent money to the level of the depreciated value of equipment, even though our major customers were big, Syncrude and Suncor in Fort McMurray. So we had to use quite a bit of cash from our business, both generated by the crane company and lines of credit from Northern Arc. Our banker at RBC was getting nervous. We could tell that.

I mentioned that to my friend at John Deere, that I could feel that the bank was mad at me financing through John Deere and that I had the feeling that they were going to call our loan. John Deere offered to help because, my friend said, they understood equipment financing, and the bank didn't. So everything was arranged to refinance, if it was needed.

> *When our banker came to see me one day, he said he was sorry, but they were going to have to call my loan. I said that's okay, I have the money to pay you out in full, and I did. I arranged to go in the next day to pay off our loans. I don't know if he was more surprised or disappointed. You'd of thought he would be happy. I am still a customer of the Royal. But I didn't have all my eggs in that basket.*

He adds, with a little smile: *They have my money; I have none of theirs.*

Gordon describes the Northern Crane days as *constant hard work* and *repetitious.* He goes on to say:

> *There was always pressure, always things to do … we had to make sure we had work, and the people to do it. We had lots and lots of equipment, and so you know, all the buying and maintaining, and all the logistics, the financing and repairs. You know we had crews and mechanics, and legal and financial and accounting people galore. We had to keep getting bigger and bigger—we were up to 140 employees when we sold out—and get larger and larger equipment.*

With Northern Crane, he was also less hands-on. He was the president, and it was the Gill family's company, but he was more a supervisor. His role was to oversee, set direction, watch out (with Treena) for mistakes, and look after the money. Gordon was involved, and the final decisions were his, but it was from a high level. And while he had good people and praises those around him as being very important to the company's success—people like general manager Leo Davis, chief financial officer Jonathan Smethurst, and many more—he didn't have the contact with the people that he had before. It wasn't work that he could immerse himself in. It seemed to be more thinking and watching than doing. It was fine, but it wasn't as much fun as when he was working alongside the other fellows. He missed the more collegial, hands-on way of working.

This was a time of huge demand for oil (bitumen) from the Alberta oil sands. The 1990s and the early part of the twenty-first century were busy; everything was on fire. Demand for the product was through the roof. Fort McMurray and the surrounding areas were (and are) the site of one of the largest petroleum deposits in the world. Self-sufficiency for Canada (given proper refining and pipeline facilities) was assured, but also huge amounts of oil were mined and shipped out of country, and it paid the companies (and governments) well. The province of Alberta particularly encouraged construction, development, expansion, Indigenous employment, and investment. Companies from around the world—Norway, France, the US, and China—rushed to build mines or take them over and expand this massive acreage of the heavy oil-saturated sands that make up this unique deposit. Royalties and taxes raised the governments' take significantly.

Workers came from all over. Large camps were located all over the area, filled with workers, coming and going. Boeing 737 aircraft flew crews in from Newfoundland and back again. This was another of the great booms, common in Canada's history, like the gold rushes in British Columbia's Cariboo, Yukon's Klondike, and Ontario's Porcupine, and other regions. It was another boom time for Gordon, like the lead-zinc frenzy near Pine Point, and the oil-and-gas exploration in the Arctic that had spurred the marine traffic and shipbuilding business in Hay River in the '70s and '80s.

Gill's crane business, a successful Indigenous company that provided good and healthy competition for the bigger companies and opened doors for Indigenous hiring, was itself becoming quite large and prominent while still locally and privately owned.

Luckily (there is that word again), Gordon chose to sell most of his interest in the company before the crash of the 2008 world financial crisis, and while he remained a director and shareholder, his role was now passive. It was time, and it was good timing. From a business point of view, how companies like Northern Crane put together the necessary capital, how they face the challenges of business and the evolution of standards, requirements, and trends, and how they innovate, grow, and stay competitive are questions of monumental weight.

In an article by Keith Norbury published in *The Globe and Mail* on October 22, 2014, the extent of growth of Northern Crane after the sale is shown by this quote:

> Established in 1986 by Gordon Gill as Northern Crane Services with two cranes and two employees, NCGS [the successor to Northern Crane] has experienced a growth in sales in the past eight years from $36.3 million in 2006 to $271.4 million in 2014. The group now has branches in the three westernmost provinces,

as well as in Idaho, Montana, North Dakota, and Texas. It has 720 employees and a fleet that includes 285 cranes ranging from six to 1,350 tonnes capacity, 78 tractors, and 300 conventional and heavy haul trailers. [It is now] one of the largest crane companies in North America.[175]

The *Globe* article addressed one of Gordon's earlier issues, his need for more flexible asset-backed loans, and his solution to the Royal Bank approach. About Northern Crane's successor, Norbury says:

To help finance [the NCSG purchases] rather than rely on covenant-heavy bank debt that could restrict cash flow, NCSG has used asset-backed loans in which the cranes and other equipment are the security… because Canadian banks have been reluctant to offer those types of loans.[176]

Gordon had used that approach to his own financing already. Ironically, it turned out that Gordon's purchaser, NCSG, was actually convincing the Royal Bank of Canada to re-consider its approach to financing this type of business. That was the same bank which Gordon suggested should accept that concept a number of years previous.

The oil sands industry eventually slowed down. But by then, Gordon was out. It is the new generation's challenge now. Oil gluts, pipeline problems, climate change, and citizen action all contributed to that. When a massive forest fire destroyed or damaged much of Fort McMurray in 2016 and 80,000 people were evacuated—virtually the whole city—there was a question of whether many would return. The oil-sands projects and plants were consolidated with two major Canadian-based companies, Canadian Natural Resources Ltd. and Suncor Energy Inc., buying out many other players. Multinational oil companies started to question the value of the oil sands amid the call for more green energy and diversification, and the value of oil-patch companies was an active point of debate. Another passing of an era, one that Gordon was quite happy to be out of.

Gordon enjoyed the exercise of selling the company, and his later role as a non-management director.

....

175   Keith Norbury, "Energy Boom Makes This Company a Growing Concern," *The Globe and Mail*, October 22, 2014.
176   Norbury, "Growing Concern," *The Globe and Mail*.

Through Stephen Kent, an experienced business consultant and mergers and acquisitions specialist, a meeting was arranged with some prospective buyers. At the beginning of the meeting, for some reason, Stephen introduced himself as a chartered accountant, stressing his educational background. The other participants, lawyers and accountants and capital guys, maybe ten or twelve people all told, followed along and introduced themselves. They too gave their educational background and talked about their business roles. They all had good educations, and many had multiple university degrees. Finally, it was Gordon's turn. *I am Gordon Gill. I have a grade-eleven education.*

> *You could have heard a pin drop. There was dead silence for some time, and then the buyers laughed out loud, long and hard. It broke the ice, and from then on, all our meetings were good.*

Here's the thing: Gordon could have said that he had his Red Seal in mechanics and welding, that he was a crane operator and engineer, or he could have put everyone in their place with just, "I'm Gordon Gill, and I own this company." But that isn't Gordon's way, it isn't likely the Métis way, and he didn't.

Gordon retained some hobbies. One was the purchase of some bush land near Fort McMurray, which Gordon and his team converted into much-needed rental property for oil-sands suppliers and contractors. That kept him in the business world of his friends working the oil sands and was like much of what he did in his life. He saw a gap and thought to fill it.

The second sideline was another one of those. Gordon explains it thus:

> *I like betting on the horse races. It was a slow pace, no pressure. There was time to do things between races. The thing was, you need information to analyze how to bet, which meant data found in programs you could buy. That was great if you were at one of the major tracks, like Northlands in Edmonton. But off-site, if you wanted to meet someone somewhere to watch and make some bets off-track, then what? There were programs sometimes, but they always seemed late, and so you couldn't get the data on the horses you needed.*
>
> *So there was a hole there, and I started thinking of how to fix that. I designed a kiosk to print information, and that led... us to figure out*

> *computer programs and the like to be able to send the printed programs,*
> *the data, to the kiosks at the off-track places, like lounges or whatever.*
> *We've done that for twenty-four years now. It is the first program for*
> *horse racing in the world like that.*

You will recognize the pattern.

CHAPTER 36:
Hay River and the Demise of Northern Transportation Company Limited

NTCL tugs with boarded up windows, the Snye, Hay River Harbour.

"Only half of NTCL's Vessels Expected to Sell: Report," CBC News.

IN 1985, ownership of NTCL was transferred to the Inuvialuit of the Western Arctic and the Inuit of the new Nunavut Territory as part of their land claims settlement. Thereafter, a number of the NT tugs, especially the "new" ones, were renamed for the most part with names showing respect for Northerners, primarily Indigenous people.

In 1999, Northern Transportation celebrated its sixty-fifth anniversary. Then-President Cameron Clement wrote:

> After the period of rapid economic development in the seventies and eighties, *we were forced to come to grips with the economic*

realities of the nineties and the dramatic effect this had on our tradi-tional markets]. NTCL had to redefine itself for the next millen-nium. [emphasis added][177]

In 2009, long after Clement retired, the company reduced staff across the North by more than twenty people, which in the North would be sig-nificant. The writing was on the wall. Change was coming to the North, as it does everywhere else.

NTCL sought bankruptcy protection in late 2016. It had been operat-ing in the North in one form or another for some eighty years. A CBC story reported in September of 2016 that:

> Only half of the vessels owned by Northern Transportation Company Ltd. appear to have value as the company tries to sell off its assets to stave off bankruptcy.
>
> In a report filed in Alberta court last week, the company's court-appointed monitor, PricewaterhouseCoopers, said that of the company's 158 vessels—mainly tugs and barges—77 are either "scrap, abandoned or out of class."
>
> Mark Fleming, the vice president of NorTerra, NTCL's parent company, said many of NTCL's assets date back decades to when NTCL was a Crown corporation.[178]

The Government of the NWT purchased the assets of Northern Transportation in late 2016, after apparently being unable to secure a private buyer. The following press release was issued at the time:

> *YELLOWKNIFE (DECEMBER 16, 2016) — Minister of Finance Robert C. McLeod confirmed today that the Government of the Northwest Territories (GNWT) has purchased the assets of Northern Transportation Company Limited (NTCL) for $7.5 million. This timely action has been taken to protect the petroleum product supply chain for NWT communities along the Mackenzie River and Arctic coast.*

---

177 Cameron Clement, *Tides* [in-house publication] (Northern Transportation Company Ltd., 1999).

178 Guy Quennevill, "Only half of NTCL's Vessels Expected to Sell: Report," *CBC North* (September 16, 2016), https://www.cbc.ca/news/canada/north/ntcl-ship-sale-1.3771750.

The Government continues to operate freight delivery services along the Mackenzie River and the Arctic coast under the name Marine Transportation Services. They are, relatively speaking, the new kid in town. Their current website reads as follows:

> *"GNWT Marine Transportation Services is your solution to move bulk petroleum and deck cargo to Mackenzie River and Western Arctic coastal destinations. With terminals located at each end of Canada's longest river and joined to Alberta by rail and road, MTS operates a fleet of eight high powered shallow draft tugboats through Canada's Northwest Territories to the Kitikmeot Region of Nunavut and the North Slope of Alaska. Fully equipped to deliver materials to unimproved shallow harbors and remote locations, MTS transports large modular and project cargo by tug and barge to resource exploration and production sites for the mining and oil and gas sectors.*
>
> *MTS offers annual scheduled service to the communities of Łutselk'e, Tulita, Norman Wells, Kasho Got'ine, Inuvik, Tuktoyaktuk, Sachs Harbour, Paulatuk and Kugluktuk. Other locations may be served on a charter basis or through alternative arrangements."*

In the winter of 2019, the old NT shipyards in Hay River were filled with derelict tugboats, sitting up on slipways, their windows covered in plywood. Piles of old equipment seemed to be strewn about. It was a sad and depressing sight.

The scene was, in some ways, a sign of the evolution of the town and the industry, and a portent of future. Most of the ships and other equipment settling into the weeds are just waiting to be scrapped for the value of the steel. Apparently, the hulls of some vessels have been salvaged and converted into houseboats that now reside in Yellowknife Harbour.

Perhaps the old ship graveyard is a metaphor for things built of steel for earlier eras and different times.

However, the shipyards appear cleaner now, and orderly, although photos of the wharf areas seem quite deserted. It isn't like the old days, like when Gordon was building ships and barges, drilling platforms, a northern ferry, and repairing anything marine and steel.

But some things remain true. NT served the North long and well, operating in harsh conditions, through ice-bound shores, heavy seas, fog, huge and unpredictable winds and waves. Its crews faced low water, early winters, late springs, and the effect of cold water and hard work on steel and engines and men. NT provided support and jobs to northern communities, especially Hay River. It also offered summer employment and northern adventure for generations of students, southern and northern alike. It is too bad that so many of the old-timers are gone and have taken their stories with them.

The stories of near deaths (and actual deaths too) and of ingenuity and sacrifice are legion, and maybe legendary. Those stories—about helping others in the face of struggles, wind, storms, and ice—are mostly gone now, evaporated like the morning mist on the big river.

Gordon's sadness at the loss of marine construction and repair work is, of course, natural. It was the place he became a man.

CHAPTER 37:
Hay River – After the Fall

Two Marine Transportation Services (MTS) tugs (formerly owned by NTCL) docked
at the Hay River wharf, July 2022, courtesy MTS.

That [NTCL's decline and bankruptcy] was just another
passing of an era. The North has seen lots of those.

DAVID MACDONALD ARRIVED in Hay River in 1980, as a young lawyer
from Cape Breton, Nova Scotia. It was for a job, work experience as a
lawyer, adventure, and supposedly only a year or two.

Forty years later, MacDonald had this to say about the present-day Hub
of the North:

Since 1987, and the decline of marine shipping business, the town has added NTPC (Northwest Territories Power Corporation) head office. That brought a hundred jobs or so and helped land development and local housing.

It is also a force for continuing and future work related to the Talston Dam Hydro works, first built in 1963, but which is now expanding. Ice roads in 2019–2020 were put in to assist the construction of more capacity, likely to triple, and tie into the electricity grid in Yellowknife, to provide an expanded and stable infrastructure.[179]

Also, even though NTCL went out of business, it has been taken over by the GNWT, so there is a new barging company running shipping now. We just had a four-engine long tanker train come in this week with lots of resupply fuel, so that goes year around.

The loss of Pine Point Mine and the town of Pine Point was, no doubt, a body blow. Then we had jet service six days/week. Now, it is only prop planes a few days a week.

We've been treading water the past decade, at least.

However, there is some business activity in Enterprise [at the junction of the highway to Yellowknife], which helps a bit here.

Also, Osisko has been doing a lot of confirmation drilling at the former Pine Point mine site and may be planning a mill out there in the next one to two years; there's a rumour they might start this year yet. If that's the case, they'd run "shift" buses from here; there won't be a town built, just a camp as there is now, plus maybe a larger administration office. I think they have at least $70 million invested, with no return possible unless they start mining again. So, we are hopeful.

There are several new buildings under construction now. All trades here are very busy, which is good. The population is just over 3,500 and has been at that level for over 10 years, I'd say.[180]

---

179 Further detail was added by former mayor Jack Rowe, in an interview with the author, 2022.

180 David MacDonald, interview with and email to the author, 2021.

It has been interesting to watch the town over the past fifty years. There was quite a large influx in the late 1940s and early 1950s. It was that initial growth that, to a large part, built the business side of town and many of those whose names adorn the streets now. Hay River was always a town of cycles, ups and downs depending on the fish catch and prices, the exploration and construction farther north, and the need for tugs and barges. Construction, mining and transportation, whether Pine Point, the railway, the highways, bridges and marine construction or petroleum exploration, affected virtually all the businesses, and indirectly at least, most of the people in the town.

Jack Rowe, a former town councilor for two terms in the 1980s and mayor from 1994 to 2000, acknowledges the cyclical nature of the town's economy in the past. Hay River is now more diversified and much more stable, according to Rowe. It is a service centre for the South Mackenzie, although that, in the grand scheme of things, is still a pretty small marketplace. But as in many small towns, people learn to do many jobs, get into different businesses, and take advantage of opportunities as they can.

Jack's father Bill Rowe, for example, first came to Hay River in 1949 from Peace Country. After mining work north of Great Slave (a long nine-month winter, he recalls), Bill drove truck, did small construction jobs, operated a gas station and repair service, ran the school bus, and raised his large family there. He and Keith Broadhead opened a mobile-home park when the new town was setup in 1963. Bill was involved in many different jobs and businesses, anything to put food on the table, and his wife, Rita, was very involved in many volunteer activities.

Their children have followed both examples. They started their own company, initially buying a couple of tandem trucks and a loader, and then built more and more businesses, which now have expanded greatly. Those children and their children are still operating many Hay River businesses, including infrastructure construction, a theatre, retail stores, hotels, restaurants, commercial and residential buildings. The B&R Rowe Centre, a modern building with offices, a theatre, and liquor store, was named for Bill and Rita Rowe. Sadly, Bill passed away in January 2022, during the research for this work.

The Rowe children and now grandchildren have been active in the community, like Rita, serving politically and otherwise. Jack's brother Greg served, for example, as the chair of the 2018 Arctic Winter Games Committee.

As a former mayor, Rowe is quick to point out that Hay River has been very fortunate to have both a sequence of old families stay on and provide new generations of leaders and a steady import of talent and new blood to the community.

Some of the original business families have moved on to bigger and better things, and some have had children and grandchildren move into other walks of life, but the business community is full of second- and third-generation leaders, names like Ashton, Jamieson, Ring, Gagnier, Mapes, King, and others too. The current mayor is, for example, the granddaughter-in-law of the Wright family, Mae and Don, who were important pioneers in hardware, insurance, rentals, and town life in general. Her predecessors as mayor include a number of second-generation Hay Riverites, mostly from that post-war influx.

The Indian Reservation (the name seems anachronistic now) is governed by the K'atl'odeeeche First Nation. The instigation for the reserve was the intended acquisition of land on the east side of the Hay River, up to the lake, by Northern Transportation. This land had traditionally been used and claimed by the Indigenous Peoples. It was where the original settlement was, and the old Roman Catholic and Anglican mission churches and residences, the old graveyard, and residences. Development of the village there has focused more education and social help in the area and promoted pride and resilience.

Recently, the local Métis association, which was just in its infancy in Gordon's time, has apparently become much more confident in recent years, placing signs proclaiming that the Métis Nation owns or at least claims that other land in the area is theirs. Possible disagreement about who controls that land, and thus what rights and interests the Métis Nation is entitled to seems likely on the horizon!

At the local level, there is an active entrepreneurial scene. Partly that is the role of the town, and partly because of the long distances to, well, anywhere. The sons and daughters and nieces and nephews of the early professionals— the pharmacist, the accountant, the lawyer, a doctor, some teachers—are now raising their own children in the community. There is construction and development, much road work, some new developments in logging, forest products, and mining, and a good local service component. And there is now the Deh Cho Bridge over the wide Mackenzie River at Fort Providence, which has removed the reliance on a river ferry in summer, an ice road in winter, and weeks of downtime in spring and fall.

The town seems to be quietly going about its business, there on the shore of the big lake. In 2018 it put on the Arctic Winter Games, hosting athletes, officials, and visitors from various polar countries and territories touching the polar seas, with visitors from Alaska, Denmark/Greenland, Russia, Norway, and others.

The Pine Point mine shutdown wasn't as devastating as it could have been. Many of the houses were picked up—often by Gordon Gill's cranes—and moved to Hay River. A good number of their residents came along. The North gets in your blood, after all.

Both MacDonald and Rowe talk about the future, and the role of the "next" generation. In addition to the new bridge spanning the Mackenzie River, and the highway extensions, new apartment and office buildings, road and water works, infrastructure, and homes are underway. It is just a question of time and money and demand.

Gordon Gill was not part of the political "class" in town in his day. As Jack Rowe says,

> Gordy just quietly went about his work. There was no bluster or bragging. They [the Gills] were good people, hard-working, and loyal. Gordy was one of the most honest individuals you would ever find. It didn't matter if things were good or bad.[181]

Then he adds,

> Even after circumstances forced Gordy and Treena to move their business south, he still bought his trucks and service vehicles from Russell King in Hay River. They were good people. And he really supported Treena and covered for her when she developed some memory problems. It always impressed me with how warm and protective he was, even just standing on the street having a chat.[182]

Gordon helped build local businesses, too, and supported others who were active in the Mackenzie Delta and Yellowknife, as a member of what

181 Jack Rowe, telephone and email interviews with the author (January 2022).
182 Rowe, interviews with author.

Yellowknifers sometimes called the "Hay River Mafia." Gordon was often involved as a shareholder and sometimes director in the hotel business, and for service companies, like Arctic Offshore, which worked the Beaufort Sea area.

There are a couple of more unusual stories about the town. One is the irony of the Mackenzie Valley pipeline. After all the fuss and delay related to the Berger Inquiry, Imperial Oil quietly and with appropriate permits proceeded with the construction of a smaller-size pipeline down the valley. While Rowe says that the pipeline—when and as it was built—didn't give the economic boom initially predicted, it did significantly help northern businesses. It has been operating since 1985. It is virtually unheard of anywhere else in Canada.

The second was international in scope and, for a few days in 1978, a matter of national importance. A Russian Cosmos spaceship was reported to be in trouble, and over the course of ten days or more, the world anxiously awaited its re-entry into the Earth's atmosphere. The craft spun out of control, apparently heading for the Northwest Territories and in fact, contrary to Russian denials, the spaceship did crash onto the winter ice of Great Slave Lake about 240 kilometres north of Hay River. Some of the remnants were found by a local fisherman out on his snowmobile. The excitement lasted for a couple of weeks. The local high school monitored the developments. Some worried about the possible danger from the crash itself, and others were nervous about potential radiation poisoning.

The feds and the military swarmed the area.

The townspeople were concerned, and, as reported by Chris Brodeur of the local *Hay River Hub* newspaper, no one was providing answers. The town called a meeting, the *Hub* ran notices for free, and the citizens of Hay River gathered to speculate and plan for their future. Brodeur thought that the Russians should take some responsibility—he was a young newspaperman in those days and a bit of a "disturber," as all good newspapermen are—and so he sent an invoice for the advertising and perhaps for the town's meeting costs to the Russian embassy in Ottawa. They didn't pay and complained to the Canadian government. Brodeur did receive a stern rebuke from the Canadian government for interfering in external relations. They didn't pay either.

Brodeur responded by sending another overdue account statement.

They still haven't paid.

So, the town of Hay River continues, but the old days, the bustle of mining booms and oil exploration and work camps, the shacks for seasonal workers, and the throb of hordes of forklifts, shunting trains, marine engines and river traffic are not likely to be seen again anytime soon.

Or so it would have seemed.

April 2022 saw the first rare-minerals shipment of concentrate leave Hay River from the first Canadian rare-earth mine, Nechalacho—one of only two in North America.[183] Perhaps this is the beginning of a new era? Of hope for a new era, this one with the rare-earth minerals industry? Fingers are crossed.[184]

As for marine engines throbbing, Maritime Transportation Services runs tugs and barges from the harbour, ready for what may come.

. . . .

183 Carla Ulrich, "'Significant Day for the North': Nechalacho's first rare minerals shipment leaves Hay River," *CBC North* (April 23, 2022): https://www.cbc.ca/news/canada/north/significant-day-for-the-north-nechalacho-s-first-rare-minerals-shipment-leaves-hay-river-1.6428596

184 First Canadian rare earth mine starts shipping concentrate from N.W.T. - https://www.msn.com/en-ca/money/topstories/first-canadian-rare-earth-mine-starts-shipping-concentrate-from-n-w-t/ar-AAXAAIV?ocid=msedgdhp&pc=U531&cvid=896a342ec6244917877ac86a12558083

CHAPTER 38:
Family and Work

Clarence as a truck driver, with young Gordon.

Dad couldn't take orders. He wanted to be left alone.

GORDON RETURNS TO the topic of his dad. Mostly his talk about his father relates to the times in northern Alberta and the move to Hay River. Clarence drops out of the picture, at least in Gordon's reminiscences. Those were always about the jobs or the things that happened when he was doing a job. But what about Clarence after the move to Hay River?

> *Dad took a job at the old Hay River Hotel and café, on the riverbank by the dock in Old Town, washing floors at night. He retired from there when the hotel closed down. He came to work for Northern Arc, doing*

the same kind of job. He was happy; he worked at night when no one was around. I sure never told him what to do.

Clarence and Armande would have Gordon and his family over for dinner and so on. It seems from Gordon's comments that they were running out of things to talk about, things in common. Perhaps it was a matter of Gordon growing along with the business and his focus on work, almost to the exclusion of anything else.

> *Dad loved to read, and Mom working in the hotel. She could bring home books that the guests left behind. Dad had rows and rows of books in stacks in his little 8-foot-by-14-foot [2.4-metre-by-4.3-metre] sheds out back of their house in Old Town. He kept giving them away and getting more from the hotel.*

> *And while Dad was well-read, he never gave advice, and he never interfered in the business. He was still a loner.*

In Hay River, most of Clarence and Armande's friends were Indigenous people, despite that shift away from things Indigenous in her earlier days. Not much changed in their life. Clarence tried fishing on Great Slave for a couple of years, not on the bigger fishing boats but by himself. It didn't work out.

And while Armande kept in touch with her parents and sisters, Clarence didn't go "home" to see his own, white family until much later in life. His daughter Mildred and her husband Ernie drove him to Saskatchewan. By that time, his parents were dead. He had not seen them since the war. Only one sister was still alive. Gordon has not made that trip.

Clarence never talked about Gordon's success as a prominent businessman in town, never offered praise or congratulations. But he must have given off a sense of pride or something, or else Gordon didn't need his father's approval. It was not an issue in his life and nothing he thought about until asked.

> *Dad didn't talk about regrets or what he should have done. What he spoke to me about were things like, "Don't trust banks." He never had a bank loan in his life, and he wouldn't co-sign anyone else's either.*

> *Because he never got a mortgage or a loan, Dad just did what he could afford at the time. In Hay River, like before, he pushed some small buildings together and joined them up to be their house.*

Once when we went back to Hotchkiss to do a spring beaver hunt when I was sixteen or seventeen, my share of the fur money was $2,200, which was lots of money then. I gave it to my dad to finish the Hay River house. It was good he could finish the house nicer.

After that, I hinted around about pooling our money together to buy a car because we didn't have one. That's when he gave me the talk about never co-signing a loan.

Father and son talked, and they lived fairly close together, but Gordon and Clarence didn't have a lot in common. The son was so focused on his work that, in Gill's words, *I was working a lot, and we visited, but there was no "shop talk," and that was hard for me.*

There is an unstated regret there, as there is about Bryan and Trent, although it doesn't seem that Gordon looks at life in the rearview mirror. He doesn't express things like guilt or regret very often. He comes across as a man who feels like he did his best and who doesn't look back.

Gordon was not a worrier. Perhaps it is innate in his personality or learned from his grandfather and mother, who had to adapt to survive as Indigenous People. Or maybe it was learned in reaction to his father.

Dad was always a worrier. He'd be bent over in pain from ulcers. He ate lots of soda in his day, which he regretted later. I swore that I wasn't going to be like that. I wasn't going to worry.

If a problem came up, I'd say, "I can deal with that tomorrow." My dad could never do that. When we went trapping beaver, Dad would be worrying about if we'd get any beaver, not just today, but he would worry about tomorrow too, fretting about things he couldn't control, like if the trap broke or something. I wouldn't do that. If we got beaver, we did. But if we didn't, well, we'd figure out why and try again. It was like that in business, like the next job. "We'll get one, don't worry," I'd say, and we most always did.

And if they didn't?

There was always something to do or fix, and the big thing was to keep the crews. We didn't want to lose them. They were such a good bunch of guys, so we'd try other things if we needed to, like repairing our own

> *stuff, or building something, like the gold dredge or doing some experi-*
> *menting. Anything to keep the guys working.*

Gordon always speaks highly of the fellows he worked with. He showed appreciation, and loyalty and he provided training.

> *Northern Arc would teach the raw new guys how to cut and place steel*
> *plates for welding in just days or a few weeks, at most. It was so good*
> *because the new guys usually went on to get their welding tickets. Many*
> *of them guys stayed with us for the long term.*

He particularly mentions Ernie Camsell, a schoolmate from Hay River, a classmate at Akaitcho Hall in the trades, and a lifelong friend. Ernie was Gordon's first hire at NTCL, and his first employee at Northern Arc. They continued working together and were partners on the Au.Nugget gold dredge up on the Liard River, until Ernie's death. Gordon says of Ernie: *He was my number one guy, all those years. He came over to Northern Arc as soon as I had enough work to be able to pay him.*

Glen Dersch is another lifelong friend and colleague. Gordon hired Glen when he walked into NT off the street at 17, green as grass, looking for work. After working with Gordon at NT, Glen followed him to Northern Arc in 1969. If Ernie was Gordon's number one man, Glen was *"a close second"*. After working with Gordon at both companies, Glen proved his loyalty and something about Gordon, too, by moving to Edmonton and continuing with Gordon at Northern Crane Services, until the end of their careers there. The two men were still close, and continued their relationship, latterly working together on a farm west of Edmonton.

Gordon isn't an effusive or outwardly sentimental man. He is generous, if not fulsome, in praise and is quick to laugh but his persona is one of containment, and control. He learned to be stoic at an early age. Yet, in the case of Ernie, and Glen, there is a sense of loyalty and friendship and caring, and now loss, that sneaks out. One can't help but wonder what true depth lies beneath the surface of this man.

> *Those guys wanted to work and wanted to do a good job. It was hard*
> *work, really hot sometimes, like if you were welding high up in small,*
> *enclosed areas. Or, if you were inside a barge, or below the deck of a boat,*
> *you'd be surrounded by that heavy steel in the summertime, and the sun*

was up all the time, and it just absorbed the heat something terrible.

And the welders themselves, they were generating all that heat with their machines, and dressed in heavy gear and a helmet. It was really tough work.

Or operating those cranes before air conditioning. Oh, my gosh. Out in the hot sun for twelve-hour days, surrounded by glass. So yeah, sometimes guys wouldn't show up. Maybe they'd get drinking or go camping. They needed a break. We didn't fire them; we took them back. Not much bad happened. That is the beauty of the union labour pool—there were lots of good people in that union hall.

Three sets of crews were ideal, it seems. One on the job, one getting to it, and the other off the job, relaxing and doing whatever made them happy.

There is pride there, quiet and calm, but it does come out—Gordon helped provide thousands of man-years of work—he and the customers, of course, the good people who helped him out, who supported him and his company.

I never wanted to be put in a corner, to be dependent on any one customer or even one industry. I didn't want to not have other work to do.

He says his drive was not for the money itself. It was for the work. He wanted to "stay in the game." They had to get bigger to do the bigger jobs. Even acquiring the huge cranes and equipment for Northern Crane to operate was "forced on us" to keep the customers happy, to ensure Northern Crane kept getting and deserving good work.

Work ethic was a factor too; leading by example. Gordon worked hard himself but calmly. His key people, he says, were the same as him—they couldn't wait to get back to work.

Another factor was praise, a close cousin of that appreciation of his fellow workers that Gordon mentions. He praises people, expressing admiration for their work in front of others, in plain sight. In meetings, he treated everyone the same, whether downtown lawyer or office cleaner, and praised them both; he appreciated that they were all people, just like him and his parents and his Indigenous relatives.

Of his grandparents and their heritage, Gordon says he looked up to them. He is proud of their independence. They were pioneers, trappers, good farmers and gardeners, honest, and hard-working.

> *Voyageurs weren't hired for laziness. They had to be physically and mentally fit.*

Gordon thinks of that as his heritage and his example. And his parents worked hard too, manual labour, trapping, subsistence farming, putting together and taking care of pretty primitive houses. Gordon learned to work, and he wanted to work.

As for Armande:

> *She had the same job for forty years. Even after work, she would be helping others. Like if she was at our place or Mildred's, she would do whatever was needed, cleaning or whatever. She was always working.*

> *She was always proud of Treena's and my success and said so. Dad was happy too, but he was never bragging around, never getting "in our way," and not "bugging us," but he let us know.*

Regarding Treena, Gordon feels he can never say enough.

> *She supported me in everything. Her job was the books and finance, and she did that great. We should really talk about her more. She was as honest as the day is long. She told me what she thought about every-thing without hesitation.*

Regarding any question about "kickbacks" or anything like that, Gordon volunteered: *Treena wouldn't have allowed anything funny. "Life is too short to go down that road"* was what she would have said.

Treena was also the parent most focused on their sons. *Treena was always there for the boys and took care of everything.* There seems some regret, as is often the case with men who work hard and long. *I was away a lot—too much.*

Gordon said another interesting thing.

> *So many people influenced me and helped me, from the very beginning. I feel like I was molded into a working machine. The way I feel about those people, I wouldn't want to leave anyone out* [of this story].

It seems that working hard and helping others was the reward Gordon offered in return. Not an intellectual and not pretentious or "full of himself,"

Gordon's path was marked by ability, curiosity, and willingness to listen. He tried to do more than was expected, more than his own job.

One final example is that as the young kitchen helper, he would also clean engine-room bilges.

> *The engine room would be cleaner, and so everyone took more pride in it, and the bosses noticed too, and the engineer liked that. And the captains, they didn't need to, but they taught me to steer the ships and to understand what they were doing. I watched, and I learned, but they showed me the way.*

CHAPTER 39:
A Life of Firsts and Lasts

Gordon

The stars kind of aligned for me.
I don't know if that will happen again.

THERE IS AN IMPORTANT intersection of life and history in Gordon's journey. Not big history, perhaps, like the invention of the internet or men on the moon, but a history of time and place in the Northwest Territories strung together in the life of one man and the things he touched. Perhaps it is all just coincidence, the play of luck and choice, and perhaps it is destiny of some kind, a crossing of talents with opportunity mixed in the bowl of experience and ambition.

This weaving of a life's tapestry or quilt connects a Cree-speaking grandfather born before the last Métis/Indigenous uprising put down by military force in 1885 to high-tech computer-operated 1,000-ton cranes and wireless horse-racing kiosks. How can that be?

Well, the connection is the Métis kid who worked hard and made good, moving from traplines to tugboats to truck-mounted "revolutionary" cranes. The thread lies in the context of much change in the "near north", and within it Gordon Gill's story of resilience, adaptation, and survival, while working and learning, with ambition, humour, and caring, and through exploration, economics, and culture.

And what are the factors?

Let's start here.

First, at a time when most people were leaving homesteads to go south to the large cities, Gordon went North. He was a half-breed when he went there and very soon a Métis—one of the first members of the local Métis Association, just when that group was finding its voice, or perhaps more accurately, just when others started hearing that voice.

Second, he went to the federal day school and then a residential school, but he did so as an older teenager, and so avoided the trauma of residential schools that is so prevalent in the news today. Gordon's circumstances allowed him to avoid the losses suffered by many others with Indigenous roots around language, culture, and innocence.

While his grandfather removed the family from their home so that his children and grandchildren need not attend a church institution, Gordon remembers his friends in Hay River thinking how lucky he was to be able to go to Yellowknife for school.

Third, Gordon learned to stake mining claims in the Pine Point lead-zinc rush and started his ship-repair career just as the better highway, the railway, and Pine Point mine were built, oil-and-gas exploration got under-way in a big way, and the freight needs of the North started to take off.

Fourth, as an employee of first YT, then NT, he was ship's engineer on the MV *Watson Lake*, which took the first drilling rig and drill pipe into the oil-rich fields of Prudhoe Bay on Alaska's north coast, and which did depth work and lent other assistance to build the first harbour at Prudhoe Bay, leading to the first rush of oil production on the Alaskan coast.

Fifth, Gordon created the first modern ship-repair business, then the first modern shipbuilding business in the NWT. It was also the first Indigenous-owned such business.

Sixth, he set up the first (and first Indigenous) crane company in the NWT, Northern Crane Service.

Seventh, as the owner of Northern Arc Shipbuilders, Gordon Gill:

- built the first (and first Indigenous) gold dredge to work the Liard River and the Mackenzie River watershed.

- built the first submersible drilling platform to be used in the Beaufort Sea, as part of the huge oil-and-gas exploration boom led by Panarctic Oils, Dome Petroleum, and the Government of Canada during the last quarter of the twentieth century.

- built the first barges used in the creation of artificial drilling islands in the Mackenzie River.

- set up the first northern (and Indigenous) company focused on ship and barge repair at the time of the construction of the first three of the "new" NT tugboats and the new big barges of the modern era.

- built the first short-throw tugboat in the NWT, the MT *Gordon Gill*, for work in the Tuk harbour and dry dock.

- built the northernmost ferry on the Mackenzie River system.

Eighth, as the owner of Northern Crane Service, Gordon brought into Alberta the first Liebherr (or any) 230- to 250-ton truck-mounted hydraulic cranes, which were quicker to set up and takedown, and which could be moved easily, without removing the crane's lattice-type booms. Previously, the standard mobile crane in Alberta was a 200-ton crawler type, with a lattice boom that had to be dismantled and carried apart from the crane in many truckloads. Gordon said that the truck-mounted cranes "revolutionized" that industry just as it started to boom. He also imported the first Spierings crane, truck-mounted with a straight rising boom and a protruding jib boom, which could do the work of some tower cranes, but with much faster access and removal time.

Ninth, another of Gordon's companies designed and set up the first technology company in the world focused on producing data information for off-track, horse-racing bettors.

And then there are the lasts, the ends of eras.

Gordon does not know if there will ever again be the kind of exploration he saw in the Arctic, the steel-based repair and fabrication industry that he was able to establish in Hay River, and the use of local contractors for such projects. He thinks he saw the last of the economic boom in the North, and the final days of major river transportation for the supply of northern and Arctic communities. Sadly, he doesn't know if the threads of history will connect the stars to align for other young Métis boys, like they did for him.

And finally, he was ship's engineer on the last wooden commercial tugboat, the *Arctic Lady*, to cross Great Slave Lake. In addition, he was the ship's engineer on the last voyage of the *Radium King*, the NT flagship tug and the last of the pre-war tugs, when it was taken to Bell Rock Camp to be retired, becoming in due course a museum piece.

All this because Gordon Gill wished to be a welder and a mechanic. All this because he knew the value and enjoyment of work, and he had the example of his grandparents and parents. All this because he had the strength and resiliency to overcome serious injuries and setbacks, the cultural impetus to adapt as needed, and a vision about improving his life.

CONCLUSION

> IT'S ALWAYS BEEN *part of me to create jobs—not for the glory—I just like doing it. And I always thought, if nothing is happening, you have to make it happen.*

Gordon Gill looks out the window of his home in west Edmonton on a beautiful morning in the middle of May 2021. He glories in the light lime-green of the poplar trees budding in the sunlight and the clear, crisp-blue sky of a prairie spring. He still marvels at the annual miracle of spring in Canada's Northwest.

It especially reminds him of the changes he has seen in his lifetime. From the life of a poor, skinny, Métis kid living in the bush, helping on his father's trapline, to ownership of a major crane and lift company, thriving in the midst of the "largest deposit of crude oil on the planet."[185] Gordon has seen much of life in Canada's North, including many firsts and certainly some lasts. He has seen life as it was in the boom times and the passing of those times. He is a man of those eras, many of which have passed on, often forgotten, often unrecorded, and usually unlamented.

Gordon is a humble man; he shows up at his office or his lawyer's office or anywhere of importance, in fact, the same way he went to work, in blue jeans and a western-style shirt. He is a good listener and a good decision-maker. The source of his success, he says, is that he surrounded himself with good people, people who knew what they were doing. He never puts on airs or holds himself up as anyone special. He is just Gordon. And he is not the one doing the talking.

In the years after moving south, Gordon and his team operated a successful crane services and transport enterprise, provided real estate for companies working north of Fort McMurray, and supported other

---

185 Canadian Association of Petroleum Producers, "What are the Oil Sands?" *CAPP: Canada's Upstream Oil & Natural Gas Industry* (2022), https://www.capp.ca/oil/what-are-the-oil-sands/.

entrepreneurs. Northern Crane grew with the times and the complexity of operating in Canada's oil sands. Cranes got bigger and bigger, and the technology and plans more and more complex. Again, Gordon found himself as the small startup, an outsider to the big boys, an Indigenous entrepreneur and business owner. He pushed forward, hired good and senior people, and competed. He made friends in the industry, and together, they succeeded. That too is magical.

Yet, despite success as a businessman starting from nowhere, when asked what the best times he remembered were, Gordon didn't hesitate. There were four:

> *Number one was when I first met Treena. How good we got along when we got married. How saving she was and that helped me save, and how willing Treena was to go along with my ambitions.*
>
> *Number two was when we had our two boys, Bryan and Trent.*
>
> *Number three was when I met Treena's sister and family and Treena's mom and dad.*
>
> *And number four was when we sold Northern Crane.*

In an age of international travel, Gordon did mention three trips to Hawaii and two trips to Mexico "with the boys." He did travel to Europe twice, but it was directly to Germany and back; he was there to buy cranes, big mobile cranes for work in the Alberta oil sands.

What Gordon likes are simple things like camping and fishing, and now some travel in an RV. He doesn't have a second home or a winter place or the common other trappings of success. He doesn't seem to need them or want them. In fact, he doesn't want to get up "high." Gordon says he has seen so many people rise and fall, good friends included, people who have lived "high on the hog," or wanted to, spending and spending, dumbfounded when things turned bad. Gordon doesn't want the fall.

That is why it isn't surprising that one of his favourite places is the campground where the Kakisa River rushes over a lovely, wide, perfectly symmetrical ridge at the 30.5-metre (100-foot) Lady Evelyn Falls. West of Hay River on the Mackenzie Highway in the NWT, before the turn off to Fort Providence and Yellowknife, the Kakisa flows "down north" from near the Alberta border. It passes through the lake of the same name, and over the Hay River Escarpment before it empties into Great Slave Lake.

The drop there, from the higher-level Alberta Plateau to the lower Great Slave Plain is about 38 metres, generally spread out over less than 6 kilometres but some of that decline is in an abrupt drop. That makes the broad expanse of boreal forest land seem to have had blocks pulled out from under its northern part, so that it just sank, straight down, leaving intact a clean wall, lowered without fuss or damage.

Kakisa has a nice campground. Gordon has photos of his boys and Bert Stromberg there. Even the case of beer shows up. In the spring, the fish swim upriver, sometimes crammed in a mass under the wings of the falls, almost thick enough to make you think you could walk on them, like a carpet. Fishing is good.

That is what you get with Gordon Gill. No talk of wealth or success. No seeking of honours or awards or naming rights, or other ways of getting his name out in public. No need for validation as is common in other circles. He genuinely doesn't care about self-promotion. He likes the simple things and has simple tastes, like the outdoors. He is calm and steadfast.

There is something both surprising and admirable that despite his background—or maybe because of it—Gordon does not require anyone to tell him who he is or what he has done. Perhaps that is only surprising to those who don't have a Métis background. He doesn't need to do the talking. Perhaps others now wish they had that kind of sanguinity.

When asked about his mother's reluctance to speak Cree, even to him, and about his father's move to a trapline, and how he faced predicaments throughout his life, things that might take anyone off a forward path, like his badly burned leg, his serious injuries in the car accident, his difficulty reading, Gordon explained it was how he was raised. He remembered the example from Granny Justine, who never stopped from morning to night, and Grandfather Noel and his own parents. But somehow, that doesn't seem to be the full answers.

What Gordon does say relates to an appreciation for others and a lot of thanks for the help he got along the way. With Gordon, you don't hear him say "I" very often. He was taught young to say "our" or "it's ours" and not "I" or "mine."

Also etched in his mind since he was very young, are his father's words,

"Where there's a Gill, there's a way; I mean, where there's a will, there's a way."

This has been a mantra for Gordon ever since. This phrase would be important to him his whole life—not saying it out loud but repeating it over and over in his mind.

His father's best gift may well have been the example of hard work and "figuring things out" but another was to tell Gordon to repeat those words whenever he ran into trouble. And Gordon did, hundreds and hundreds of times throughout the years, when he was having doubts or facing a difficult problem. He credits that a lot. It kept him going, finding a way, finding his way.

Gordon consciously thought that part of his job was to help others look good. He wanted to be helpful and if he didn't know what to do, he knew who to ask. It was his way, and the Northern way to help others, and they helped him in return, *many times over*, Gordon says.

In the midst of the passing of time and place, we all have connections. We may not recognize the connection as such until it is too late, or until someone tells *our* story, but it is there.

In Gordon's tale, the thread of history is there, subtle and probably just coincidence, or so he says… but the Métis kid became what he always wanted, a mechanic and a welder. He took that ambition and made a life. He faced much change and many challenges. For Gordon, it was a case of continuous work and effort, trying new things, innovating and adapting. He was open to opportunity, and he succeeded. When we talked about his story, he wondered out loud, "What story?" The answer was, and is, pretty clear: "Well, you were a Métis kid born in the bush; you were poor, living by trapping, and hating school. Now you can look back on flying by Learjet to meetings. You had a very successful business career, doing what you wanted.

"Your father was a trapper in the bush and gone for most of your first fifteen winters, yet you learned a lot, got involved in different businesses and investments, and served on the boards of a number of good companies.

"You were raised by your Indigenous grandparents and mother in tough conditions at a time when your family was losing its language and history. You had two bad accidents and many challenges in business, and yet you prevailed, stayed calm, and married. And you got to travel the North and try new things. And you have a list of firsts and lasts and mosts that anyone in the country would be proud of. All of that."

Gordon's reaction was typically to downplay his role in all of that. That seems cultural to many. And unusual in the business world.

All success was due to help from others. My whole life people have been willing to help me. They piled work on me, and I liked it, and did it. It was how I learned.

As for Gordon personally, he misses Treena "every day." His house is still "Treena's Cave." *At this point everything and I mean everything in the house Treena bought and placed. Even my clothes. One of these days I will have to get some new clothes.*

He says the best thing to say about Treena is: *"What a partner she was."*

Otherwise, Gordon is semi-retired, visiting his sister in the North Country and working some farmland just west of Edmonton.

Kind of a circle, it seems to me.

He expressed surprise that anyone would think this special. Well, I did, and I hope you do too.

POSTSCRIPT

GORDON GILL is too busy. He's been building a barn with long-time friend Glen Dersch, doing the dirt work with bobcat and backhoe. And he was shoveling gravel. Then he was going to drive his motorhome up to see Mildred and Marvelle for his birthday. Gordon turned eighty-one in June, 2022.

Family and friends, farming, and hard, physical work.

Yup, kind of a circle.[186]

----

186 Sadly, Glen Dersch passed away in June of 2022. Gordon misses him greatly, and wishes he could have lived to see this book in print.

EPILOGUE

SUCCESS ELUDES MANY, especially when that success is defined by others.

Gordon's story touches the major events and trends, booms and busts affecting the near and not-so-near north over the last half of the twentieth century. From life on a trapline with bush trails and quagmire roads, wooden tugboats, staking claims, and northern travel, he advanced to marine construction, oil-and-gas exploration, and cranes. He involved himself in technology for horse-race fans, searching for gold, stock trading, and land development and management. Business was his method; hard work, choice, and chance his ammunition. Some things worked, some did not. But he worked hard, helped others, and has had a good and interesting life. He is still soft-spoken, and true to himself. He did not seek credit, accolades, or recognition; rather, he sought to serve, learn, and succeed. And, importantly, Gordon Gill lived the transition from an era where people like his mother tried to hide their "Indigenousness" to a business world where companies "hungered for Native content" in those businesses.

By any definition of success, Gordon Gill seems to have achieved it.[187] He travelled much farther than most. He has seen a lot. More important to him, however, are the people he has lost, the close friends and loved ones.

Gordon does not presume to advise others; he doesn't think there is a message in his success. If pushed, Gordon would say he worked hard, learned what he could, and was thankful. He had a wish for the future and put in the effort to win that future. He tried new things. He moved when he

187 Napoleon Hill defined the major attributes of leadership in his 1937 book, *Think and Grow Rich*. They are: unwavering courage; self-control (self-discipline); a keen sense of justice; definiteness of decision; definiteness of plans; the habit of doing more than paid for; a pleasing personality; sympathy and understanding; master of detail; willingness to assume full responsibility; and, understand and apply the principle of cooperation. Gordon seemed to know this instinctively. He never heard of Hill or the book.

had to and gave more than was required. He doesn't think he is remarkable but that the "stars aligned" for him in a way that may never happen again.

You can be the judge of that, and what role life as a half-breed has played in the life of Gordon Gill, Métis shipbuilder.

ACKNOWLEDGEMENTS

I ACKNOWLEDGE with great appreciation the continuous patience, humility, and sense of fun that Gordon Gill has brought to telling his remarkable story. His understated and quiet good humour and his generosity of spirit were constant companions on this journey, which I hope shine through in the writing. So too, do I acknowledge the effort and care that Gordon's niece, Marvelle Kobbert, has put into transcribing Gordon's words, consulting on family history, sourcing material and photographs, and helping get this work to publication.

Gordon's words in this book, shown in italics throughout, were in response to the writer's questions, posed in person and by email. They have been used as they were said. That questioning and the transcribing of Gordon's memories took place in the late winter and spring of 2021 and were followed up by the writer for expansion, clarification, and explanation over the rest of 2021 and the first half of 2022.

Thanks beyond words go out to Loretta Bertol for her enthusiasm, probing questions, constant encouragement, editorial and research efforts, reminders, corrections and advice. Without her collaboration in concept, writing, approach, proof reading, and publishing, this work would be so much the poorer and incomplete.

Laura, Barbara and Cam at Friesen Press have been very caring and helpful resources.

I am grateful to those many friends who have listened to me go on (and on) about the book, offered information and suggestions, and asked deep and thoughtful questions. The depth of encouragement, technical help, and advice has been crucial and proof of friendship beyond expectation. Many are quoted in the text, but among my village of unsung heroes are Chris Brodeur, Amal Chaaban, Kyler and Cameron Clement, Andrew Coates, Chuck Davidge, Anne Dixon, Tracy Elofson, Peter Flynn, Afsheen

Javid (AJ) at Canada House Gallery, David MacDonald, Patrick McKenna, Professor Emeritus James Morrison, C.M. of Saint Mary's University, Halifax, Word and wording expert Susan Rockwood, Jack Rowe, and others. Donna Oliver taught me about the existence and legacy of residential schools, and much more.

A note of appreciation is necessary, too, for the questions raised by Senator Patti Laboucane-Benson during an early conversation that helped focus the research on matters Métis, which inform this book and which, as Andy Sims QC (long-time lawyer for the Metis Settlement Appeal Board of Alberta) says, show there is not just one Métis story in our country, but many.

Professor John S. Milloy answered, in his deep and thoughtful book, *A National Crime: The Canadian Government and the Residential School System, 1879 to 1986*, my anxious and nagging personal question: "Who am I, an older white, Anglo-Saxon, nominally Protestant man of privilege, to write about a Métis life?" Milloy writes,

> I, too, began with misgivings, feelings of trespassing upon Aboriginal experience, but… [the story] represents in bricks and lumber, classroom and curriculum, the intolerance, presumption and pride that lay at the heart of Victorian Christianity and democracy, that passed itself off as caring social policy and persisted, in the twentieth century, as thoughtless insensitivity. The system is not someone else's history nor is it just a footnote or a paragraph, a preface or chapter in Canadian history. It is our history, our shaping of the "new world"…
>
> As such, it is critical that non-Aboriginal people study and write about the schools, for not to do so, on the premise that it is not our story too, is to marginalize it, as we did Aboriginal people themselves, to reserve it for them as a site of suffering and grievance…

While this story is about one unique man and not residential schools, except in a very small and unique situation, Professor Milloy's words speak to me about my effort to share the story of Gordon Gill, knowing that the discrimination against and separation of the Indigenous people in our country in my own time is something I can only help express but never know.

The photos used in this book are, unless otherwise credited, from the Gill/Kobbert Family Archive. Marvelle Kobbert has done such important work, in difficult times, in gathering and identifying the family photos. She has also been resourceful, and very helpful in her many insights, her interviewing and transcribing skills, and her advice on matters Métis in her extended family,

The wonderful painting by Laura Harris, which serves as the focal point for the cover of this book was a revelation and a bridge, and is used with permission from the artist. While I see a foggy channel down a river or lake, Gordon sees birchbark, and others see boats, or canoes, or storms. The title of the painting, *It's Like Searching for Gold*, symbolizes this story, and Gordon's life, figuratively and literally. Thank you to Laura Harris (lauraharrisartist.com) and Canada House Gallery of Banff, Alberta for their cooperation and assistance.

I have attempted to refrain from offering opinions or judgements on matters not in my experience and to present the history of the life and times of Gordon Gill and current reading as fairly as I can. Any errors, omissions, or just lousy interpretations are my own.

Gordon Gill's story of upbeat perseverance and his unpretentious wisdom humble me. They remind me of the blessings and life lessons gifted to me by my darling daughters Stephanie, Virginia, Keltie, and Heather, reflected in words framed and given to me by Stephanie:

All the things
I didn't know
I didn't know.

How true.

BIBLIOGRAPHY AND SOURCES

GORDON GILL'S COLLEAGUES called him "The Godfather." Nothing was in writing. As a result, while there are photos, no diaries or letters exist on which to base this work. The primary source for this story is the oral history compiled through verbal and email interviews conducted by Gordon's niece, Marvelle Kobbert, and the author. Other interviews conducted by the author include Chuck Davidge, Chris Brodeur, David MacDonald, Jack Rowe, Jonathan Smethurst, Kyler and Cameron Clement, and others mentioned in the text.

Historical Sources

Beattie, Owen, and Geiger, John. *Frozen in Time: The Fate of the Franklin Expedition* (London, UK: Bloomsbury Publishing LLC, 2004).

Berger, Thomas R. *Northern Frontier, Northern Homeland: The Report of the Mackenzie Valley Pipeline Inquiry* (Ottawa, ON: Mackenzie Valley Pipeline Inquiry, 1977).

Berton, Pierre. *The Arctic Grail* (Toronto, ON: McClelland and Stewart, 1988).

Brodeur, C. J. H., publisher and editor. *Hay River Hub* Newspaper, various editions.

Canadian Geographic. "Métis," *Indigenous Peoples Atlas of Canada* (2018), https://indigenouspeoplesatlasofcanada.ca/.

Clement, Cameron. "NTCL 65 Years," *Tides* [in-house publication] (Northern Transportation Company Ltd., 1999).

Collins, Eileen. *I've Been Here Ever Since… An Informal Oral History of Hay River*, edited and compiled by Eileen Collins (Hay River,

AB: Tourism Advisory Committee of the Town of Hay River, June 1999).

Ens, Gerhard J., and Sawchuk, Joe. *New Peoples to New Nations: Aspects of Métis History and Identity from the Eighteenth to the Twenty-First Centuries* (Toronto, ON: University of Toronto Press, 2016).

Fitzpatrick, Alfred. Unpublished manuscript "Schools and Other Penitentiaries" c.1933, National Archives of Canada, --File: "Schools and Other Penitentiaries" MG28, I 124 Volume 1 courtesy, Professor James Morrison, C.M., St. Mary's University, Halifax, NS.

Gough, Barry. *First Across the Continent: Sir Alexander Mackenzie* (Norman, OK: University of Oklahoma Press: 1997).

Gower, Lewis Neil. *Go North Young Man: A Memoir.* Unpublished Manuscript.

Guthrie, Jim. *A Photo Essay*, June 23, 2021, courtesy of Jim Guthrie and Charles (Chuck) Davidge.

MacFarlane, John M. "Vessels Built by Northern Arc Shipbuilders Ltd.," *Nauticapedia* (2015), http://www.nauticapedia.ca/Articles/Vessel_Builders_Northern_Arc.php.

Milloy, John S., *A National Crime: The Canadian Government and the Residential School System, 1879 to 1986* (Winnipeg, MB: University of Manitoba Press, 1999).

Morin, Gail. *Northwest Half-Breed Scrip – 1885* (Scotts Valley, CA: CreateSpace Independent Publishing Platform, 2018).

Morrison, James H., C.M., The Right to Read; Social Justice, Literacy and the Creation of Frontier College. The Alfred Fitzpatrick Story. Nimbus Press Ltd, 2022.

Morrow, William J. *Northern Justice: The Memoirs of Mr. Justice William G. Morrow* (Toronto: University of Toronto Press, 1995).

Newman, Peter C. *Company of Adventurers,* Volume 1 (Toronto, ON: Penguin Books Canada Ltd., 1985).

Ootes, Jake. *Umingmak: Stuart Hodgson and the Birth of the Modern Arctic* (Vancouver, BC: Tidewater Press, 2020).

Raibman, Paige. "A New Understanding of Things Indian": George Raley's Negotiation of the Residential School Experience," *BC Studies* 110 (1996): 69–96, https://ojs.library.ubc.ca/index.php/bcstudies/article/view/1343/1386.

Ross, Campbell A. "Teaching in Northern Alberta Communities; The Importance of Place, Past and Present"; 2016, era.library.ualberta.ca > items > 6990bb77-0ff0-4617, Instructor Emeritus, Grande Prairie Regional College.

Ruzicka, Bob, writer, "Northland Destiny," track 6 on *Straight North*, featuring Ted Wesley, vocalist, PET-MAC BMI 1972.

Ruzicka, Bob, writer, "The First Barge," track 8 on *Straight North*, featuring Ted Wesley, vocalist, PET-MAC BMI 1972.

Ruzicka, Bob, writer, "Winds of Change," track 7 on *Straight North*, featuring Ted Wesley, vocalist, PET-MAC BMI 1972.

Sharp, Florence. *Saga of the Battle River* (Battle River, AB: Battle River Historical Society; Inter-Collegiate Press, 1986).

Sibbeston, Nick. *You Will Wear a White Shirt: From the Northern Bush to the Halls of Power* (Vancouver, BC: Douglas & McIntyre, 2015).

Sissons, J. H. *Judge of the Far North* (Toronto, ON: McClelland & Stewart, 1968).

Teillet, Jean. *The North-West is Our Mother: The Story of Louis Riel's People, The Métis Nation* (Toronto, ON: HarperCollins, 2019).

Wilson, Garrett. *Frontier Farewell: The 1870s and the End of the Old West* (Regina, SK: University of Regina Press, 2007).

Zaslow, Morris. *The Northward Expansion of Canada, 1914–1967* (Toronto, ON: McClelland & Stewart, 1988).

Selected Online Sources

Buffalo Airways, https://buffaloairways.com/

Canadian Association of Petroleum Producers, https://www.capp.ca/

The Law Society of the Northwest Territories, https://lawsociety.nt.ca/

The Nauticapedia, http://www.nauticapedia.ca/

North of 56, https://northof56.com/

Canadian Association of Petroleum Producers, https://www.capp.ca/

Report of the Truth and Reconciliation Commission of Canada (December 2015) https://rcaanc-cirnac.gc.ca/eng/1450124405592/1529106060525

Wikipedia, https://en.wikipedia.org/

INDEX

This index lists only selected Persons, Places, and Vessels for quick reference.

Some names and places are repeated so many times throughout the book that a full index would be meaningless. Accordingly, certain names are not shown in this index, including Gordon and Treena Gill, Clarence and Armande Gill, Mildred Gill Kobbert and Marvelle Kobbert, Gestur Gudmundson, Bryan and Trent Gill, Noel and Justine L'Hirondelle, Chief Akaitcho, Sir John Franklin and Kookum Gray. Certain writers or commentators quoted or referred to are omitted, especially if they are referred to in footnotes.

Common places, or those repeatedly referenced, are also omitted, including Hay River, and Yellowknife, NWT, Great Slave Lake, Great Bear Lake, the various mountain ranges in the NWT, the Peace, Mackenzie, Slave, Athabasca, Saskatchewan, Nahanni and other rivers, Hudson Bay, Arctic Ocean, Beaufort Sea, Mackenzie Delta, Alaska, (and some of its islands, outposts and waters referred to in news stories), Edmonton, Calgary, Regina, Vancouver and Winnipeg.

The tug MT Gordon Gill, and the marine transport services, Northern Transportation Co. Ltd, and its nicknames NT and NTCL, and Marine Transport Service, and its nickname, MTS, as well as government departments, have likewise been omitted.

PHOTO CREDITS

All photos (including a few post- and photo-cards without attribution) are from the Gill/Kobbert family collections unless otherwise indicated. Thank you to the NWT Archives for preserving and permitting use of the northern photos identified by the letter N throughout. Kendall Townend [https://www.kendalltownend.com/end] enhanced the photo of Gordon so that the "eating jay" could be seen, a blue bird against blue workman's clothing. Cameron Clement found and delivered YouTube and other social media information on Northern Transportation Co. Ltd. Chris Brodeur was very helpful in advising on, and providing context for, the photos, and articles which appeared in the *Hay River Hub* newspaper. David MacDonald and Tom Maher of Hay River were good enough to take or find photos of present-day Hay River, and current boats of the Marine Transportation Services (MTS) fleet.

ABOUT THE AUTHOR

NEIL GOWER, KC, loves the North, the area around Great Slave Lake, and old tugboats. He holds a BA in history and an LL.B from the University of Alberta. Gower has worked extensively in the North, beginning with four summers working for Northern Transportation Co. Ltd., and then practising law (primarily as a legal aid defense lawyer) in Hay River (1975–1977) and for business clients throughout the NWT thereafter.

A strong supporter of northern business and Indigenous learning, Gower is a fifth-generation western Canadian whose great-great-grandfather came to Pile o'Bones Creek (now Regina, SK) in 1882. Gower's family has been involved in and focused on the history of the great northwest ever since.

Gower's love of northern history and admiration for Gordon Gill's initiative and dedication fueled his desire to tell this unique story. Gill's life of struggle and success, opportunities seized and lost, and continuous adaptation mirror the tremendous changes in Canada's North over the last half of the Twentieth Century. Gower reveals the remarkable "life and times" of a pioneering métis entrepreneur against the backdrop of significant historical transitions in Northern development, lifestyles, marine transportation, mining, and petroleum exploration.

Now retired, Gower is a writer living in Edmonton, AB. He was the lawyer for and a long-time friend of Gordon Gill, metis shipbuilder.